The Imagination of
Early Childhood Education

The Imagination of
Early Childhood Education

Harry Morgan

BERGIN & GARVEY
Westport, Connecticut • London

Library of Congress Cataloging-in-Publication Data

Morgan, Harry, 1926–
    The imagination of early childhood education / Harry Morgan.
        p.   cm.
    Includes bibliographical references and index.
    ISBN 0–89789–594–0 (alk. paper)
    1. Early childhood education—Philosophy.   2. Early childhood
education—History.   3. Early childhood education—Curricula.
4. Montessori method of education.   I. Title.
LB1139.23.M67   1999
372.21—dc21   98–38309

British Library Cataloguing in Publication Data is available.

Library of Congress Catalog Card Number: 98–38309
ISBN: 0–89789–594–0

First published in 1999

Bergin & Garvey, 88 Post Road West, Westport, CT 06881
An imprint of Greenwood Publishing Group, Inc.
www.greenwood.com

Printed in the United States of America

The paper used in this book complies with the
Permanent Paper Standard issued by the National
Information Standards Organization (Z39.48–1984).

10 9 8 7 6 5 4 3 2 1

This book is dedicated to the pioneers of early childhood education, who include, but are not limited to, Caroline D. Aborn, Felix Adler, Henry Barnard, Barbara Biber, Susan Elizabeth Blow, Anna E. Bryan, Ruth Burritt, Horace Bushnell, Sarah B. Cooper, Abigail Eliot, Mary J. Garland, Elizabeth Gilkeson, Barbara Greenwood, William Nicholas Hailmann, William Torrey Harris, Elizabeth Harrison, Caroline T. Haven, Patty Smith Hill, James Hymes, Jr., Josephine Jarvis, Harriet Johnson, Maria Kraus-Boelté, Matilda Kriege, Margaret McMillan, Rachel McMillan, Emma Marwedel, Lucy Sprague Mitchell, Anna Ogden, Hortense Orcutt, Keith Osborne, Anne L. Page, Elizabeth Peabody, Susan Pollock, Caroline Pratt, Alice H. Putnam, Pauline Agassiz Shaw, Margaret J. Stannard, Lucretia Treat, Nina C. Vandewalker, Sylvia Ashton-Warner, Catherine R. Watkins, Lucy Wheelock, Edna Noble White, and Kate Douglas Wiggin.

Contents

Introduction

This is a book about children, parents, and teachers. If there were a single entity that could integrate these three groups into a passion for childhood education, it would be imagination. A scholarly view of childhood experiences captures this imagination while dispelling the notion that young children are learning only when teachers are teaching.

Early childhood education requires teachers who are knowledgeable about young children from infancy through age eight. It also requires parents who are willing to accept the responsibilities associated with the idea that they are the child's first teachers. And early childhood education requires an informed public willing to act upon the idea that high-quality early education is essential for future generations.

Traditionally, the ages of birth through eight are more associated with developmental concerns that emerge from basic human reflexes at birth than from grade assignments during schooling. Early childhood teachers are therefore more concerned about the learner's stage of development than the designation of a school grade level.

This book also examines historical features that are important to early childhood scholars. These features began to take shape hundreds of years before the recorded birth of Christ, beginning with Aesop's fables—fables that were not originally intended for children but found a welcome place in children's literature. Only recently have scholars noted the contributions of the slave Aesop to Western thought. Previously, discussions of Western education commenced with studies of philosophers like Socrates, Plato, and Aristotle, and little attention was given to philosophers like Aesop who appeared centuries before them and significantly influenced their ideas.

This writing explores Greco-Roman and Judeo-Christian influences on the development of education from antiquity through the medieval period and up to the present day. Education of boys was usually assured, but education for girls was given last consideration, or none at all. Here, the role of the church was critical in making education available. The grip of religion on learned matters gradually lessened, and eventually European countries took the lead in state-sponsored education for children six years and older.

The idea that graded schooling for young children should start at the age of six can be traced to Plato and members of his academy, including Socrates and Aristotle, who contemplated the mysteries of life with their young pupils. Socrates did not have a classroom, as other teachers of his time did; students followed him to the marketplace and the streets, where he used what came to be known as the "Socratic method" of disseminating information. The power of knowledge gained from experiences, not solely school encounters, is seldom recognized in today's views of how young children acquire knowledge and construct wisdom.

In ancient Rome, youth who attended school had a slave, not far behind, carrying their writing materials and the lyre that they learned to play to accompany their singing. At one point in his life, Aesop the fabulist was such a slave and was thus enabled to sharpen his wit. It proved to be a dangerous talent for his time and status.

John Comenius, a Moravian minister, proposed that like young plants, infants need a nurturing parental environment in which to experience healthy growth. It was the imagination of Jean Frederic Oberlin, however, who in 1767 founded the first school for children under the age of six and developed a type of curriculum and style of teaching suitable for the very young. Since this was the first, it took an inspired imagination to formulate a curriculum and successfully recruit practitioners who shared his philosophy in fulfilling the learning needs of young children from working-class families.

The "how" of learning was the primary concern of Oberlin, who founded his school in a working-class community in France. Classes were led by women who sat among the children, telling stories from their imagination while they were knitting. These centers were called "knitting schools" and their teachers "conductrices." The curriculum fostered in the knitting school served as a model for the early German kindergartens and followed a different historical pathway than did grade schools. By the mid-1800s these schools (also called "infant schools") were throughout France and included instruction in reading, writing, and arithmetic.

Public schooling in a step-wise, graded sequence was formalized in the United States by Henry Barnard, who in 1867 became the first federal commissioner of education. Early public schools emerged from tutorial models for the well-to-do, private school practices, and religious schools. Teaching and learning in them was a didactic enterprise replete with rote exercises.

In 1807, forty years after Oberlin's first knitting school, three remarkable black men who could neither read nor write founded a school, and hired a white teacher, to educate young black children in Washington, D.C. Because of the political climate, and the fact that most blacks in Washington were slaves, it took great imagination to make their school a reality. The school survived a few years in a city with thousands of blacks—only 500 of whom were free. In 1820, Annie Marie Hall, a black woman from Prince Georges County, Maryland, opened a school for black children in the District of Columbia, on what is now known as Capitol Hill. Though she had access to few curriculum models, graduates of her school ultimately became teachers, lawyers, and other professionals.

Influenced by his friendship with kindergartner Susan Blow, William T. Harris, superintendent of public schools in St. Louis, Missouri, encouraged her to open the first public kindergarten in 1873. Blow had been trained in Froebel's methods while attending a school in New York City that was owned and operated by Maria Kraus-Boelté, one of Froebel's German students. This was in the midst of a long period of special training for preschool teachers that would set these "kindergartners" apart from elementary school teachers.

The first public school teachers were not much more educated than their students. In the mid-1800s, a fourth-grade education could qualify an adult to be hired as a teacher. During the early 1900s, graduation from a "normal school" (approximately high school) was required to qualify as a teacher.

During this same period, teacher training institutions were primarily occupied with supplying graduates to teach grades for which school districts were willing to pay reasonable salaries. Prior to 1900, teacher education institutions had little interest in preparing teachers for employment in relatively low-paying nursery schools. Working parents and others in need of care for their preschool-age children were required to seek low-cost or free services in private, religious, or philanthropic venues where workers' salaries were considerably lower. These services, more often than not, were called "nursery schools" or "infant schools," or consisted of child care provided by women in their homes.

Between 1900 and 1960, university education for teachers of preschoolers was provided in academic areas related to child growth and development, family studies, or home economics; it usually was not in the education department.

In the early 1900s, efforts of Jacob Riis and Jane Addams, through the settlement house movement, assisted impoverished immigrant families and migrant black families from the South. They organized child care and free milk programs in neighborhoods close to the populations in need. Such efforts helped stem the tide of children doomed to poor nutrition and school failure. Within the philanthropic tradition, Susan Blow, Horace Mann, Elizabeth Peabody, and Ralph Waldo Emerson campaigned for kindergartens in public schools. As a result of their efforts, kindergartens were opened in poor communities under the sponsorship of religious groups and missions. Church leaders viewed these programs, together with their established Bible school programs, as a forum for expanding their religious following. The philanthropists' ultimate mission, however, was a full acceptance of preschool education by the public sector as a right, not a privilege. Settlement house programs sought volunteers and graduates from normal schools and university programs to assist with the needs of the urban poor. The university fields of nursery school, child care, early childhood education, and social work grew out of these needs.

Maria Montessori, an Italian physician and childhood education theorist, toured the United States in 1913–1914, advocating a cooperative role for parents and teachers in the early education of their children. She spoke of new ideas related to the training of the senses that she had introduced in Casa dei Bambini, a school she had founded for young children living in impoverished conditions. Montessori had followed the theories of Sicard, Séguin, and Froebel. Many schools in the United States adopted her recommended curriculum, and greater emphasis was placed on parents supporting the work of the school. Many believe that her work contributed to the founding of parent-teacher organizations.

In the mid-1960s, Head Start was founded to remove poor families from the cycle of poverty that had started during the 1920s when immigration of poor families from Europe and the migration of Southern blacks to urban areas succumbed to the national economic collapse. The depressing conditions that still lingered with some families in the 1960s inspired President Lyndon Johnson's War on Poverty and sparked the founding of Head Start. Head Start became the new community-based nursery school, intended to reduce the effects of poverty on the children of immigrant European and black migrant families that had first appeared over sixty years earlier.

Early childhood education has been enriched by the efforts of many professionals who focus on the special needs of the young. Studies in the 1970s reported that more than 80 percent of children with handicapping conditions were not receiving educational services they needed. The National Advisory Committee on the Handicapped and the Bureau of Education for the Handicapped supported the passing of Public Law 94–142 in November 1975. By 1978, all states were required to "assure the free, appropriate public education of all handicapped children." This culminated a long history of inconsistent services offered for intellectually and physically challenged young children. This history can be traced to Roche-Ambroise Cucurron Sicard (1742–1822), who opened a school for deaf children in Bordeaux, France, in 1782. His work influenced Edouard Séguin (1812–1880), a pioneer of modern methods of teaching severely challenged children. Sicard also inspired Thomas H. Gallaudet, who learned Sicard's methods at the Royal Institute of Deaf-Mutes in Paris prior to implementing his own curriculum at what later became Gallaudet College in Washington, D.C.

Universities focusing on early childhood education assumed the natural academic area for the study of women and children was one that emphasized health, nutrition, childhood, and family. Therefore, the study of child development and nursery school practice was assigned to departments of home economics, human ecology, child and family studies, and nursing schools. It was not until the 1960s that most schools of education established early childhood programs in their graded teacher education divisions. This transition followed the replacement of earlier normal schools by state teachers' colleges.

By the 1990s, schools of education have brought early childhood programs into their traditional settings, and only a few early childhood programs remain as independent entities within universities. The few that remain as stand-alone academic units are often called departments of child and family studies, human ecology, or child development.

In many ways, the history of early childhood education can be followed through the development of its curriculum. The nurturing qualities stressed by Froebel flowed from the philosophy of John Comenius, and the work of Sicard and Séguin inspired Maria Montessori's inclusion of parents as the child's first nurturers. This was followed in the 1920s by the influence of psychosexual theory employed by Sigmund Freud and his followers. Behaviorists like John B. Watson, B. F. Skinner, and Edward Thorndike were influential through the 1950s. This historical process culminated in Erik Erikson and Jean Piaget's identification of stages of development that provided significant milestones. The dissenting views of Skinner, Thorndike, and G. Stanley Hall also were examined.

Play is a primary source of development in young children, and play is children's work. Theorists have attempted to define play by humans and animals as an activity from which participants derive pleasure. Lev Vygotsky pointed out that while play is the leading source of development in young children, defining play as a source of pleasure misses the mark. Vygotsky identified various types of childhood activities—like sucking on a pacifier—that would not be singled out as play. He also suggested that certain games commonly identified as play are pleasurable to children in the United States only when they are winning. We also know that some children can be engaged for hours in play with a few simple toys, whereas other children engage in play for only a short time with a great variety of toys and other objects that are visible and accessible. There also are children who gain more pleasure from sitting and listening to adult conversations than from engaging in what adults define as "play."

Throughout the philosophy and theories of Froebel, play is described as essential to the living organism. Froebel's concept of play involves a natural interaction between children and objects of play. Certain objects of play, according to Froebel, have shapes and physical properties that appear to be attuned to the developmental needs of children. He sees children as deriving a sense of being by participating in the world through symbolic play, and the objects of play (he called them "gifts") are attuned to the needs of growing children. The ball, according to Froebel, is shaped for a specific purpose. As a sphere, it provides tactile sensations when children handle it, and these sensations provide foundations for conceptualizations in mathematics and geometry later in life. For Froebel, the pleasure that play provides children contributes to their making meaning of their world and is not solely for fun—although fun can be an enjoyable accompaniment.

With the emergence of federal programs supporting early education and various states making kindergarten a requirement, extensive advances have occurred in early childhood education. Early childhood practitioners have two learned societies: the National Association for the Education of Young Children (NAEYC) and the Association for Childhood Education International (ACEI). These societies hold annual meetings at which political policy, professional practice, ethical issues, and research are discussed.

The Woman's Education Association, founded in England in 1872 to work with people in poverty, sponsored the work of Abigail Eliot, the first director of the Ruggles Street School in Boston. The association also participated in the founding of Radcliffe College, a Boston Montessori program in 1915, and the Boston Children's Museum. The wife of Henry G. Pearson headed the group's nursery center committee and was not satisfied with the curriculum that Abigail Eliot was implementing at the Ruggles Street School. In 1921, Margaret McMillan was hired by the association to work with Eliot, an experienced social worker, by helping her infuse child development practices into their nursery school curriculum.

Through the 1920s, there was considerable disagreement about curricula and programs for preschool age children. The powerful nursery school group emphasized nurturing and observation without direct intervention until it was called for. Montessori's followers encouraged intervention and direct instruction as a staging point for learners and labeled the classroom teacher "directress" to reinforce this concept. In the early 1900s, the state of Rhode Island adopted the Montessori approach for its school system.

John Dewey was among the first to recognize the rigidity in Froebel's curriculum. Dewey attributed this to characteristics associated with the German way of life. Dewey's followers suggested that children in all grades should be allowed complete freedom to explore an environmentally rich classroom designed to foster such activity. He was not talking about the teacher being absent from the experience; rather teachers would make judgments about which of the many projects and interests could be the most useful for enabling children to reconstruct their own knowledge. Because of his affiliation with teacher training at the University of Chicago, many thought that Dewey had the greatest opportunity to influence schooling.

In public schooling, Dewey's Progressive Education movement did not do well because many schools had hired teachers with the equivalent of a high school education; they had heard about Dewey but had never read or understood his writings. Also, his methods were very different from the training the few well-prepared elementary school teachers had received. Progressive Education was very successful in private schools, where many teachers were university-trained and had studied Dewey's theory with enough understanding to incorporate its principles into their practice. The Peninsula School in California, an exemplary Dewey model founded around 1900, is still in operation.

Because many early public schools had not accepted the responsibility and costs associated with educating children under the age of six, many teacher education centers ignored this group of children. Exceptions were Atlanta University, the University of Chicago, Columbia University, the University of Iowa's Child Welfare Research Station, and Harvard University. By the 1920s normal schools accepted the responsibility of teacher education for nursery school and kindergarten teachers.

In the early 1930s, Dewey and Froebel's theories were modified in laboratory schools to accommodate scientific "child study." This accommodation was created to include the work of psychologists like Guthrie, Skinner, and Thorndike. Thorndike administered a behavioral observational model at prominent private schools in New York City. From this, he developed a study program of behavior reinforcement. This was followed by the work of G. Stanley Hall, who stressed *what* children should be taught.

Teacher education at the university level was a means, in a gender-specific society, to keep services for families and children in a single center run by women primarily for female students. Colleges of education did not become interested in preschool teaching until public schools adopted kindergarten and kindergarten teachers were being paid on par with public school teachers. In the mid-1960s, during the early days of Head Start, many programs paid regular teacher salaries before funding was reduced by the federal government.

In the early 1990s, universities lumped early childhood education, nursing, and human ecology (home economics) in the same department; elementary education (K–6) was a stand-alone program along with secondary education, special education, and various subject areas. These separate programs often had a center for student observations designed to support course work. These units of the university were sometimes called departments of child and family studies, of human ecology, and of early childhood education. With higher salaries for nurses, nursing programs for the most part are stand-alone programs in a separate university facility.

Within the recent past, reorganizations at institutions of higher education have often incorporated early childhood into the same department as elementary education, thereby making early childhood more a part of the regular education system and obtaining similar salaries for its graduates. This has caused, in most cases, a reorienting of the early childhood curriculum away from child development concerns and toward a more graded academic curriculum, rather than influencing teachers in upper grades to utilize a more developmental early childhood curriculum. Influenced by the grade school philosophy, many university teacher education programs in the 1990s are changing their names to early childhood/elementary education.

Church-supported child care centers, proprietary public child care, and philanthropically supported care for children up to the age of five pay lower salaries and attract "teachers" who have not completed college. Occasionally, university-trained teachers take these positions as temporary employment. Too often, Head Start teaching positions fall into this underpaid category.

Some states have attached services for four-year-olds to their regular school systems and thus have made regular teacher salaries available to teachers of this age group. In the early 1990s the Presidential Commission on Education proposed that "children should start school ready to learn." This statement focused more attention on Head Start and programs for children five and younger.

Psychologists who were the first to study child development—many through university courses in early childhood education—have informed us that learning starts at birth, and that what children experience in their early years is critical for later knowledge acquisition. During the early years children acquire language, the knowledge needed to make meaning of their environment, and basic characteristics that form their personality and cognitive style at a highly accelerated rate. This makes early education the phase of teaching and learning that lays the foundations for healthy, learning children. It gives a critical role to nursery schools, early childhood programs, and Head Start, since psychologists have reported that the environment is the most critical feature in child growth and development. Characteristics that were previously thought of as basically genetic (inherited) are stimulated and often emerge developmentally through early environmental interactions.

As municipalities adopt school services for children of younger ages— say two- and three-year-olds—nursery schools and early childhood centers will gain strength as a regular part of the public education system. The risk here is a loss of early childhood identity in the rush by school systems to create "academic" preschools in an attempt to accelerate rote learning and improve test score performance.

Some state departments have organized their community-based systems as early childhood (preschool–grade 4); middle grades (grades 5– 8); and secondary (grades 9–12). Other state systems have organized as elementary education (kindergarten–grade 5); junior high (grades 6–8); and high school (grades 9–12). Even within these systems, some communities are encouraged to experiment with other variations, sometimes because of the racial composition of schools and occasionally because of unusually large populations within a narrow age range.

States control the right to work in public schools, and to a lesser degree in private ones. Teacher certification can be issued only by the state education department (sometimes the city equivalents as in New York City and Buffalo, New York). Some states automatically issue teaching certificates to those who have successfully completed an approved program. Some states require graduation from an approved program and the passing of a test. The state's control of the test that is used can be a discreet control of teacher preparation. There are also special certification programs for nontraditional trainees who are placed on a fast track because they already have a degree in a field like mathematics, science, or English. Universities, more often than not, orient their teacher education curriculum to match the state's latest requirements, regardless of the soundness of the policy.

For example, in Georgia in the 1990s, early childhood teachers are certified after successfully completing a test designed by the Educational Testing Service (ETS) for elementary education teachers. ETS has a national test available for early childhood teachers, but the Georgia Education Department decided not to use it because its clients—school superintendents and local administrators—prefer that grades 4 and 5 be taught by teachers with early childhood training rather than teachers educated to teach elementary or middle grades.

Historically, persons trained in elementary education, unlike those trained in early childhood education, have received various certifications—including kindergarten–grade 6; grades 1–6; grades 1–8; preschool–grade 8; and variations of these levels—depending on the political climate in the state department of education at the time of certification. Efforts to unify, and in the process modify, early childhood education so that it becomes more like elementary education can be traced to two University of Chicago professors in the early 1900s and is described in Chapter 1.

In a capitalist economic system where the right to work can be controlled by certification, professional work rules and salaries are subject to the laws of supply and demand. Practitioners are encouraged to shift to other work opportunities when their first choice is diminished or closed to them. It is possible that an increase in work opportunities can occur in a single age range, say, preschool, because of marriage and childbearing patterns. As this group moves through the system, greater or fewer teaching opportunities can be created along their pathway. The state departments of education can be encouraged to modify their certification patterns to accommodate these surges if they get requests from their clients, the local superintendents and school administrators.

In 1998 confusion reigns between direct instruction, which might yield something that can be mass-tested, and how schooling can enable early learners to experience their own reality through a planned reconstruction of knowledge. This is the first year the state of Georgia will ignore three-year-olds by combining early childhood education with elementary education, and test all prospective teachers of lower grades with the ETS Elementary Education Test. This new group of teachers will be certified P–5 (preschool through grade 5). In contrast, the state of Ohio will certify early childhood candidates entering universities in 1998 to teach children who are age three through grade 3, as designated by the NAEYC and the ACEI as the early childhood period.

Despite these differences between universities involved in teacher education and state certification entities, the early childhood professional societies, NAEYC and ACEI, have been consistent over the years, designating children through the age of eight (preschool–grade 3) as the early childhood client population. This age range is not attached to grades of schooling, but to child growth. This makes early childhood education fundamentally different from elementary education in terms of how professionals are taught, and of how the needs of young children are perceived and met.

In early childhood education, the NAEYC and the ACEI have insisted that early childhood encompass studies and practices that focus on the growth, development, and education of youth from birth through age eight. Teachers of elementary and middle grades have an important but different mission. This distinction was made clearly in the 1996 report of the Carnegie Task Force, which stated that the age span of three to ten is "crucial for children's optimal learning and development."

REFERENCES

Adams, G., & Sandfort, J. 1994. *First Steps, Promising Futures: State Kindergarten Initiatives in the Early 1990s*. Washington, DC: Children's Defense Fund.

Bredekamp, S., & Copple, C. 1997. *Developmentally Appropriate Practices in Early Childhood Education*. Washington, DC: NAEYC.

Carnegie Task Force. 1996. *Years of Promise: A Comprehensive Learning Strategy for America's Children*. New York: Carnegie Corporation of New York.

1

Historical Imagination

The history of childhood is a nightmare from which we have only recently begun to awaken. The further back in history one goes, the lower the level of child care, and the more likely children are to be killed, abandoned, beaten, terrorized, and sexually abused.
—Lloyd deMause

The history of education is a story that should start with the first humans, because it is teaching and being taught that defines the meaning of humanity. The definitions that set humans apart from animals are embedded in the ability to learn, and to teach others, how to make and use tools to enrich existence. L. S. B. Leakey, born in Kenya and member of a family who devoted their lives to the study of anthropology, has told us:

The problem of trying to locate the place of origin of man and the higher primates has been discussed in many books and scientific papers, ever since the works of Darwin and others made it clear that the story of the Creation must be replaced by something that was in accordance with our general knowledge about the evolution of all forms of life, and that man could not be treated as though he was the one exception to all laws of nature. Darwin himself, with little to guide him except the present day distribution of the living great apes and many old world monkeys, expressed his belief that Africa would eventually be proved to be the birth-place of man. (Leakey 1969, p. 2)

Western civilization has been studied from the perspectives of its history, geography, philosophy, and literature. It is a story of two traditions during the early centuries, Greco-Roman and Judeo-Christian. As these civilizations emerged, African societies had already risen, flourished, and waned, approximately 5,000 years before the flowering of the Greco-Roman and Judeo-Christian traditions. It was the transition of cultural activity from southern Africa to Egypt that inspired many Greco-Roman and Judeo-Christian developments. (See Table 1.1 for a timeline of notable influences on early childhood education through the ages.)

ANCIENT GREECE AND ROME

The history of education usually starts with the life of Socrates, who lived thousands of years *after* the great teachers and philosophers of Africa had flourished and passed on. Since the preponderance of our culture has its roots in Europe, our studies of Western civilization continually ignore the influences that previous cultures had on the thinking of Socrates, Plato, and Aristotle.

In every country that one visits and where one is drawn into conversation about Africa, the question is regularly asked by people who should know better: "But what has Africa contributed to world progress? . . . not the wheel, not writing, not mathematics, not art . . . not this, not that and not the other thing. . . ." These critics of Africa forget that men of science today are, with few exceptions, satisfied that Africa was the birth-place of man himself, and for many thousands of centuries thereafter Africa was in the forefront of all world progress. (Leakey 1969, p. 1)

The early Greeks and Romans inherited many of their "achievements" from African societies, including monotheism. Religion was central to early Judeo-Christian and Greco-Roman societies. Laws were deemed sacred commandments handed down by God. Religion explained the laws of nature and morality, relieved the fear of death among people, and was central to the aesthetics of art and literature, and the principles of science.

Approximately two centuries before Plato, Socrates, and Aristotle, a slave named Aesop had created hundreds of parables and fables that were expressed through the oral tradition. Among other things, Aesop's fables helped to define morality. In a time when concern was given to constant changes in nature, Aesop proposed that human encounters involving living things require that such things as honesty, fairness, and respect for others should remain permanent. To express a pragmatic understanding of permanence, he used events and issues, and in the process gave voices to humans and animals.

Demetrius of Phaleron, a Greek political figure, collected the fables of Aesop about 300 years after Aesop's death. The collection, *Assemblies of Aesopic Tales*, was translated into Latin 300 years later by a freed Greek slave, Phaedrus. In the second century, Babrius, a famous writer of the period, translated the fables into Greek.

Games and community activities of that time involved children and adults in the same groups, and Aesop's fables were viewed not as stories for children but as fables for all. Artworks created during this time depict village festivals in which children and adults engaged in dancing, eating, and group play in the same general areas.

After the general acceptance of monotheism by the Hebrews and Greeks, it came to be believed that this single source of power bestowed upon humans the moral freedom to choose between good and evil. The Hebrews indirectly raised the awareness of individuality, moral freedom, and the essence of self. They expressed the idea that individual moral autonomy, the *self* (or *I*) could accept or reject God's law. This idea of individual power, expressed in the choice of good or evil, became the moral foundation of Western Christian civilization.

In Greek thought, it was generally agreed that individuals created problems for themselves and society; therefore, individuals must resolve problems. Humans should create laws to control behavior and discourage problems from overwhelming society. In this view, it was not reasonable to expect God to resolve all human problems. To the Greeks, laws were an important achievement for humanity; this characterization gave rise to the democratic process and issues concerning political freedom. These basic ideas set the stage for philosophers to encourage freedom of experience in various venues.

Independent city-states emerged in Greece during the fifth century B.C., through the freedom of experiencing the democratic process. By the sixth century B.C., Greek philosophers had examined religious issues and elements of nature to the extent that many myths were being questioned. They concluded, among other things, that patterns in nature were organized around certain principles and were not necessarily created by the gods or through mystical processes. This opened the way for studies in the applied sciences, the collection of data, and the systematic study of natural phenomena. Thus, philosophers and practitioners applied empirical reason, rather than religion, to an understanding of how things are ordered in the world. In the first nonreligious traditions, the Greeks studied mathematics and established geometric laws, and their physicians relied more on rational assessments than on mystical thought and magic.

THE MIDDLE AGES AND THE RENAISSANCE

Historians have suggested that during the Middle Ages there was no period called childhood. The concept of childhood can be traced from

Table 1.1
Influences on Early Childhood Education, 560 B.C.–1990

560 B.C.	300 B.C.	1500	1600	1700	1800	1850
Aesop 560 B.C.	Socrates 470–399 B.C.	John Comenius 1592–1670	John Locke 1632–1704	Jean-Jacques Rousseau 1712–1778	Johann Heinrich Pestalozzi 1746–1827	Margarethe Schurz 1832–1876
	Plato 427–347 B.C.					Charlotte Forten 1837–1914
				Johann F. Oberlin 1740–1826	Friedrich Froebel 1782–1852	
	The Republic 396 B.C.					Ivan Pavlov 1849–1936
	Aristotle 384–322 B.C.					Anna Bryan 1858–1901
						U.S. Office of Education 1867

Transcendentalists

William E. Channing
1780–1842

Horace Mann
1796–1859

Bronson Alcott
1799–1888

Ralph Waldo Emerson
1803–1882

Nathaniel Hawthorne
1804–1864

Elizabeth Peabody
1804–1894

Henry Barnard
1811–1900

Henry David Thoreau
1817–1862

					1800	1850
					Industrial Revolution 1820–1860	U.S. Civil War 1861–1865
						Emancipation Proclamation 1863
						Freedmen's Bureau established 1865

Table 1.1 (continued)

1900	1920	1940	1960	1980	1990
William T. Harris 1835–1909	G. Stanley Hall 1844–1924		James Watson 1878–1958		
Susan Blow 1843–1916	Sigmund Freud 1856–1939		Anna Freud 1895–1982		
Kate Douglas Wiggin 1856–1923	John Dewey 1854–1952		Jean Piaget 1896–1980		
Rachel McMillan 1859–1917 and Margaret McMillan 1860–1931	Harriet Johnson 1867–1934		Erik Erikson 1902–1997		
Ella V. Dobbs 1866–1952	Alfred Adler 1870–1937		B. F. Skinner 1904–1990		
Patty Smith Hill 1868–1931	Maria Montessori 1870–1952		J. McVicker Hunt 1906–1991		
Alice Temple 1871–1946	Lucy Sprague Mitchell 1878–1967		Benjamin Bloom 1911–	**Child Abuse Prevention Act 1973**	
Lucy Cage 1876–1945	Lev Vygotsky 1896–1934		***Brown v. Board of Education 1954–1955***	**Education for All Handicapped Children Act (PL-94-142) 1977**	
U.S. Children's Bureau 1912			**Elementary and Secondary Education Act (PL-89-10) 1965**		
		Works Progress Administration 1933–1943	**Project Head Start 1965**	**Gifted and Talented Act 1978**	
		Lanham Act 1941–1945	**Bilingual Education Act 1965, 1974**	**Federal Preschool & Early Intervention Program Act (PL-99-457) 1986**	
			Project Follow Through 1967		

European Immigration 1880–1917	Great Depression 1929–1939	World War II 1939–1945	U.S. Invasion of Vietnam 1965	U.S. Bombing of Cambodia 1970–1973	U.S. Invasion of Grenada 1983
African-American Migration 1900–1940	Harlem Renaissance 1930–1940		Civil Rights Movement 1960–1970		U.S. Invasion of Panama 1989
World War I 1914–1918					

the thirteenth century, and most of what has been recorded from that period has been gleaned from adults' diaries, poetry, literature, and religious writings that discuss children incidentally. Art of that period that depicted children with adults portrayed children as adults drawn in smaller dimensions. "Medieval art until about the twelfth century did not know childhood or did not attempt to portray it. It is hard to believe that this neglect was due to incompetence or incapacity; it seems more probable that there was no place for childhood in the medieval world" (Aries 1962, p. 33).

The execution of Socrates sent Plato into self-exile around the Mediterranean, and he did not return for ten years. Shortly after his return, Plato founded the Academy and wrote his views concerning education in the *Republic*. In Plato's view, children should be spared the self-serving interests of parents by their government, which should place the most promising children in schools financed by the state.

During the time of Socrates and Plato, children remained with their parents until the age of six. From that age, the sons of affluent families attended elementary school. Plato suggested that children's experiences should be free of violence, pornography, and vulgarity; such things were often found in myths and legends told to children by their nurses and mothers.

Younger boys studied reading, writing, gymnastics, and music. Their music instruction consisted of learning to sing and accompany themselves on the lyre. Plato intended education for children of the upper classes to prepare them for leadership roles in the military or government. While their children were being educated at government expense, their parents could be employed in occupations serving the public good.

Upon contrasting the schools of Athens and our schools today, one would find remarkable similarities. Athenian schools were set up by individuals as private enterprises, and parents made choices based upon costs and the schools' reputation for turning out scholars. This pattern is similar to the private school structure in the United States today. It was Plato's view, however, that schools should be constructed and maintained by the state. The state also should select teachers and pay them.

In thirteenth-century England, grammar schools were maintained by guilds. Usually a priest was appointed to each guild, and he was expected to teach in its grammar school. Later, grammar schools sprang up in towns under religious sponsorship, and on occasion the town fathers were involved as well. The founding of grammar schools was followed by song schools in which very young children were taught Latin through memorizing hymns. These schools, called Latin schools, were attended primarily by sons of affluent families.

During this time, there were attempts to develop common or vernacular schools for boys and girls from families of modest circumstances.

These schools taught grammar for use in business dealings, legal papers, and court matters, as well as arithmetic.

Besides Latin schools for the children of affluent parents, and vernacular schools for boys and girls of the ordinary folk, there was a need for apprentice education. In Germany this need gave rise to a group of educators called *Rechenmeisters*, who taught a seven-year course in bookkeeping, arithmetic, and writing. Its graduates were known as journeymen, or *Schreibers*, and instructed assistant teachers. As job openings occurred, persons eligible for the *Rechenmeister* level filled them.

By the sixteenth century, this group of teachers had become very influential because of their exclusive license to teach to certify others. In most instances, by the 1800s writing and arithmetic were provided along with the regular program in European schools, and the guild lost its monopoly outside of commerce and business. (Even in the late 1800s in Boston, some schoolchildren's parents were charged for writing and arithmetic to be taught to their children by a special guild teacher who came for that purpose, or someone on staff if there were enough pupils to warrant hiring such a teacher.)

Also in the sixteenth century children's dress took on a specialized design that distinguished it from adults' attire. This change first appeared among children of middle-income and affluent families. Children from poor families continued to wear clothing designed for adults for sometime thereafter. The new style of clothing was worn by boys during a period when middle- and upper-class adults were demonstrating an interest in uniforms. Special childhood clothing for girls did not emerge until much later.

THE SEVENTEENTH AND EIGHTEENTH CENTURIES

France

From diaries kept by Heroard, the doctor who attended Louis XIII and his family in the seventeenth century, we have learned details of nursery talk, playtime activities, and habits of the king's children. Heroard's writings reveal that at the age of seventeen months, Louis XIII was given a violin, an instrument still thought of by peasants as a common fiddle played at dances and festivals. A ball was also among Louis's many playthings, and by the age of two, he played with many toys that were common to children in affluent families. Two centuries later, Froebel would point out the ball, as a geometric sphere, an essential element in child development.

Little attention was paid to formal education for female children. It was thought that upper-class women might need some religious education, and all girls should be informed enough for religious conversion and how to participate in church rituals. It was also accepted that they should know enough not to confront their husbands, how to keep house and care for children, and have a proper understanding of the language. This knowledge, it was surmised, could be passed on to them by mothers and other older women. Few were willing to go on record in support of formal education for girls. A clergyman of that period might ask, "For what purpose?" Women could not be religious leaders, heads of state, military leaders, or professors.

One of the most unusual educational documents circulated in the late 1600s was a small book entitled *On the Education of Girls*. On the basis of this book, its author, François de Salignac de la Mothe Fénelon (1651–1715), was contracted by Louis XIV to tutor his grandson, who later became the duke of Burgundy. Fénelon, a member of a noble family that devoted itself to the Catholic Church, was the priest assigned to direct a sisterhood of new Catholics in Paris. His work with young women was remarkable, and the Church hierarchy was pleased with the many new converts.

His success did not go unnoticed by the duchess of Beauvillier, who, after recognizing Fénelon's success in converting girls to Catholicism, sought his help with her eight daughters. *On the Education of Girls* was written in response to her request. He was also successful as the tutor of Louis XIV's grandson, a troubled child who had been a great discouragement to others who attempted to tutor him. Fénelon followed the recommendations in his book originally written for the education of girls.

Fénelon's work with girls was more of a service to the Church than to women. He was far from being an advocate of equal rights for women, believing that women were frivolous, vain, and enjoyed repeating simple stories. His greatest contribution was that he believed education should start very early in a child's life, even before she or he could communicate by means of language. In his view, as infants acquire language, they should be given direct, simple answers to their questions. This should be followed by simple questions put to them by the adult, to make them aware of what they do not know, as an inspiration for them to seek more advanced information. Fénelon was among the first to discuss the role of the brain in learning. It was his belief that children should not be forced to study Latin at an early age because their brains are not yet stable, nor should they be expected to study reasoning because their factual information is too meager to apply the principles of reasoning.

Fénelon's belief in indirect teaching, and the teacher's response to a child's description of experiences as a basis for teaching, are similar to ideas expressed by Jean-Jacques Rousseau. Fénelon's purpose, however, was unlike that of Rousseau in that Rousseau espoused learning in a free environment that fostered inquiry for the child's purpose, whereas Fénelon's primary purpose was to protect the child from evil in the theological sense. He wanted to direct the child's attention to a sense of morality, and these values could be promoted through education. He saw storytelling as an important aspect of early learning, for example, and thought that Bible stories should be used for this purpose.

In 1767, Jean Frederic Oberlin (1740–1826) started the first school for children age six and younger. At his own expense he established the school in rural France for children from working families. Oberlin recruited teachers—whom he called "conductrices"—to sit among small groups of children and encourage language interaction through storytelling and start-up points for art and small construction projects, while the conductrices completed their knitting. (Hence the school was called a "knitting school.") Such gatherings, sometimes called "rug meetings," are still conducted in preschool and regular school programs in early grades.

The conductrices instructed children in reading and language studies in part by placing labels on classroom objects (table, chair, etc.) that were written in both the community patois and standard French. This was done to enable children to associate their negatively valued dialect with standard French and to integrate this language activity with all other learning activities. It remains common practice in classrooms today; kindergarten teachers will affix names to classroom objects as a staging point for standardized language development.

Oberlin surmised that the inability to speak standard French would make it difficult for these children, as adults, to be accepted into French society or employable in cities. This notion is widely accepted today in U.S. schools with large percentages of Southern white and African-American children. Some of these schools have found it necessary to train teachers to understand black English (often referred to as Ebonics) and the dialect of Southern whites as a second language and as a staging point for teaching standard English.

Prussia

Prussia was the site of many educational reforms in the seventeenth century. Its scholars were influential in education, philosophy, and psychology. It was ahead of the rest of the world in providing education for all classes, including the children of peasant families. By 1620, Prussia required school attendance for both boys and girls.

Located on the southern coast of the Baltic Sea and north of the Danube, it was a society characterized by many as literate, militaristic, and arrogant. The ruling classes were identified as particularly harsh and despotic. Yet from this environment, two relatively benevolent and education-minded Prussian kings, Frederick William I and his son, Frederick the

Great, emerged as supporters of nonsectarian public education years before such ideas were expressed in the rest of the world.

In 1717, Frederick William I decreed that all Prussian children of elementary school age must attend school. In the years that followed, the king contributed land and money to create schools for children from poor families. This was a major shift in public policy; a state official, the king, was assuming it to be the duty of the state, rather than the family or the Church, to provide for the education of children.

This step in the development of secularized schools in Prussia was continued by his son, Frederick the Great, who in 1763 enacted the General Code of Regulations for Rural Schools. Several matters in the decree are pointed out by many historians as landmarks in the education of young children. An examination of selected items, however, will reveal that despite the decree, the Church still retained a significant influence over education. The decree ordered the state, local officials, clergy, and families to provide for the following:

1. The education of all children between the ages of five and fourteen;

2. The learning of the principles of Christianity, reading, and writing by all children and their receipt of an official completion certificate issued by the teacher, preacher, or inspector;

3. School attendance at least three days a week during periods when children are required to help with farm work;

4. The education of all unmarried young citizens beyond school age, in continuation schools held by the schoolmaster on Sunday;

5. Payment from Church funds for families too poor to pay the tuition;

6. Inspection of all schools in each administrative district by the Lutheran superintendent in charge of that district; and

7. Inspection of individual schools twice a week by the village preacher, who will hold conferences with teachers as to how instruction can be improved.

Rousseau's novel *Emile* had profound effects on the transition of Prussian education from a system controlled and dominated by religion to a secular, state-controlled system. Except for the peasant class, Prussia was a well-read and well-educated society with an organized system of elementary schools.

Under the influence of Rousseau's writings, Johann Bernard Basedow (1724–1790) initiated a popular view that started the development of secularized Prussian schools. Using Johann Comenius' *Orbis sensualium pictus*, the first children's book to match narrative with pictures, as a student critically influenced his views on the education of young children. This approach enabled children, after hearing the story several times, to repeat the story by looking at the pictures.

Basedow stressed the senses as an essential aspect of knowledge acquisition, and the expansion of the learner's experiences as important. He liked to characterize his ideas on education as new and not dependent on the theories and philosophies of others. He based a major portion of his approach on children's play, and on language development as emerging from the natural conversations of children.

Some historians disagree on the extent to which Basedow's reading of Rousseau contributed to this transition, but the fact remains that he was an ardent reader of Rousseau and made it known that he supported his philosophy at a time when Prussia seemed ready for a change in its educational system.

Joining Basedow in his attack on the formalized religious Prussian educational system were Baron von Rochow (1734–1805), who refined teaching methods in rural schools for peasant children, and Christian Wolff, a professor at the University of Halle (1707–1723) who lectured in German—in contrast to the established practice of lecturing in Latin (the sectarian vernacular). After complaints from Wolff's religious colleagues, Frederick William I banished Wolff from the country for his "aesthetic" influence on students.

Some historians claim that the coming to the throne of Frederick the Great, the son of Frederick William I, was the turning point toward educational liberalization in Prussia. Among other things, Frederick the Great did not discourage intellectual confrontations between religious orthodox and reform groups. He recalled Wolff from exile to be chancellor of the University of Halle (1741–1754). These and other liberal acts were major steps toward nonsectarian education in Prussia.

Some historians have suggested that Basedow was too intellectually modest to be considered a main force in this transition. However, during Rousseau's literary attacks on the French education system, it was Basedow who popularized these ideas in Prussia.

In major cities like Hamburg and Altona, and in the academy where he lectured, Basedow condemned the oppressive religious influences on education and general society that were experienced by the ruling classes to some degree, and by the peasants to a greater degree. Within this context, Basedow in 1768 issued a written and spoken appeal, *Address to Philanthropists and Men of Property on Schools and Studies and Their Influence on the Public Weal*. In it he presented two important elements in the public and private debate over education. He called for the establishment of a national council of education and stated that education should be free of religious influence. Basedow's *Address* also included curriculum suggestions taken primarily from the writings of John Locke, Comenius, and Rousseau.

Basedow's appeal received a tremendous public response that brought financial contributions from peasants, the rich, and all religious groups. It seemed that the entire country was ready to free its educational system from the grip of religious control. The funds enabled him to publish manuals on educational curriculum. One of them included a hundred engraved illustrations for teachers of science and nature to follow in teaching children.

Basedow used some of the funds to develop a model school in Dessau, the Philanthropinum, to demonstrate his principles of educational freedom. Some historians have suggested that Basedow was great with start-up ideas but poor with continuing management, and for that reason, his schools did not last very long. It was also reported that the Philanthropinum was treated as a fad and exploited by some to enrich themselves.

By 1774, Basedow had published *The Elementary Work*, consisting of four volumes with over 100 illustrations. A school that followed Basedow's manuals was started by Christian Saltzman (1744–1811), who had taught in Basedow's original school. Saltzman's school was opened in 1784 on a picturesque site of rolling hills, valleys, lakes, and streams. It was a natural setting for nature walks, artistic appreciation, and geographic and geologic studies as described in the writings in Rousseau.

Carl Ritter, whom some credit with the founding of modern geography, was one of Saltzman's first students, and Christoph Frederick Guts Muths, often referred to as the "grandfather" of German gymnastics, was his instructor for recreation and gymnastics.

In Saltzman's school, on a typical day approximately fifty residential students awoke in the early morning, engaged in planting and cultivating, tended to farm animals, ate, spent one hour in formal physical exercise and several hours in games and play, and devoted eight hours to academic studies. These residential schools were primarily for children from wealthy families, but their curriculum soon found its way into schools established for children from peasant families and those of modest means.

Baron von Rochow, owner of large estates, as a result of his service in the Royal Prussian Guard, was a great proponent of holding the poor responsible for their condition because, in his view, they were ignorant and imprudent regarding the economics of life. He believed, however, that their financial circumstances could change through education, and unlike others with such views, he intended to act upon his ideas.

Intrigued by current views concerning education as described by Rousseau and Basedow, Rochow investigated various systems to find a method that might ease the plight of the peasant classes. His search for the best means of enlightening the poor occurred at a time when Basedow was organizing citizens to promote a more liberal education system for Prussian citizens, to be financed through philanthropy. Like many others during that time, he was greatly influenced by Basedow, and he thought what was being discussed could be the system for which he was searching. Rochow read the writings of Basedow, and a short time later published a work of his own that was intended for teachers of peasant children.

Rochow's *A Schoolbook for Country Children, or for Use in Village Schools* was designed for the teachers he hired for a "Basedow"-type school built on one of his estates. The school housed over seventy children in a relaxed environment where teachers and children engaged in Socratic exchanges, and followed a curriculum much like the one found in Saltzman's school. Following academic explorations through methods he described in his published intellectual discussions with Socrates, Plato revealed a means of extending understanding through posing strategic questions designed to elevate thinking. This became known as the Socratic method. In Rochow's school, teachers sought to orient these Socratic discussions toward the practical nature of their students' life experiences.

The education establishment was surprised by the success of Rochow's schools and the social changes they effected in the family life of the children who attended. To advance his influence in other schools, Rochow began to describe his curriculum in books of short stories that used topics describing farming, citizenship, religion and domesticity. Non-Christian groups found offensive his inclusion of Christianity and prayers for children to memorize, and they ridiculed his work as a subterfuge for Christian teaching.

Elementary schools of that period required the memorization of the catechism. This was done to develop memorization skills as well as to teach the content, and the content was supported by schools and teachers. It was viewed in Rochow's schools as a part of moral training rather than theological teaching. His books, *The Peasant's Friend* (1773) and *The Children's Friend* (1776), were in such demand for teacher training that they were provided for teachers, and also given to young children, for the following fifty years.

In 1779 Rochow published *The Improvement of the National Character by Means of Popular Schools*. In this writing he was among the first to propose a national education agency, not merely for the elite and affluent but for all common folk, called Volksschulen. He suggested that Germany lacked a means to project its national character among all citizens, and a national education system could serve such a purpose. Rochow's schools promoted Christian morality which, by the time *Improvement* was published, had became the hallmark of curricula in United States' schools and universities. (Using the national school system to establish a national character was practiced in Germany during the late 1930s during national anti-Jewish campaigns of hate, and eventually led to the Holocaust. There is no evidence that Rochow would have supported such activity.)

After the death of Frederick the Great, and following a suggestion previously made in a speech by Basedow, a central board was created in 1787 to direct all educational affairs. (A similar board had been set up for and by the Lutheran Church in 1771.) The central board was designed to complete the transfer of the power to control common education from the church to the state. In 1794, the Prussian legal code designated schools as state institutions.

This development brought together scholars from all over Germany to complete a published document that was finally issued in 1794. This document, designed to cover fundamental Prussian civil law, had one chapter devoted to education. It decreed that all schools and existing universities were to become state institutions, and new institutions could be founded only with the knowledge and consent of the state. All such institutions were subject to inspection.

Switzerland

The concept that early childhood teaching and learning require approaches different from those of elementary school grades was introduced by Johann Henrich Pestalozzi (1746–1827), a native of Zurich, Switzerland. His influences can still be recognized in Montessori, Emilio Reggio, and the many programs that acknowledge the influence of Jean Piaget and John Dewey. For instance, the idea that hands-on experiences are essential for children's learning is fundamental to the curriculum espoused by Montessori practitioners. Pestalozzi's observation that human learning and development are essentially an internal process was at variance with tabula rasa concepts and with the Lancasterian methods of organizing schools that were prevalent during that time. Pestalozzi created controversies during his time because his approach aligned teaching methods with his child development theory.

Pestalozzi's methods were the first to have a recognizable psychological framework. His teaching methods, which followed the models that display freedom of experience, were revolutionary for their time. Pestalozzi believed that learners needed freedom within a system to advance their own worth and dignity, and that growing children continually make meaning from their environment. It was his view that experiences in an encouraging environment can serve as a rich source for childhood learning, and teachers can best serve learners by expanding their experiences. The knowledge that children acquire, Pestalozzi believed, emerges primarily from their own observations and interpretations of social situations, observing the behaviors of others, and observing relationships between objects and the environment. Controlling learner experiences would, in Pestalozzi's view, inhibit moral, intellectual, and physical development. He suggested that children's acquisition of knowledge flourishes in an environment encouraging freedom rather than control.

Pestalozzi's ideas gained international recognition through his work at an orphanage in Stans, Switzerland. He invested a great deal of his life in his theory of freedom and experience, abandoning careers in law and the ministry, for which he had been educated. In 1774, he converted his farm into a school for children from poor families and refined his ideas about how children learn. Twenty-five years later he founded schools in Burgdorf and Yverden, and this work influenced his reputation as a "pioneer of modern education." Pestalozzi influenced other well-known theorists, many of whom continued his work. He frequently advised philosophers, psychologists, and educators who planned curricula and materials for early education.

THE NINETEENTH CENTURY

Germany

Friedrich Wilhelm August Froebel (1782–1852), born in Thuringia, Germany, continued the work of Pestalozzi in a school that he opened in the little German village of Blankenberg after teaching in one of Pestalozzi's schools. Two years later, in 1839, he called this institution *Kindergarten* (child's garden).

Froebel's early childhood philosophy could be said to have emerged from experiences in his own childhood. His father was an educated member of the clergy, and his mother died soon after his birth. His older brothers were away at the university, and because of his father's career, Frederich was alone during most of his early childhood. By the age of four it was apparent that Frederich did not have a sense of balance that would be expected of a child his age. This may have resulted from a lack of opportunities to run and romp; his father had confined him to the house—because of his clumsiness. Viewing these restrictions as harmful to Frederick's development, his uncle obtained permission to raise Frederick in his home, where he could roam about the home and grounds. Since the contrasts between these environments reveal a critical change from controlled restrictions to freedom of experience in his life, one can understand that these experiences could be critical in helping form Froebel's theory of child development.

At the age of sixteen, Froebel was apprenticed to a forester because of his attraction to the freedom of working outdoors. His teacher allowed him to go his own way in the forests. Later he was sent to Jena as a university student, but had to discontinue because of financial reasons. By the time he was twenty-seven, Froebel had heard about the ideas of Pestalozzi and approached him for a teaching job. He was hired to work in one of Pestalozzi's early schools. The more he learned about Pestalozzi's ideas, the more he thought about the possibilities for preschool children. (Interestingly, although Froebel followed the work of Pestalozzi in developing his kindergarten, it is he, and not Pestalozzi, who is considered the father of the kindergarten movement).

Timing was also on the side of Froebel. He was most active in organizing programs for young children during a period when family life was changing from home and farm family work in small villages to work in coal mines and factories, and urban living. These transitions called for a shift in the roles of family members as they related to a larger society.

When Froebel opened his own kindergarten in Blankenburg, he designed objects for use in the classroom. He called these childhood materials "gifts." Each gift was designed to accommodate Froebel's theoretical approach to kindergarten.

Froebel had to describe his kindergarten and its principles to a population that included many who had ignored early childhood as an important period for learning. In the first two years of his kindergarten's operation, he started to write and disseminate his philosophy concerning activities and popularize the idea of kindergarten. Initially, the Prussian government prohibited the establishment of kindergartens because they were characterized as revolutionary.

Froebel's writings were not always clear to the public, and either he or someone he trained had to describe the practice to new converts. It was not uncommon for someone to be attracted to the ideas as articulated by Froebel, only to be disappointed upon facing children in the classroom setting. In some ways this served as a useful screening device, in that only those who understood the philosophy and practice would remain as kindergartners (the term used for teachers of the young) and their trainers.

One was never sure whether Froebel was describing his philosophy for humanity or his philosophy for early childhood education. His ideas concerning humanity and nature were appropriate for all ages and reflected transcendentalist idealism. His deep religious convictions were more generic than denominational. The symbolism inherent in Froebel's ideas was transformed into practical classroom applications.

An example of the practical side of idealism was that the children freely constructed items from their own experiences without the teacher directing their work toward a project chosen by the teacher. In this free environment, one child might build a battlefield with blocks as bunkers and hills, possibly because books read at home dealt with war and captured his imagination. The teacher would engage the child in a discussion concerning the choice of constructions and battles, and simultaneously enlarge the child's use of language, vocabulary, interests, and concerns. The block-building activity might be followed by an art project, writing, or clay modeling, each with child/teacher and child/child interactions. The free selection of project and subject embodies Froebel's philosophy of "natural" development.

In educational thought today, this is seen as enabling children to experience their own reality. For example, a child in Froebel's classroom might select soldiers and a battlefield (because a book read at home was the reality of his experiences). Today, a child from the housing projects might decide to build a high-rise with a playground. The teacher supports this choice by engaging the child in a conversation concerning the characteristics of her reality.

Froebel's educational thought can be found in the philosophies of Johann Gottlieb Fichte, Immanuel Kant, and Georg Wilhelm Friedrich Hegel. Their ideas sought to identify reality and attempted to locate a practical means by which it could be experienced. They attempted to define the basic relationship between nature and the individual. In their view, the meaning of existence can be found in the compatibility of nature and individuals. Differences that exist are merely subunits "under the umbrella" of the nature/man relationship. Teaching is a means of enabling individuals to understand the relationship between themselves and their environment. This conceptualization has been called the Law of Unity.

Froebel suggested that before children are of kindergarten age, parents should engage them in active play at home, with common household items having the shapes of cylinders, balls, circles, squares, and triangles. No attempt should be made to name these items as such; the labeling—according to Froebel—should be done later, during kindergarten, when the teacher employs systematic methods for introducing related concepts. (These ideas, and materials similar to Froebel's "gifts," were later espoused by Maria Montessori, but she wanted the teacher [directress, in Montessori's words] to control their use in order to promote learning.) Eight basic principles formed the foundation for Froebel's approach to kindergarten teaching and learning:

1. Education of the very young requires that they be assisted in their natural development. This education begins at birth.

2. Earliest education has a direct influence upon the later development of the whole child; therefore, the early years are the most important phase of child development.

3. Physical and emotional development in childhood are not separate entities but are closely integrated.

4. Early education should focus upon physical development and should influence emotional development through the senses.

5. A natural basis for education should be sought through the sense organs and the natural development of their skills through exercises.

6. The natural inclinations of the child are destined to be reasonable in their expression of physical and emotional wants. Education must satisfy both.

7. Education's first attention should be to the limbs through the development of movement.

8. The child's soul is awakened in the beginning through physical impressions. These impressions should be systematically regulated through the work of a caring adult.

Froebel's objects, which he called "gifts" (see Figure 1.1), were designed to support the principles. Variations or replicas of them can be found in early education programs today (prominently in authentic Montessori programs). Some of the more significant gifts are the following:

1. Six different-colored balls constructed from heavy cloth with a string attached to each ball. A frame is provided for hanging the balls (see Figure 1.1.a).

2. A wooden sphere, cube, and cylinder, each two inches in diameter and designed to hang on a frame that is provided (see Figure 1.1b.).

3. A two-inch cube divided into eight one-inch cubes.

4. A two-inch cube divided into eight brick-shaped blocks, each two inches long, one inch wide, and one-half inch thick.

5. A three-inch cube divided into twenty-seven pieces, three of which are divided in half diagonally, and three others into fourths by two diagonal cuts.

6. A three-inch cube divided regularly into thirty-six pieces, eighteen of which are blocks of the same size and shape as those in the fourth gift. Six of the remaining pieces are cut in half. Three others are cut in half lengthwise, making six square prisms.

7. A box of thin, colored cardboard in geometric shapes accompanied with tablets of the same shape and size. This is essentially a matching process that allows the cardboard shapes to be placed in a similar-shaped indented tablet.

8. A collection of square, colored sticks.

Figure 1.1
Froebel's Gifts

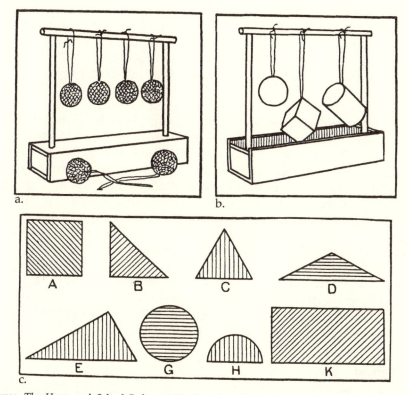

Source: *The Home and School Reference Work*, vol. 9 (Chicago, IL: The Home and School Education Society, 1917), 3228, 3229.

9. A collection of rings made of silver wire cut into quarters and halves.

10. A collection of wood or cardboard triangles and oblongs, gummed paper squares and circles, and colored paper cut into squares for folding projects (see Figure 1.1.c).

Froebel suggested that the child should be encouraged to study one gift at a time. He also recommended child-size furniture; if it was not available, the legs of adult-size tables and chairs could be shortened to make them more suitable for children.

Froebel's gifts, and his approach to developing preschool activities for children, were featured prominently in the kindergartens of the early 1900s, mainly because they were established by practitioners who had studied with Froebel or his followers. It is not unusual that Froebel's materials are common to Montessori programs. There are, however, important differences in the introduction and use of materials. Froebel's gifts are available in classrooms for young children to choose among them. Montessori directresses control the introduction and use of materials for their real-life function, whereas Froebel supported free use of materials for play activities. The Montessori definition of play was incompatible with the views of Pestalozzi, Froebel, and, later, Piaget.

In the United States by 1830, kindergarten supporters were quite familiar with Froebel's theories, the direct influence of his own childhood, his work in Pestalozzi's school, and the indirect influence of Rousseau's philosophy. Publications concerning childhood during this period reflected a gradual change in attitudes toward the behavior of young children, from strict religious expectations to a lessening of that structured conformity. Expectations for child behavior were becoming less harsh as adults acknowledged the possible benefit of play.

The impact of Froebel's theories and Rousseau's philosophy were reflected in writings about child-rearing practices in the United States. To an audience of informed mothers, *The Mother's Book*, written by Lydia Child in 1831, recommended a thoughtful selection and use of toys. An 1835 follow-up, *The Father's Book*, by Theodore Dwight, recommended a greater focus on the improvement of children's toys and games in order to improve their specific potential for learning.

England

In the early 1800s, Pestalozzi's philosophy inspired philanthropic works in England. Among those who were inspired was Robert Owen, who owned a factory inherited from his father, that employed as many as 500 children. He established an infant school in Lanark, Scotland, for children under six, and an elementary school for children seven to twelve. In the evening the mill was turned into a social center that offered education for the adult workers. Within ten years, Owen's Pestalozzi-based model was being visited by observers from all over the country, but within twenty years it had ceased to exist. It was unlikely that other mill owners, reaping huge profits from following capitalistic principles, and municipal authorities would allow socialistic principles to flourish in their midst.

The conflict between socialism and capitalism appears to be the reason for the failure of Owen's American experience. With world recognition of his successful Pestalozzi-designed educational experience in England and Scotland, Owen's enthusiasm for early education brought him to the United States. In 1824, he purchased property along the Wabash River in Indiana and attracted more that two dozen scholars to assist in the

development of an ideal community with an infant school for children
ages 2–5; a middle school for children 6–12; and an evening school for
those who were over 12 (this age group would also be factory workers).

The formation of this exceptional community, New Harmony, was directed by Joseph Neef, a teacher from Pestalozzi's school in Switzerland.
The diversity of the 1,000 members gave rise to various commitments to
assist in community development. Some of the adults became disgrun-
tled and expressed disappointment that equal benefits flowed to all regardless of individual levels of labor. Faced with increasing complaints,
a disenchanted Owen withdrew his support and the community failed.

Pestalozzi's ideas, however, took root in England and in 1824 fostered
the founding of the London Infant School Society (later the Home and
Colonial School Society). The latter group hired a teacher/trainer who
had worked with Pestalozzi to help teach personnel for 150 schools that
were opened in England by 1835.

From this start, the growth of public education in England was slow.
By 1840, in at least one-third of working poor families, were homes
where everyone was illiterate—and their children would grow up illiterate as well. Although England provided for schools at all levels, there
was no centralized, regulated system, and the average length of schooling was two to three years. Reading was the major subject of study,
followed by writing, basic arithmetic, religion, surveying, and occasionally geography.

The United States

Education for Black Children

In 1704 the Society for the Propagation of the Gospel in Foreign Parts
hired a private tutor, Alice Neal, to teach in the first school established
for black children in the United States. Other schools were established
by the society in both Northern and Southern communities to teach an
understanding of the Bible. Black children as young as six and as old as
sixteen attended these schools, but the distinction between early childhood education, elementary education, and secondary education was yet
to be made. The Society of Friends, also known as Quakers, was the most
active group in establishing schools for blacks, as a part of their abolitionist philosophy. In areas where it was not specifically unlawful to
educate blacks, other groups established schools for the teaching of
Christianity.

The first Quaker school for young black children appeared in 1735.
Even though the school operated only one day a week, it was hailed by
abolitionists and condemned by slaveholders, who were supported
by other Christian groups. With Benjamin Franklin's support, Quaker

Figure 1.2
New-York African Free-School, No. 2

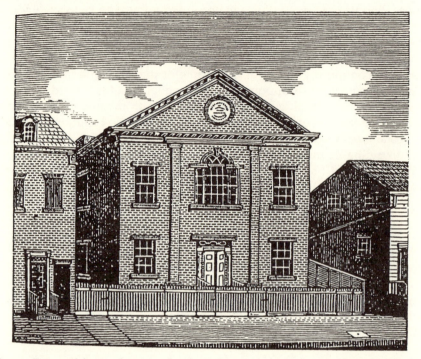

Source: Engraved from a drawing taken by P. Reeson, a thirteen-year-old pupil. C. C. Andrews. *The History of the New-York African Free-Schools* (New York: Negro Universities
Press, 1830, 1969).

groups in Philadelphia and New York City formed the Manumission
Society to ward off gangs of Southern whites who roamed the streets of
Northern cities, kidnapping blacks who would be taken to Southern
plantations. In 1787 the Manumission Society founded the New York
City African Free School to develop an educated black population ca-
pable of taking their rightful place in society after the abolition of slavery
(Figure 1.2).

The New York African Free School hired Cornelius Davis, a white
man, as its first teacher. To raise both funds and worldwide awareness
of its existence, Davis invited dignitaries to visit the school. He was
proud of student performance and anxious to display their work to prospective contributors. The school opened with forty students of various
ages. In 1791 a female teacher was hired for the girls.

The board of trustees consisted of twelve influential whites, including
Alexander Hamilton, one of the authors of the *Federalist Papers*, and John
Jay, one of the framers of the Constitution and the first chief justice of

the United States from 1789 to 1795. Jay had held antislavery views for some time and suggested that slavery diminished the American character. George Clinton, later vice president under Jefferson and Madison, was also a trustee.

The teaching and management system of Joseph Lancaster, adopted for use by the African Free School in 1809, appeared to be an economical means for running the school with its increasing number of pupils.

> Through the space of about twenty years, the school continued to give satisfaction to its friends; the number of scholars varying from forty to sixty, until the year 1809, when the Lancasterian or Monitorial system of instruction was introduced . . . and a teacher was employed, who understood that system, who appeared to feel an interest in the improvement of the children under the care of the Board of Trustees and still continues in their employ. The introduction of this excellent plan produced a very favorable change in the school, and in its affairs generally; the number of pupils soon increased, and their order and general decorum became objects of favorable remark, even among those who had previously been in the habit of placing but little to their credit. (Andrews 1830, pp. 17–18)

The Lancasterian system enabled a single teacher, through the use of older students in a monitor system to look after groups of ten to twelve students, to oversee more than 100 children. The monitorial system was not a new idea; the Brothers of Common Light were the first to use it, and Jesuit groups utilized similar systems. In a common version of the system, monitors took charge of all routine matters like recording attendance, assigning new students to proper class placement, and taking charge of slates and books. They were also responsible for other matters according to their abilities: direct instruction, examining and promoting, finding out the reason for a pupil's absence, and tracking books and supplies. In a well-organized Lancaster system, teachers had little to do. Early childhood educators of the time were severely critical of the militaristic manner in which children were constrained and herded from one group activity to another. Some children at an early childhood age did occasionally demonstrate benefits derived from the Lancaster system. A seven-year-old pupil at the African Free School made the following presentation to a group of visitors:

> I am just seven years old, and I think I have learned considerable since last examination. I was then entirely ignorant of writing; I now present you with these humble specimens of my attainments

in that art. I was then also unacquainted with the use of figures; I have since gone through simple addition, subtraction, multiplication, and division; I have some knowledge also of the compound rules. I say not these things to magnify my little self into something great, but in the credit of the Lancasterian plan of instruction, and for the encouragement of all my little school-mates to improve the time while they have the advantage of an early education. (Andrews 1830, p. 44)

Lancaster described his monitorial system in his book *Improvements in Education* (London, 1803). After schools in the United States adopted this system in varying degrees, he published *The Lancaster System of Education with Improvements*. It became apparent that Lancaster's methods involved much more than a system of monitors. Following the details in Lancaster manuals, one could organize, under the management of a single trained teacher, a well-organized school for as many as 800 children.

In November 1817, a letter to the editors of the *Atlantic Monthly Magazine and Critical Review* appeared concerning the African Free School.

Messrs. Editors,

Permit me through the medium of your valuable Miscellany, to express the pleasure which I lately experienced at the annual examination of the African Free School of this city. The subject of education has excited so much enlightened curiosity of late years, that, so far as the general theory is concerned, little seems to have been mistaken or overlooked. The more practical spirit of modern metaphysical philosophy, has laid the ground work of the improvements in the plans of education, and the freer institutions, and intelligent public spirit of modern society, have given opportunity for common sense and philanthropy to execute their favorite designs for the benefit of the community, by the more careful and thorough disciplines and instruction of the lower orders.

It would be superfluous, at this time to enter into an exposition of the principles of the Lancasterian system, or undertake a detail of its advantages; if these were necessary, one attendance at the annual examination of the African Free School of New-York, would speak more than volumes on this subject. At the visit which I made, I saw enough to convince the most skeptical, that the colored race is abundantly endued by nature with every intellectual and moral faculty, and capable of repeating the most assiduous culture. Indeed if my eyes had not told me otherwise, I should have thought myself in one of the best regulated and best taught schools, composed of the fairest hued children in the land. (Andrews 1830, pp. 48–49)

Figure 1.3
The Daily Intelligencer (Washington, D.C.), August 18, 1818

A SCHOOL,

FOUNDED by an association of free people of color of the city of Washington, called the " Resolute Beneficial Society," situate near the Eastern publc school, and the dwelling of Mrs. Fenwick, is now open for the reception of children of free people of color, and others that ladies or gentlemen may think proper to send, to be instructed in reading, writing. arithmetic, English grammar, or other branches of education, applicable to their capacities, by a steady, active and experienced teacher, whose attention is wholly devoted to the purposes described. It is presumed, that free colored families will embrace the advantages thus presented to them, either by subscribing to the funds of the society, or by sending their children to the school; the terms in either case being remarkably moderate. An improvement of the intellect and morals of colored youth being the leading object of this institution, the patronage of benevolent ladies and gentlemen; by donation or subscription, is humbly solicited in aid of the fund——the demanas thereon being heavy, and the means at present much too limited. For the satisfaction of the public, the constitution and articles of association are printed and published. And, to avoid disagreeable occurrences, no writings are to be done by the teacher for a slave, neither directly nor induectly to serve the purposes of a slave, on any account whatsoever. Further particulars may be known, by applying to any of the undersigned officers:

WILLIAM COSTIN, President.
GEORGE HICKS, Vice President.
JAMES HARRIS, Secretary.
GEORGE BELL, Treasurer.
ARCHIBALD JOHNSON, Marshal.
FRED. LEWIS, Chairman of the Com.
ISAAC JOHNSON, ⎱ Committee.
SCIPIO BEENS, ⎰

N. B. An evening school will commence on the premises, on the first Monday in October, and continue throughout the season.

☞The managers of Sunday schools in the Eastern District, are thus most dutifully and respectfully informed, that on Sabbath days the school-house belonging to this society, if required, for the tuition of colored youth, will be uniformly at their service.

Prominent African Free School graduates included Martin DeLaney, who went on to graduate from Harvard Medical School in 1852; Ira Aldridge, who became an acclaimed Shakespearean actor on the European stage; James McCune Smith, a graduate of the University of Glasgow Medical School, who became the first black pharmacist (and later director of the Colored Orphan Asylum in New York City); and John B. Russwurm, who went on to graduate from Bowdoin College in Maine and become editor of *Freedom's Journal*, one of the first black newspapers in the United States.

In 1807 three remarkable black men—George Bell, Nicholas Franklin, and Moses Liverpool—who could neither read nor write founded a school for free black children in Washington, D.C., and hired a white teacher. The political climate, and the fact that most blacks in Washington were slaves, required great imagination and ingenuity to create such a school. The founders advertised that the school would not admit any black child from a slave family who did not have the consent of the person who owned the slave. The school survived a few years in a city with thousands of blacks—only 500 of whom were free.

After several years as educational innovators in a city with few who could pay for their services, the men reopened their school in 1818 with a new means of financing their endeavors. Their new approach started with the formation of a foundation that appealed to affluent blacks and whites to support a school for young free blacks. A widely read newspaper of the time printed an article describing their appeal (Figure 1.3).

In 1829, a black woman named Annie Marie Hall, from Prince Georges County, Maryland, opened a school for black children in an area of the District of Columbia now known as Capitol Hill. Hall, as a free black, had attended an integrated school in Alexandria, Virginia, where she received a traditional education. The death of her husband left her with little income and she needed to provide for her small children. After several years on Capitol Hill, she moved her school to A Street. Its graduates went on to other schools, and as adults became successful teachers, lawyers, and other professionals.

Members of the Society of Friends (Quakers) continued to open schools for black Americans in conjunction with their manumission work and the education of a black population prepared to promote their own interests in a free society.

After the Civil War and the abolition of slavery, Quakers continued to establish schools for blacks. *The American Freedman*, a publication of the Freedman's Union Commission, reported the work of the commission to the public and dealt with public perception that occasionally the benefits flowing to ex-slaves placed them in a position superior to that of poor whites. The commission was founded to focus on equal rights as they enabled the recovery of the South from the Civil War. An important report appeared in the February 1867 issue of *The American Freedman* regarding the work of Quakers in cooperating with the work of the commission.

Philadelphia Institute for Colored Youth

Among the various influences which have combined to bring about the present meliorated state of public feeling, in this country, toward the colored people, none has been more potent than that exerted by the above named institution, Before the schools of Port Royal were even dreamed of, and, of course, before the other freedmen's schools, which the success of the Port Royal experiment brought into existence, had commenced their demonstrations, "the Institute for Colored Youth," in Lombard Street, in Philadelphia, had furnished ocular proof to thousands of skeptical whites of the capacity and educational susceptibility of the colored people.

Rarely have requests been more wisely made, or more judiciously administered, than those made by Richard Humphrey and Jonathan Zane, and administered by Marmaduke Cope, Thomas Wister, Benjamin Coates, and the rest of "thirty persons," members of the Society of Friends, who constituted themselves an association or board, for this purpose. The facts are these:

In 1832, Richard Humphrey died, leaving $10,000 for the "education of colored youth in a school of learning, in order to prepare and fit them to act as teachers." In 1844, Jonathan Zane died, leaving $18,000 for a similar purpose. Other small legacies were left, to take the same direction; the whole constituting a fund of about $30,000. The money was variously and usefully employed, in the line of its purpose, until 1851, when the school building was erected in Lombard Street, Philadelphia, and a school opened in it in 1852, which has been from that time to this a successful operation. (*The American Freedman*, February 1867, p. 165)

Philadelphia Institute for Colored Youth. The Philadelphia Institute for Colored Youth hired black teachers, who were well educated for their time, to teach black youth who aspired to become teachers of other blacks. Two of the institute's first teachers graduated from Oberlin College in Ohio. Several others completed their work at the New York African Free School. In 1902, the institute moved several miles from the city and opened as the Cheyney Training School for Teachers. In 1925, Cheyney became a Pennsylvania state institution, and in the 1990s it survives as Cheyney University, the oldest institution of black higher education in the United States. Its primary mission remains teacher education.

During the Reconstruction period there was a great deal of activity among educators and social planners to assist the South in its recovery.

In 1865, the U.S. Congress had established the Freedmen's Bureau, officially known as the Bureau of Refugees, Freedmen, and Abandoned Lands. Following the war, a poorly organized group of government workers and a justice system that was slow to act created problems for volunteers and those appointed to aid with reforms in the South.

The work of the Bureau of Refugees, Freedmen, and Abandoned Lands—to promote basic education and provide for the safety and welfare of black and white citizens in the South—actually commenced in 1862. In an area of the country where blacks had been considered property, this mission did not endear them to the white population. The commission's constitution directed that its paid workers and volunteers should "aid and cooperate with the people of the South without distinction of race or color, in the improvement of their condition upon the basis of industry, education, freedom, and Christian morality."

> The first public effort for the relief of freedmen, was in February 1862. At that time the Proclamation of Emancipation had been issued. Those of Generals Freemont and Hunter had been rescinded. In spite of an act of Congress, runaway negroes were frequently returned to their rebel masters. In other instances they were refused admission within the army lines. The influence of the Border States was still predominant. The fiction of a divided South whom emancipation would unite was not yet dispelled. The emancipation of the negro was demanded by a few; earnestly deprecated by many. (*The American Freedman*, November 1866, p. 117)

In 1862, General Thomas Sherman and Commodore Samuel Dupont made a special appeal to Congress for the implementation of legislation, and to Northern citizens to increase their volunteerism. A short time later organizations started forming in the North and began to take names of those who were willing to volunteer in the South. For example, the Contraband Relief Organization was founded in Cincinnati, and in Chicago, the Northwestern Freedman's Aid Commission was established. Following public meetings in New York, Boston, and Philadelphia, similar organizations were invigorated. In the initial stages, the scope of the work was not fully understood, but groups were responding to articles in *The American Freedman*. One of them suggested:

> Horseless, naked, unfed, without homes, opportunities of industry, or means of support, the most pressing demand was for immediate physical relief. But in this inception of the enterprise far-sighted men perceived the deeper needs and more permanent work. They proposed not to support the negro, but to render him self supporting; to help him for the moment; to provide him means of self-

support; to give him tools, land, and the opportunity of labor; but, above all, to send him the teacher and the school-book; these were the objects proposed by the founders of this work. (November 1866, p. 117)

The commission requested volunteers from Northern communities to go to the South as teachers, and the response from competent blacks and whites was more than sufficient. Volunteers went into communities where black populations were living in overcrowded shacks, and many families, as well as children, were wandering and homeless. The volunteers reported to offices set up to aid in the transition and assumed tasks related to teaching as well as chores necessary to stabilize a population long enough to establish a school. They assisted with clearing ground, construction, food preparation, and serving health needs.

Charlotte Forten, one of few black women who answered the call for volunteer teachers, wrote about her experiences with volunteers and the children they served in a two-part article published in the *Atlantic Monthly* in 1864. She described their fears, the dangerous environment in which they all lived, and the eagerness of black children to learn.

It was on the afternoon of a warm, murky day late in October that our steamer, the *United States*, touched the landing at Hilton Head. A motley assemblage had collected on the wharf,—officers, soldiers, and "contrabands" of every size and hue: black was, however, the prevailing color. The first view of Hilton Head is desolate enough,—a long, low, sandy point, stretching out into the sea, with no visible dwellings upon it, except the rows of small white-roofed houses which have lately been built for the freed people. . . . Little colored children of every hue were playing about the streets looking as merry and happy as children ought to look,—now that the evil shadow of Slavery no longer hangs over them. Some of the officers we met did not impress us favorably. They talked flippantly, and sneeringly of the negroes, whom they found we had come down to teach, using an epithet more offensive than gentlemanly. They assured us that there was great danger of Rebel attacks, that the yellow fever prevailed to an alarming extent, and that, indeed, the manufacture of coffins was the only business that was flourishing at present. (1864, pp. 587–588)

Born into an affluent black family in Philadelphia, Charlotte Forten (1837–1914) graduated from the Higginson Grammar School in Salem, Massachusetts, and completed one year of teacher training at the Salem Normal School. Her father, a member of the Anti Slavery Society, was active in the abolitionist movement. John Greenleaf Whittier encouraged Charlotte to volunteer to teach the newly freed citizens.

The bureau made it clear in local newspaper reports and descriptions in their newsletters that because of limited funds—the support of the local military and of cooperative Southerners—its monetary assistance to communities that wanted to establish schools where none previously existed was modest. In a country where few people in need of help could read newspapers, rumors of the extent to which the bureau could be helpful exaggerated its resources. In its publication, *The American Freedman*, the commission found it necessary to make clear its role in helping communities build new schools. The following instructions were published in *The American Freedman Journal*.

When a school is wanted in a village or neighborhood, let the people organize themselves into a school society. They may then get a school-house as well as a school by taking hold with energy. They may go to work in this way:

1. Call a public meeting of all persons interested, without distinction of race, color, or former condition, and let the notice go widely circulated beforehand.

2. Secure good speakers so as to have the object of the meeting, and the benefits to be derived, ably set forth; so what the people should do, and what the Bureau may do to aid them.

3. What will be expected of the people is this: After organizing their society, they should secure, by gift or purchase, the perfect title to a lot of land, of not less than one acre, to be held by the board of trustees for school purposes. They should next secure good pledges of labor, and money enough to provide for all the work required in the erection of the building, fences, grading the lot, etc.

4. The Bureau makes no pledges in advance in any case. The Assistant Commissioner has some funds to use in the erection of school-houses, and desires to spend the money so as to extend the greatest good to the greatest number. He will generally endeavor to supply all the lumber, nails, etc., needed for the construction of the building.

5. No funds will be expended on private estates, nor on property of doubtful title. The land must be held by the Trustees, as before stated, and the title be perfect in them. Evidence of this must accompany each application to secure attention at headquarters.

6. Every application must stand upon its own merits, and will be acted upon according to its deserts, and the ability of the Bureau to aid at the time.

7. The people should understand distinctly that the Bureau is only acting as a friend to help them make the start in the right direction. They must rely upon themselves for every thing they can. In making the application the following terms, in addition to the above, must be complied with:

8. The lot for the school-house should be centrally located, so as to accommodate those who should attend. It must be in a pleasant, quiet, retired, dry but not dusty, airy, and healthy situation. Shade and ornamental trees and shrubbery must be planted from time to time in and around the school lot. Especially must privies be provided in separate yards for boys and girls, not less than one hundred feet distance from the school-house. Also, a well or cistern on the lot, unless there is good water nearby to which access may be had. The ability of the people to support a teacher, wholly or in part, and to provide books, should be stated. (September 1867, p. 277)

The idea of self-help was reinforced in a variety of ways for blacks after the Civil War. Modest help could be expected from the commission only if communities initiated the work of residents as school trustees according to the above-cited rules of the commission.

The circumstances surrounding local government assistance for free public education in the South for free blacks were described in the following communication to the Freedmen's Bureau from its representative in Georgia, Captain J. E. Bryant. It was printed in *The American Freedman* and is thought to depict conditions throughout the South.

It is evident that the ruling class at the South will not provide for the education of the freedman. A law has been enacted recently by the Georgia Legislature establishing a system of common schools for white children only. The bill provides who may be scholars as follows: "That any free white inhabitant, being a citizen of the United States and of this State, and residing within the limits of any county or school district, organized under this act, between the ages of six and twenty-one years, shall be entitled to the instruction in the Georgia schools in said county or district, without charge of tuition or incidental expenses." The laws of Georgia are, we believe, as liberal as any of those of Southern States. It is evident, therefore, that the work of educating the freedmen must now be undertaken by others besides the ruling class of the South. The Northern educational associations do not, we believe, propose to establish schools in every county and neighborhood at the South; but they propose to establish first-class schools at the central and important points, schools that shall be models. "Then when these states come to establish a system of their own, they will find one furnished to their hands, and a much better one than they would ever or could ever have provided." It is estimated that some 90,000 persons at the South have been taught by various missionary and denominational societies. When we remember that four millions of colored persons and other millions of white persons there are ignorant, the work already done seems small. There are in Georgia 131 counties. Schools have been established by northern associations in less than 15 counties, and yet quite as much, we believe, has been done in Georgia as in most of the Southern States. We cannot expect that the northern societies will do much more this year than they did last. It is, therefore, evident that the great mass of colored people at the South must remain in ignorance unless they assist in their own education. (February 1867, pp. 171–172)

Education of White Children

Among several creative endeavors to develop early education in the United States was an important one by Robert Owen in the first half of the nineteenth century. The little town of New Harmony in Indiana was founded in 1814 by George Rapp as an experiment in Utopian living. By 1824, the "Rappites," or "Harmonists" as they were sometimes called, sold their community to Robert Owen, Pestalozzian admirer, and William Maclure, a wealthy Scot. It was to be their site for a "New Moral World" and "Community of Equality," surrounding common folk with "people of exceptional knowledge."

Among the original settlers, the people of exceptional knowledge included John Chappelsmith, artist; French naturalist Charles A. Lesueur; Samuel Chase and his wife, Martha, teachers of chemistry; Marie Fretageot, a progressive educator, and her son, Achille; American zoologist, Thomas Say; agriculturist William Price, and his wife; John Spaakman, pharmacist; Joseph Neef, Pestalozzian educator, recruited to run the schools; Gerald Troost, geologist and physician; Cornelius Tiebolt, engraver; Frances Wright, social activist for women's rights; Stedman Whitwell, architect; and Phiquepal d'Arusmont, teacher. This group was joined by friends, relatives, and promising students and totaled approximately thirty people who traveled on a large boat up the Ohio River to the Wabash River and into the town of New Harmony, Indiana. Maclure financed the building of a large boat in Pittsburgh to carry passengers and crew up the Ohio River and on to the Wabash. Called the "Boatload of Knowledge" by journalists of the time, Maclure named the boat "The Philanthropist."

Records are not clear as to whether Joseph Neef, the teacher who employed Pestollizzi methods, came with the original group or traveled from his native Kentucky, arriving at about the same time. In 1826, Neef and Maclure organized the New Harmony school system into three divisions—an infant school for boys and girls ages 2 through 5; a middle school for boys and girls ages 6 to 12; and an adult evening school for persons over the age of 12. Following the principles of Pestalozzi and progressive education, Neef taught classes and supervised the boys and Marie Fretageot taught classes and supervised the girls. Phiquepal d' Arusmont, Lesueur, Say, and Troost taught in the subjects for which they were noted.

By 1826 the school system was well organized and operating. This cannot be said for the rest of the community. Robert Owen decided not to reside in New Harmony, and original residents were somewhat resentful of new arrivals who appeared to relocate in New Harmony primarily for its benefits after the hard work of establishing the community was done.

Maclure and Owen's philosophical disagreements concerning the social direction of New Harmony ultimately led to Owen selling out and returning to England. The site exists as a state memorial center, and some descendants of the original New Harmony settlers remain in nearby communities.

It remains today as a reminder that the first kindergarten (1826) and the first infant school (1826) in the United States were founded at New Harmony, Indiana. Owen's four sons and daughter remained in the United States and became notable in their own right. Richard Owen was the first president of Purdue University, David Dale Owen became a geologist, and William Owen was an author.

Historically in the United States children were viewed as a church and/or family responsibility. Children born to poor families were raised by the family, abandoned to institutions for the poor, or cast into the street. This was also the fate of many unwanted children, some who were mentally or physically disabled. For these children, modest aid was available from philanthropic organizations and the church, and little from the state. It was within this context of social and political individualism that public schools in the United States emerged. After 1820, in many states of the northern United States, people started to vote for taxation to support public schools. It was considered unwise for black families to send their children to these schools because tax-supported schools were viewed as institutions for paupers. Abolitionists thought it would jeopardize their fight to outlaw slavery if free black children were viewed as burdens to the state.

Education in the United States closely followed the philosophy of the Englishman John Locke. The American version of Locke's thought had its own Calvinistic and other religious practices and interpretations. In the 1830s, Bronson Alcott, an American transcendental philosopher, put forward views influenced by Rousseau's romanticism. Many transcendentalists, including Alcott, had grown up on farms where children were welcomed as workers to assist with never-ending chores. There were few labor laws to protect children from long working hours and other forms of exploitation.

The transcendentalists worked for a childhood that was free of exploitation and materialism, and defined childhood as saintly. This was at great variance with the Calvinist philosophy, which viewed humans as born in sin, and childhood as being the period closest to this condition of depravity. Calvinists placed the burden on parents to raise children in a strict religious manner in order to relieve them of original sin.

The transcendentalists did not intend their free "common school" (like the European model) to be a school for common folk, but rather to be a "common" school that would eliminate distinctions. They proposed a common educational experience that would eliminate racial, ethnic, and social labels. Such schools would provide, free for all children, an educational experience that engendered a sense of a community, civic pride, and morality.

In 1848, during a period when new perspectives concerning play in childhood were being popularized, Horace Bushnell, a minister in Hartford, Connecticut, published several of his sermons and some thoughts concerning Christian education as *Views of Christian Nurture*. His works showed similarities to the views of John Comenius (the Moravian minister and educational philosopher who wrote about family life and education in the 1600s) and Rousseau's *Emile* (in the 1700s). Comenius sought to integrate thought about education with a religious family life. Rousseau pleaded for a less harsh environment in which children were allowed to develop—in an environment that, in his view, was more natural for childhood. From this perspective, play in childhood was proposed as a natural phase of human development.

Bushnell counseled that play through self-selection was a perfect childhood activity. His view of the symbolic nature of play parallels descriptions of this activity offered by Frederick Froebel that swept the kindergarten movement in the United States sixty years later. Bushnell was addressing an American population of the 1830s that was concerned about the "idleness of childhood," which left young children vulnerable to the devil. It feared that activity not directed by adults would allow children to succumb to their devious nature that being "born in sin" left them with. It was also important to family members that children, as soon as they were physically able, share in the arduous chores of farm life.

Being a recognized minister, Bushnell articulated his views concerning the essential value of play in a manner that made the idea of play acceptable to an informed Christian population. He was among the first to call children's play "work," an analogy still used in the 1990s. Like Comenius, Rousseau, Pestalozzi, and Froebel, Bushnell supported a free flow of childhood experiences without adult interference. He suggested that childhood experiences that were allowed to occur could be shaped by adults without undue restrictions, but he did not believe that children should be left completely alone, to be observed by adults in the Rousseau tradition. He also did not perceive original sin as a lingering factor; in his view, infancy was free of any overwhelming tendencies to sin and was ripe for the moral and civic influences of caring parents.

In 1855, Margarethe Meyer Schurz (1832–1876), a German immigrant who had studied with Froebel, opened the first school for children that was called "kindergarten" in the United States in Watertown, Wisconsin. It is often not considered the first kindergarten in the United States because the children were taught in German. Elizabeth Peabody (1804–1894), inspired by Schurz, is frequently credited with starting the first kindergarten in the United States (in Boston in 1860) because it was the first kindergarten taught in English. It was Joseph Neef, William Maclure, and Robert Owen, however, who established the first school for kindergarten-aged children in New Harmony, Indiana, in 1826. Throughout her career, Peabody was a proponent of Froebel's infant education philosophy, a transcendentalist, and a major figure in the establishment of public kindergartens in the United States.

Peabody raised funds to support the free kindergarten movement, gave lectures, and edited *The Kindergarten Messenger*. In 1863, she and her sister, Mary Tyler Mann, wrote *Guide to the Kindergarten and Moral Culture of Infancy*. It was considered the authoritative publication on the theory, philosophy, and methods of the kindergarten movement through the 1890s. Peabody also published a series of teacher guides and historical treatises that reflected her transcendental philosophy.

Elizabeth, her two sisters, and her brother were born in Billerica, Massachusetts. Her Harvard-educated father had been a teacher at the Phillips Andover Academy, and her mother, Elizabeth Palmer, was the head mistress at North Andover Seminary for Young Ladies. The Peabody children attended a school founded by their mother in Salem, Massachusetts. Elizabeth, an outstanding student, was encouraged to study Greek with Ralph Waldo Emerson and philosophy and history with William Ellery Channing. It is believed that their influence encouraged her to embrace transcendentalism.

By the age of fourteen, Elizabeth was assisting in her mother's school, and at the age of sixteen, she had her own class of young learners. After teaching in several schools in Maine and Massachusetts, in 1825 Elizabeth and her sister Mary founded the Beacon Hill School in Boston. In 1860, she opened a kindergarten in Boston.

As more children started attended her kindergarten, Peabody realized the need for higher-quality programming and a broader imagination to keep such an enterprise lively and productive. These demands became too much for her and her small staff to sustain over time, and it became obvious to her that she needed further instruction. She eventually closed her kindergarten in Boston and moved to Germany for further study.

The kindergarten movement began to grow rapidly. At first kindergartens were private. Matilde Kriege, a student of Baroness von Marenholtz-Bulow, and her daughter, Alma Kriege, were invited by Peabody, during her German visit, to join the staff of the Pinckney Street Kindergarten in Boston. The Krieges opened their own kindergarten in Boston in 1868, and one was founded about 1873 by Maria Kraus-Boelté in New York City for children from affluent families. Elizabeth Peabody was a staunch supporter of the Krieges' kindergarten and raised funds by giving lectures on transcendentalism and other philosophical topics. Also in the 1870s, Pauline Agassiz Shaw financed thirty-one kindergartens throughout the Boston area.

In the South, Susan Pollock opened the first kindergarten for young white children in Washington, D.C., in 1870. Susan was brought to the kindergarten movement through the influence of her mother, Louise, who initially was influenced by her reading of *Moral Culture in Infancy and Kindergarten Guide* by Elizabeth Peabody and Mary Mann.

Maria Boelté, a student of Froebel, married John Kraus, an intellectual in his own right. They were encouraged by Peabody to bring their imagination for kindergarten and their Froebel knowledge to the United States. From an inspiring lecture by Peabody in Chicago, Alice Putnam was attracted to the kindergarten movement because of her young daughter's education and her enthusiasm with Peabody's work. Peabody inspired Putnam to study kindergarten education with Susan Blow. These studies were followed with advanced work with Maria Boelté-Kraus. In 1874 Putnam opened a private kindergarten for children from wealthy families in Chicago.

. In 1873, near St. Louis, Susan Blow (1843–1916) opened the first kindergarten in a public school system. It was housed, at no cost, in a room in a public school, on a trial basis. Susan Blow was a strong supporter of Froebel's methods. She had grown up in an affluent family; her father had served as U.S. minister to Venezuela, minister to Brazil under President Grant, and later a commissioner of the District of Columbia. She spent a privileged childhood in the St. Louis suburbs. Her teaching experience started as a paid teacher of Sunday school classes, an occupation that was common for well-to-do Christian women of her time. By middle life, however, she could not resolve differences between the philosophical literature to which she was exposed and the limited freedom allowed women in her Presbyterian faith. She joined the Episcopal Church in search of a more liberal view of what women could accomplish.

Her awareness of the German kindergarten movement led Blow to seek training from one of Froebel's teachers in New York, Maria Kraus-Boelté. After spending time in New York, she returned to her home in Carondelet, a suburb of St. Louis, and sought William T. Harris' assistance in acquiring space in a public grade school. Harris, a well-read educator who was aware of the kindergarten movement, provided the facilities that Blow requested; thereby the first kindergarten in a public school was opened in the Des Peres School in Carondelet. Blow taught in the kindergarten and trained new teachers. Among the first were Mary Timberlake, a primary grades teacher eager to learn kindergarten methods; Cynthia P. Dozier, a New York-trained kindergartner; and Sally Shawk, a local teacher. Their vision for this merger to introduce the philosophy of Frederic Froebel to grade-school teachers met with great disappointment; the St. Louis public school system appointed an elementary-trained teacher to supervise their kindergartens. The complete story is detailed in Chapter 7.

In San Francisco between 1880 and 1885, John Swett, superintendent of public schools established two experimental kindergartens. By 1886 Swett established kindergartens as an official part of the San Francisco public school system.

Following the theories of Froebel and her own training under Kraus-Boelté, Susan Blow planned a training curriculum that consisted of "mother-play" songs accompanied by music, versions of Froebel's gifts and occupations, and stories from Greek myths, Shakespeare, Dante, and Faust.

Blow was a pioneer in establishing mothers' meetings (precursors of parent-teacher associations), trips to cultural sites by pupils and teachers, planting gardens, and homework. In 1874 she moved to Boston, the center of kindergarten philanthropy, antislavery, and women's suffrage activities. There was also an emerging group of writers and intellectuals who were active in studying and practicing transcendental philosophy.

Under the leadership of William N. Hailmann, kindergarten was added to a regular grade school in 1874. As superintendent of schools in LaPorte, Indiana, from 1883 to 1894, he established public kindergartens in LaPorte in 1888. Eudora Hailmann, his wife, conducted a training school for kindergarten teachers in LaPorte from 1885 to 1894. The public was made more aware of the kindergarten movement at the Centennial Exposition in 1876. There the public was able to observe a model kindergarten conducted by Ruth Burritt. The pupils were eighteen children from a Pennsylvania orphanage, the Home for Friendless Children.

Using Froebel's methods and Milton Bradley products, Burritt conducted a full day of kindergarten activities with a break for lunch. The Milton Bradley Company was invited to demonstrate its line of Froebel's gifts. Featured were building blocks that, it was claimed, had educational value that turned many wasted childhood hours of boredom into hours of intellectual stimulation. Ernst Steiger, another retailer of children's toys, joined over twenty other toy exhibitors promoting kindergarten materials, maps, and globes. Steiger owned a New York publishing company and had been encouraged by Elizabeth Peabody to publish materials related to early schooling.

The Milton Bradley Company, which had earned a reputation as a supplier of educational materials to schools and parents, also exhibited materials with more direct teaching potential; Sentence Builder, Language Tablet, and Word Builder. To retain its claim as original suppliers of Froebelian materials, they marketed The Original Kindergarten Alphabet and Kindergarten Blocks.

Bradley and Steiger passed out written materials at their Centennial exhibits, both claiming the endorsement of leaders in the kindergarten movement. Bradley claimed the endorsement of Peabody and Kriege, and Steiger noted that Maria Kraus-Boelté and other well-known Froebelians demonstrated the ease with which gifts and occupations could be used by parents with their young children. This marketing strategy was aimed at easing the anxiety of parents who were reluctant to turn their children over to an institution at such an early age. They were thought to look more favorably upon exposing their children to kindergarten "gifts and occupations" at home. Encouraging home teaching by informed parents significantly expanded the market.

By now, there were several factions of the kindergarten movement in the United States; one major division was between those who concentrated on classroom curriculum (German and U.S. versions of Froebel) and those who focused on kindergarten as a way to rescue children from poverty. Without a national consensus, the Froebel Society of Boston and Elizabeth Peabody shared in the promotion, planning, and fund-raising necessary to maintain the exhibit.

Publications and reporters hailed the model kindergarten a great success. Peabody believed that the Centennial kindergarten would stimulate American mothers to organize neighborhood study groups and parents' unions as a forum for parent involvement in the movement. She dedicated a journal that she edited, *The Kindergarten Messenger*, to the cause. When the exposition closed in 1877, Susan Blow, who managed one of the kindergarten displays, was invited by school authorities to start a kindergarten in Philadelphia.

Alice Harvey Whiting Putnam (1841–1919) was educated by tutors in her home in Chicago. Her interest in kindergarten was kindled by one of Elizabeth Peabody's lectures about the virtues of early education. Her enthusiasm led her to organize a group of parents to discuss the merits of Froebel's principles. From this group, Putnam founded the Chicago Kindergarten Club (1883); it met regularly to stimulate interest in the kindergarten movement.

Putnam's enthusiasm for more knowledge about early childhood encouraged her to enroll in a training school in Columbus, Ohio, that was founded by Anna J. Ogden for the purpose of educating kindergarten teachers. Returning to Chicago after two years, Putnam opened the first kindergarten in her home. This program formed the basis for her opening a "pioneering school" for the teaching of young women who wished to enter the early childhood profession.

During this endeavor, Putnam became associated with Elizabeth Harrison, the director of the Cook County Normal School. In 1890, Putnam became president of the Chicago Kindergarten Club, and president of the International Kindergarten Union in 1901. Harrison and Putnam together founded the Froebel Kindergarten Association, which was granted permission to open the first kindergarten in public schools in Chicago in the Brennan School (1886). This led to the gradual opening of other kindergarten classes in Chicago's public schools.

For a considerable period of time, the most important work for sponsors of the kindergarten movement was giving talks to interested groups, fund-raising, and being active in various communities—not classroom teaching.

It was not until almost 1900 that the general public viewed kindergarten as belonging in regular schooling. Prior to that it was thought of as the work of neighborhood settlement houses, church missions, and other philanthropic institutions that served impoverished families. Some even viewed it as a child-care opportunity for wealthy families. However, there were informed parents who bought kindergarten materials from companies like Milton Bradley to teach their children at home. Maria Montessori, coming to the United States in 1913 to give public talks, further advanced the parent's role in teaching young children.

By 1870, William T. Harris (who later became the U.S. commissioner of education), as superintendent of St. Louis schools, started grouping children in that city in grades 1 through 12. This arrangement had originated in 1850 with Henry Barnard, who had been head of the Connecticut state education system and was then chancellor of the University of Wisconsin in 1858. In 1854, after visiting the kindergarten of Berthe Meyer Ronge in London and seeing a demonstration of Froebel's methods and "gifts," Barnard was convinced that the kindergarten philosophy opened educational thought to the most original and sound perception of early child development. He regarded Froebel's as the most vital of all philosophies of education—by far the most original, attractive, and philosophical form of infant development the world had yet seen.

Earlier, despite efforts to prevent an organized state system of free education in Rhode Island, several oratory events staged by Barnard convinced a previously reluctant legislature to hire him to organize such a system.

After becoming U.S. commissioner of education in 1867, Barnard reported to Congress in 1869 that the District of Columbia should be among the municipalities to provide early education for the "play period of childhood," and that "all children should have a kindergarten experience." He was among the first to propose that kindergarten should be a part of the graded educational systems provided by states. In the late 1880s, he published a complete encyclopedia of child culture and development intended for teachers and parents. He published philosophical papers for distribution among teachers, community leaders, and the legislature entitled *Papers for Teachers*. Barnard drafted the first laws for free public schools, promoted equal education for females and males, proposed the first teachers' organization, and established the first state system of public libraries.

During the early days of the kindergarten movement, pupils in the few private kindergartens were from well-off families, primarily because they had the money, but also because the parents were inspired by philanthropists who were often their business colleagues or friends. These philanthropists were actively seeking subsidized kindergarten services for children from poor families.

One essential difference between the work of philanthropic kindergartners and regular schoolteachers lay in home visitations. Especially in the homes of the poor, kindergartners were often received and trusted. Regular schoolteachers did not conduct home visits even among the affluent, and they were fearful of poor neighborhoods. They preferred to summon parents to the schools when information-sharing was necessary. Kindergartners, on the other hand, were often trained in nursery school traditions, social work, and related fields, in which home visits were common practice.

By 1875, the kindergarten movement had reached the west coast. This group was comprised of dedicated Froebelians. Through the pioneering work of Emma Marwedel and her student Kate Douglas Wiggin, the San Francisco Public Kindergarten Society was founded in 1878, the year the first free kindergarten, the Silver Street School, was established in the west. The first children served were from families in a nearby ghetto known as Tar Flat.

The board of directors of the kindergarten society invited Felix Adler, New York City director of the Ethical Culture Society, to help raise funds through the sale of life memberships. The Ethical Culture Society had already established the Adler Free Kindergarten in New York City.

A private kindergarten had been established in California in 1873 by

Bertha Semler, who had studied under Froebel. In 1876, Emma Marwedel arrived in Los Angeles to establish a kindergarten for wealthy families and a training center for kindergarten teachers. Marwedel taught Kate Wiggin.

Wiggin opened her own private kindergarten in Santa Barbara, California, in an old house known as "Swallows' Nest." Kindergartners were on the lookout for just the right piece of property, the proper atmosphere, and the perfect environment to replicate Froebel's "children's garden." Wiggin's Santa Barbara location had some of the characteristics, but not all of them, of the kindergartens run by philanthropists in Eastern and Midwestern cities.

We were a very happy family in the Swallows' Nest that summer, and we taught one another more than any of us realized. The only lack that I ever felt was that I longed consciously for a larger group of children, and I had a vision of how wonderful it would be to plant a child-garden in some dreary, poverty-stricken place in a large city, a place swarming with un-mothered, un-defended, under-nourished child-life.

This was the vaguest of visions, for I had never had the smallest experience with crowded neighborhoods, or with any but carefully brought up, well trained, silk stockinged children, not even having attended a large public school with its varied types of foreign birth or foreign parentage. (International Kindergarten Union 1924, p. 28)

In 1880, after the work of Kate Wiggin and Emma Marwedel became well known and respected, Wiggin founded the California Kindergarten Training School, to teach Froebel's theory and philosophy to young women who wanted to become kindergartners. Observers from the state university and normal schools in California often visited and took careful notes on the Froebel theory in practice. Over the next few years, Wiggin's school graduated more than 390 kindergartners.

In 1883, Wiggin and Marwedel founded the California Froebel Society. Their work became nationally known, and they were now being invited to other communities to help establish kindergartens, to present papers at Froebel Society conferences, and to speak at teachers' conventions. By 1910, there were thirty-two kindergartens in San Francisco, and at least one kindergarten in thirty-three other California towns.

The free kindergartens were financed through contributions, kindergartner's personal funds, and philanthropic groups' fund-raising efforts. The social work philosophy of the kindergarten and settlement house movements was not readily accepted by supporters of local taxation for public schools. Especially in South, the education of children was viewed as a family responsibility, and the use of public taxes to fund schools came late to many of these communities. Their inhabitants viewed kindergarten as a luxury that was the responsibility of individual families.

In Toronto, at the 1891 annual meeting of the National Education Association, A. S. Draper, the state superintendent of schools for New York, proposed that kindergarten become a part of all school systems. The proposal was approved and paved the way for the National Kindergarten Association, which worked for the passage of laws related to early education in many states.

In the West, Sarah Cooper led a campaign in California to establish free kindergartens for the poor. In her view, the "scientific" methods of Froebel served as a useful foundation for religious proselytizing among families. As a Sunday school teacher, she used Froebel's principles to teach her class, rather than the common procedure of reading and teaching from Bible stories. In rejecting strict Christian orthodoxy in favor of Froebel, Cooper intended to reform Sunday school teaching by helping other teachers understand the relationship between Froebel and Christian principles. Church authorities visited her free kindergarten and were disappointed that there was no mention of Christ in the songs, games, and other Froebelian activities.

This placed Cooper in direct confrontation with the elders of her church, and she asked for a hearing. This event brought national attention to kindergartners in general and to members of the free kindergarten movement of San Francisco who were asked to testify. In their view, Froebel's principles were on trial. The testimony and compelling arguments presented on Cooper's behalf by local kindergartners led the church to drop the charges. Cooper nevertheless left the church and joined the Congregational Church. Here she continued her crusade to integrate Froebel's principles with those of Christianity. The hearing provided good publicity for the kindergarten movement but caused a break between the free kindergarten movement and various churches. Cooper, along with her Bible class, opened the Jackson Street Kindergarten in San Francisco. Other kindergartens followed and were incorporated as the Golden Gate Kindergarten Association. To increase the number of kindergartners available for the rapidly increasing market, Cooper founded and operated the Golden Gate Free Normal Training School without salary.

Jane Addams and Jacob Riis, founders of the settlement house movement in Chicago, were supporters of the free kindergarten movement because of its focus on the poor. Neighborhood centers were established in urban areas to assist immigrant and migrant groups' understanding of voting procedures and to teach both basic academic and social skills, such as how to complete job applications. In the same urban centers, recreational games, free lunches and milk for children, and child care for working mothers were often provided. It was natural that settlement house advocates would find kindergarten an essential service for the poor. In addition, settlement house workers had completed training programs that were closely related to university programs recommended for kindergartners before specific courses were established. Workers in the Hull House and Elizabeth Peabody House kindergartens were college-trained and lived in the settlement house. In New York City, the Neighborhood Guild offered kindergarten as its first stable program in its new center in 1887.

In several parts of the country, urban school systems with large immigrant populations offered unattractive vacant facilities to kindergarten advocates. The latter were nonetheless pleased at the offers, because they saw this as a means of encouraging schools to establish their own kindergartens on public premises sometime in the future.

At first, the schools that accepted kindergarten children required philanthropic organizations to pay teachers' salaries and the cost of materials, and in some cases even rent for the space. Kindergartners accepted these conditions. As more and more schools in major cities established kindergartens as a part of their regular services, school systems assumed the housing costs and salaries of preschool teachers, which were eventually raised to match those of regular teachers. This transition called for more preschool-trained teachers.

THE TWENTIETH CENTURY

Private schools influenced by John Dewey opened for those who could afford them. They included campus laboratory schools offering kindergarten at the Hampton Institute in 1893; at Atlanta University (organized by African-American faculty and parents) in the late 1800s; at Tuskegee Institute (preschool organized for African-American children of faculty and community), also founded in the late 1800s; at the University of Chicago (organized in 1915 by faculty wives); and at Columbia University in 1921 (to support training of Teachers' College students).

In the early 1900s, the Peninsula School, including preschool age children and reflecting the theories of John Dewey, was started in California. The Child Development Foundation was founded in New York City in 1915 to promote the theory and practice of Maria Montessori. One of its first schools opened in the same city and was directed by Eva McLean.

Through the New York City Board of Education's Bureau of Educational Experiments in 1921, Lucy Sprague Mitchell and Harriet Johnson, a nurse, and Caroline Pratt, a nursery school adherent, established the City and Country School. This endeavor laid the groundwork for Bank Street College, which today, with a children's school and graduate school, is a model for early childhood studies. Also in 1921 a Boston social worker, Abigail Eliot, who trained with Margaret and Rachel Mc-Millan in London, opened the Ruggles Street Nursery School.

In 1921, Lucy Cage opened a training center for early childhood teachers at Peabody College for the education of teachers in the South. The following year, Edna White opened a laboratory school in Detroit as a child development center. Barbara Greenwood opened a nursery school for the University of California at Los Angeles in 1923. The first nursery school opened as a part of a regular public school was in 1924.

As a part of the Progressive Education movement, Patty Smith Hill started a campus nursery school at Columbia University's Teachers College in New York City in 1921. With the increasingly wide range of views about child care, institutions where teachers were being taught attempted to centralize theory and practice. In 1925, Hill invited a group of people to meet at Columbia University's Teachers College to discuss the current status of nursery schools in the United States. In 1926, this group formed the National Committee on Nursery Schools.

Phillis Jones Tilly, of the home economics department at Hampton Institute in Virginia, opened a nursery school for the children of faculty and community families to support the teacher training program in 1929. In 1930, a similar school was started at Spellman College in Atlanta, under the leadership of Pearlie Reed. Home economics departments at other black institutions followed their lead.

It was not until the 1930s that education beyond the equivalent of a high school diploma was required for teaching. Teacher training institutions during that time were referred to as normal schools, and even though such schools provided a pool of well-trained people, the appointment of teachers was so political at the local level that often completely untrained people were assigned to teach the "little ones." Some normal schools went to a tenth-grade equivalent, while others went to the eleventh or twelfth grade. Advanced study was considered one additional year, much like the freshman year of college.

Two major organizations were formed to establish policy for this new academic area. The National Association for the Education of Young Children (NAEYC) and the Association for Childhood Education International (ACEI) established birth through the age of nine as the group to be covered by the philosophy, theory, and practice of early childhood education.

Efforts to Merge Preschool and Elementary Curricula

The approach to curriculum development in early childhood education has traditionally embodied a voice for children. The articulation of this voice guides the teacher in the introduction of projects and ideas, many of which emerge from the imagination of children. The kindergarten and nursery school curriculum ensured pupil freedom, starting with the beginning of each day. Then the teacher and children met as a group to establish the date, the names of the day and month, and the weather (by looking out the window). The teacher wrote this information on a large piece of newsprint and placed this with other information displayed in the room for the remainder of the day.

There was little or no direct instruction or memorization of the words used in the narrative, nor was a "times table" to be memorized in the early childhood classroom. The elements of literature awareness, reading, and/or math were included in all class projects (planting a garden; making a purchase in a post office; constructing, serving customers, or making a purchase in a grocery store, etc.). This program was promoted in nursery schools and kindergartens in the early 1900s, and similar patterns are visible today. Early childhood-trained teachers of the late 1990s follow a consistent version of this general approach.

When teachers trained in elementary school education (usually K–6) are assigned to teach in an early childhood setting (grade 3 and below), one may observe considerable direct teaching of "academics," rote performance by pupils, and frequent testing to assure the teacher and/or the principal that learning has taken place. This is often referred to as "back to basics." The result of such an approach is that a period of childhood usually devoted to imaginative aesthetic exploration is instead one of direct instruction.

For pupils in the elementary education context, there is less adventure and reflection for them to discover important aspects of of their lives for themselves. Children who bypass kindergarten and nursery school are less likely to engage teachers in conversation in later grades or become active participants in group projects. Early childhood programs are built upon child/teacher interaction as a means for developing language and other skills, enabling children to understand the complex nature of their world and how it works.

Tension between professionals in early childhood education and in elementary education tends to surface at intervals and to have predictable resolutions, but the conflict is seldom completely resolved. This conflict has its origin in the early 1900s when kindergarten was merged with public school's primary grades. The merger was deemed essential by the founders of the kindergarten movement in the United States in order to break the generation-to-generation cycle of poverty among urban immigrants and Southern rural migrants who relocated in cities. It was also the goal of philanthropists in the movement to pay the costs of nursery schools and kindergarten with public taxes by attaching them to regular schools.

Early Advocates of the Merger

It appeared that the worst examples of child neglect occurred before children reached school age. Margaret McMillan (1860–1931), with the aid of socialist associates, was elected to the Bradford School Board in London. In that post she initiated programs of health support for children from poor families. She concluded, however, that school age was too late to intervene in the lives of poor children, so in 1918 she and her sister Rachel founded their own day and night nursery school for children ages one to six. They were influenced by Margaret Mitchel, who in 1904 had published a very influential book, *Education Through the Imagination*, that inspired nursery school and kindergarten workers to expand the aesthetic aspects of working with young children.

> Children are emotional. And memory has its heyday in them, so that it seems as if they are in just the state which makes fantasies natural. In a sense children seem to be more original than grown-up people. Just as a little child will perform a hundred movements in an hour and run about all day, as a grown-up person cannot do, so he will not tire of "making-up" stories and dramas, and inventing fantastic tales to explain everything. But all this does not prove that a young child has greater muscular strength than an adult, or a greater power of imagination. It only shows what power he has is not under any rigid control. He moves as a child, imagines as a child, and has a certain kind of freedom only because he has not won an other and higher kind of liberty. Imagination is, as Goethe said, the forerunner of reason, just as movement of any kind is the forerunner of Will. (1904, p. 21)

Children in the McMillans' nursery school were given baths in high-sided tubs, clean clothing, and nutritious meals. These services were integrated with medical and dental care, as well as learning activities that included the children working in the school's vegetable and flower gardens, and playing in gravel piles, sandboxes, and piles of trinkets. The school was called "open-air" because the construction left one side of the building open to admit large amounts of fresh air.

After the death of Rachel, Margaret continued her socialist activism, teacher training, and promotion of nursery education and work in their school. The writings of Charles Dickens (1812–1870) that depict the lives of London children in the nineteenth century offer excellent descriptions of children from the social class who were served by the McMillan sisters. Dickens was an advocate for the poor, and through writing about impoverished children for adult readers, he influenced significant changes in children's literature of his time.

In a very influential 1925 book, *Unified Kindergarten and First-Grade Teaching*, S. C. Parker, professor of educational methods at the University of Chicago, and Alice Temple, associate professor of kindergarten and primary education at the University of Chicago, detailed the merging of kindergarten with first grade. As trainers of elementary school teachers, they criticized kindergarten teachers for emphasizing the stages of development and the symbolic representation in children's thinking.

Parker and Temple stressed that they were utilizing a *scientific* approach to the consolidation of early childhood and elementary school curricula. Preschool education was the domain of parents, nursery school teachers, and kindergarten teachers. Teachers with elementary school training were referred to as preschool teachers and, frequently with envy, as "kindergartners," which was perceived by the general public as applying to all preschool child care workers. This resulted in discord between kindergartners and elementary school teachers. To some degree, Parker did little to discourage this enmity, and occasionally used the discord to sequester aspects of the early education curriculum while advancing traditional elementary school curriculum in her newly combined model.

The Use of Testing

For their "scientific" influence, Parker and Temple turned to the work of Lewis M. Terman. Terman's *The Intelligence of School Children* was a perfect supplement for Parker and Temple's approach to the merger. Schools had already been established along the lines of annually admitting six-year-olds and having them progress from grade 1 through grade 12. These graded stages made it relatively easy to mechanically note each child's performance by grade and age. Instruments like IQ tests referred to *expected* pupil performance by grade, based upon an index determined primarily by the measured performance of all schoolchildren in the nation. An index called "mental age" emerged from Terman's work that was used in classifying pupils.

> It is necessary that the reader should at the outset arrive at a correct understanding of what the term "mental age" is and is not intended to signify. . . . the real meaning of the term is perfectly straight-forward and unambiguous. By a given mental age, we mean that degree of general mental ability which is possessed by the average child of corresponding chronological age. (Terman 1919, pp. 6–7)

An examination of sample test items reveals the bias in favor of experiences common to children from English-speaking northern European and upper-income American families. It was also common for early intelligence "experts" to confuse knowledge for intelligence. A child is asked, among other things, to recognize a table lamp. Rarely in homes of poor immigrant families was there electricity in the early 1920s. And before 1930 the same was true of homes in rural or other nonurban areas. Thus, such a test item is clearly more a measure of knowledge gained from experiences common to upper-income U.S. and European families than of innate intelligence.

Terman drew upon all of the major workers in the field of IQ to assist in making the label "scientific" fit the movement to merge kindergarten and first grade. This group of psychologists included Sir Cyril Burt in England, Carl Brigham of Princeton University, John B. Watson (considered the father of behaviorism in the United States), Robert Yerkes (for whom a research lab has been named at Emory University), and Henry Goddard. It was Terman, however, who led the charge from his position in various eugenics societies organized to protect society from the proliferation of "mental defectives."

Terman's work was already having an effect in schools that took the kindergarten/first grade merger seriously. He proposed that all kindergarten children be screened by testing them for fitness to advance to the first grade.

> The first task of the school when it gathers its newcomers together should be to give each child a mental test to determine the nature of his endowment. . . . In the schools of Council Bluffs, Iowa, all the pupils of the kindergarten and the first grade are tested, and entrance to the first grade from the kindergarten is based entirely upon mental age. (Terman 1919, pp. 64–65)

Terman and his colleagues were interested in sorting children by performance scores, race, and ethnicity. At that time black Americans were not of much interest to researchers because it was virtually impossible for them to advance up the vocational ladder outside of selling services to other blacks.

In the eugenics societies of which Terman was a member, there was great interest in immigration policies relating to the numbers of persons being allowed to enter the United States from "undesirable" countries. The eugenics community seldom missed an opportunity to use IQ scores to advance the interests of white Americans and northern Europeans. In 1919, Terman, working with some of his graduate students, published IQs based on race for five groups of children in the first grade.

Race	Number	Median IQ
Spanish	37	78
Portuguese	23	84
Italian	25	84
North European	14	105
American	49	106

Source: From L. M. Terman, *The Intelligence of School Children* (Boston: Houghton Mifflin, 1919), 56.

He went on to report that desirable traits were highly correlated with IQ. Among them were sense of humor, power to pay sustained attention, persistence, initiative, accuracy, willpower, conscientiousness, social adaptability, leadership, personal appearance, cheerfulness, and cooperation. In other reports of intelligence Terman was less equivocal:

It is interesting to note ... the level of intelligence which is very, very common among Spanish-Indian and Mexican families of the Southwest and also among negroes. Their dullness seems to be racial, or at least inherent in the family stocks from which they come. The fact that one meets this type with such extraordinary frequency among Indians, Mexicans, and negroes suggests quite forcibly that the whole question of racial differences in mental traits will have to be taken up anew and by experimental methods. . . . They cannot master abstractions, but they can often be made efficient workers, able to look out for themselves. (Terman 1919, pp. 91–92)

This was not the first time that the work of the school was placed under scrutiny by psychologists. G. Stanley Hall, who had studied with Wilhelm Wundt in Germany, had conducted a two-year survey of children in free kindergartens and the primary grades in the 1880s. He reported that children in urban areas were not very knowledgeable about objects and animals common to rural life. This provided support for proponents of Pestalozzi and Froebel's "natural" settings as being superior to the "artificial" experiences prevalent in city life. Philanthropists who had been active in the Froebel kindergarten movement solicited farm families to accept poor city children as two-week members of their family in order to provide a natural environmental experience. (The work of G. S. Hall will be discussed in greater detail in Chapter 2.)

The idea of an intelligence test to determine school performance can be traced to Théodore Simon and Alfred Binet, who in the early 1900s were contracted by the Paris minister of public instruction to devise a test to identify children suspected of being mentally retarded, so that they could be properly placed for special attention (Binet & Simon 1916). These early diagnostic measures were based upon assessing various factors related to reasoning skills, and it was assumed that these intellectual abilities (factors) contributed to a single general intelligence (g). Binet cautioned that his instrument should not be used to advance the interests of political or ethnic groups. No single element in the defining and measuring of intelligence has survived with greater persistence than the theory that intelligence can be determined by a single factor—the g factor (Spearman 1904; Terman 1916; Burt 1940; Cronbach 1949).

The concept of general intelligence as it relates to school performance was introduced in the United States by Terman in 1916. He used the Binet and Simon instrument as a basis for developing the well-known Stanford-Binet test of intelligence. This instrument, which has undergone modifications since its introduction, is currently the most widely administered test of intelligence (Thorndike et al. 1986). As with the Binet and Simon instrument, the Stanford-Binet test of intelligence purports to determine general intelligence from selected factors determined to be essential to intellectual performance (Terman & Merrill 1973).

After Stanford-Binet, the Wechsler Intelligence Scale for Children–Revised (WISC–R) is the next most commonly used instrument (Wechsler 1974). Both are designed to be administered individually, with the Stanford-Binet emphasizing verbal responses more than the WISC–R. The WISC–R is designed for children ages six to sixteen, and consists of twelve subtests (two are optional). Half of the items are verbal, and half do not require verbal responses.

It is expected that the more recent version of the latter, the Wechsler Intelligence Scale for Children–III (WISC–III), as well as the Wechsler Preschool and Primary Scale of Intelligence–Revised (WPPSI–R), will become equally popular tests for screening gifted children (Kaufman 1992). The widespread use of these traditional instruments occurs at a time when information-processing theorists and others are suggesting alternative approaches, and in the process are creating a receptive scientific environment for imaginative and inventive constructs.

Spearman (1904) constructed intelligence tests in such a way that the concept of a single factor, g, would be assured. He started with the idea of a principal component, using a single axis, with other abilities projected at right angles being rotated for the highest potential. By selecting a principal component, and projecting each vector (subordinate factor) onto the axis, Spearman could always obtain a single factor. He conceded, however, that there might be a specific factor unique to a particular test.

L. L. Thurstone was among the first to suggest that the human organism is far too complex for intellectual activity to be determined by a single factor. In 1938 he developed what he called "primary mental abilities" and introduced multivariate analyses to operationalize his theory.

Thurstone's test batteries were developed for three age levels with approximately six tests designed to measure a separate ability. He suggested that intelligence cannot be determined by measuring a single ability; rather, multiple factors like verbal ability, deductive reasoning, spatial ability, and perceptual speed are essential to a unified theory of intelligence (Thurstone 1938; Thurstone & Thurstone 1946). Thurstone rejected the principal component approach to factor analysis, and proposed a rotated factor axis that in essence eliminated g (Gould 1981).

Despite Thurstone's new approach, it still remained the view of Spearman and his followers that Thurstone's "set of abilities" contained an underlying element common to all measures of ability that could be defined within the framework of g. There is some dispute as to the original inventory of factor analysis. Burt claimed this distinction, but most writers give the credit to Spearman. The work of these early theorists dominates a great deal of today's scholarly thought on intellectual performance and IQ testing.

Despite the persistence of g theorists, intelligence testing began to incorporate Thurstone's multifactor analyses. Following his publication of a test battery to measure primary mental abilities (1938), others started to develop multivariate instruments to measure separate abilities. Arnold Gesell (1949), for example, developed an age scale to measure infant development. His developmental schedules defined four areas of behavior but did not claim that these were measures of intelligence. They were adaptive behavior (subject's reactions to objects); motor behavior (subject's control of body); language behavior (vocalizations and speech, bodily expression), and personal-social behavior (interpersonal relations). Many of Gesell's followers, however, using his model, developed instruments to assess these behaviors and labeled their instruments measures of "intelligence." At several points in the history of assessing intelligence, single-factor theorists have had to defend against assaults on the concept of g (Hunt 1961; Cattell 1963; Horn & Cattell 1967; Zigler 1970; Elkind 1971; McClelland 1973; Charlesworth 1976).

In their presumption of a "scientific" approach to developing an argument for the unification of kindergarten with elementary education, Parker and Temple (1925) turned to IQ testing. In addition to testing, which was used to bolster their arguments for including kindergarten in the regular grade sequence, they sought to integrate the kindergarten project-method of study into the grade 1 curriculum, and to impose some of the grade 1 curriculum upon kindergarten. They suggested that the best elements from kindergarten and grade 1 could be blended into "curriculum and methods continuous and delightful."

In such a unified program there is no break between the two grades in curriculum or in methods. Plays and games, construction and drawing, and the study of social life and nature, which were once considered peculiar curriculum of the kindergarten, now continue through the first grade. On the other hand, reading, once considered unsuited to kindergarten children, is introduced in the kindergarten as early as the mental ages of the individual pupils assure successful learning of this useful art. The reading which is taught, however, is not the "scourge of infancy," as Rousseau called it in 1762. (Parker & Temple 1925, p. 1)

The Transitional Period

The nurturing qualities of the nursery school had over the years led to development of a special curriculum scaled to the developmental needs of young children. Educators like Parker and Temple were well aware of these qualities and had mixed feelings about them. On the one hand, they ridiculed the talk about symbolic learning, while at the same time they wanted to have some of these teaching and learning qualities displayed in grade 1 classrooms. For pupils in the 1920s, grade 1 presented factual knowledge to be memorized. Parker and Temple's proposal to fuse kindergarten into first grade sought to preserve what they considered the attractiveness of both grades.

> High-sounding Froebelian symbolism kept kindergarten isolated. Froebel himself was an expert in this sort of mystical juggling of words. . . . Under the title of "symbolism" such quotations from Froebel became the central factor in the kindergarten creed for many of the earlier enthusiasts. Eventually, however, these beliefs became the rock on which kindergartners divided into two sects— the conservatives, who believed in "symbolism," and the progressives, who opposed it. As long as the "symbolists" held the field, the kindergarten tended to remain isolated, uncoordinated with the first grade in which the common-sense purpose of giving practical skill in reading, writing, and arithmetic stood in such marked contrast to the physical ideals of symbolism. When the progressive common-sense kindergartners, however, acquired greater influence and control, cooperation and coordination with the first grade was greatly facilitated. (Parker & Temple 1925, pp. 13–14)

Parker and Temple were well aware of, and acknowledged, the Progressive Education movement that was emerging from the philosophy of John Dewey, their colleague at the University of Chicago. Dewey and his wife had founded the Laboratory School there in 1896 and conducted it for eight years. The "progressives" that Parker and Temple mention above wanted change in the moribund U.S. system, but they were not the "progressives" who were identified with John Dewey's philosophy.

Dewey's progressives were more in line with Rousseau and Froebel, espousing a nurturing curriculum that was free and open to pupils' imagination. Dewey sought more content, not less. Schools attempting to become more "progressive," however, did little to further Dewey's aims. Parker and Temple's progressives were more inclined toward a fusion of didactic teaching and some elements borrowed from Dewey's approach.

Through the 1920s, women and men with an elementary school completion certificate were eligible to take the certifying test for kindergarten teacher. Often, an examination wasn't necessary, as when the superintendent of schools was a political appointee. Graduates of elementary schools were encouraged to pursue one or two more years of education in a "normal school." At a time when efforts to unify kindergarten and grade 1 were at their peak, Alice Temple and her colleagues at the University of Chicago forged ahead with a two-year university training program for graduates of normal schools.

During the first years of the program's existence, the College of Education of the University of Chicago, like other teacher training schools, offered its undergraduates one general curriculum for the training of elementary school teachers and one special curriculum for the training of kindergartners. In other institutions, the training of kindergartners was left to departments of home economics or family and child studies, and even schools of nursing.

> There are two chief reasons for the existence of this practice in normal schools. In the first place, the kindergarten was maintained in this country as a private and philanthropic institution for many years before it became a part of the public-school system. Teachers for these early kindergartens were trained in private kindergarten training schools established for that purpose, and for a number of years these same private normal schools were able also to supply the gradually increasing demand for kindergarten teachers in public schools. Hence when the public normal schools finally found it necessary to train kindergartners they, naturally enough, simply added a special curriculum similar to those prevailing in the private training schools and employed one or more kindergartners to teach most of the subjects.
>
> In the second place, the controlling principles, methods, and materials of the early kindergarten were so different from those of the early primary school that a special type of teacher-training seemed to be absolutely essential. (Temple 1920, pp. 498–499)

The major forces in the nursery school and kindergarten movements were very protective of the nurturing aspects of their curricula. The philanthropists that supported the kindergartens were pleased that they would be moved into public schools paid for through public taxation. Normal school-trained kindergarten teachers were hopeful that the early education curriculum inspired by Rousseau, Pestalozzi, and Froebel would be a stronger influence on elementary education, and that the "scientific" approach to elementary education would not greatly influence their domain. It was clear by 1920 that the scientific approach would bring a curriculum requiring rote memorization and instruments that tested for memory and IQ.

In the midst of this transition, the work of Jean Piaget emerged. Piaget had observed and interviewed young children, including his own, in various settings. Through his careful observations, data collection, and analysis, Piaget's concepts of logical thinking in children, and the symbolic value derived from their play, started to become known among early childhood professionals in the United States by 1950. Fundamental to his writings was the reintroduction of concepts associated with symbolism and imagination in children's construction of meaning.

> The appearance of symbolism . . . is the crucial point in all the interpretations of the ludic function. Why is it that play becomes symbolic, instead of continuing to be mere sensori-motor exercise or intellectual experiment, and why should the enjoyment of movement, or activity for the fun of activity, which constitute [sic] a kind of practice make-believe, be completed at a given moment by imaginative make-believe? The reason is that among the attributes of assimilation for assimilation's sake is that of distortion, and therefore to the extent to which it is dissociated from immediate accommodation it is a source of make-believe. This explains why there is symbolism as soon as we leave the sensori-motor level for that of representational thought. (Piaget 1951, p. 55)

Because of the genetic tilt to the academic discussion regarding the processing of information, scientists like Piaget found obstacles to the acceptance of their qualitative data collection and interpretation. Professionals in the early childhood community accepted Piaget's work as a welcome reinforcement for their commitment to the value of experience espoused by Rousseau and Froebel.

The scientific community at that time, however, had captured the attention of other educators. It was influenced primarily by empiricists who observed the responses of pigeons and rats to various stimuli, then generalized human learning from their animal investigations. Their methods were driven by models derived from Pavlov's studies of conditioning. This approach to measuring learning dominated theory and studies in psychology in the United States until 1960.

Educational professionals in public schools were attracted to this approach and designed specific "objectives" to match psychology's "response" concepts. Parker and Temple, on the basis of their positions and reputations at the University of Chicago School of Education, prepared the model for most early education programs in the United States. In their influential writings, behavioristic "objectives" were seldom left omitted. "Since the term 'objectives' has come into common use recently among educators and sometimes seems to be a better term for focusing attention on the specific ends or purposes toward which education is directed, we have entitled the chapter 'Social and Psychological Objectives in the Unified Program' " (Parker & Temple 1925, p. 31).

Early Childhood Education and the Civil Rights Movement

The 1960s was a tumultuous time in civil rights for the United States. Organizing in the black community centered around the work of Malcolm X and of Martin Luther King, Jr. It was almost a replay of the differing philosophical views of Booker T. Washington and W. E. B. Du Bois in the late 1800s.

Washington, the president of Tuskegee, an institution in Alabama for black students, held the philosophical position that all blacks should seek to provide their labor for the good of the country, and set aside their pursuit of equal opportunity. He surmised that equal opportunity would come to blacks gradually, as whites observed their industrious, cooperative spirit. Du Bois proposed that blacks should be granted the rights of citizenship and opportunities that should flow from their basic rights. He proposed that at least 10 percent of the black population had achieved a level of scholarship despite the hardships, and this "talented tenth" could be cultivated to provide guidance and leadership for the rest.

In 1905, Du Bois organized a meeting in Buffalo, New York, to denounce Washington's conciliatory speech at Atlanta in 1895—the "Lay down your buckets where you are" advice to blacks—and indicated to an audience of predominantly white businessmen that blacks should be cooperative workers in their industries and servants in their homes. In New York City in 1909, on the centennial of Lincoln's birth, the Niagara Movement (founded by Du Bois at Buffalo in 1905) became The National Association for the Advancement of Colored People (NAACP). Jane Addams, John Dewey, Du Bois, William Dean Howells, and Lincoln Steffens signed its original charter. The following year, Du Bois published the first issue of *The Crisis* magazine, intended for the homes of enlightened black families. The first printing was 1,000 copies; by 1920, more than 10,000 copies were printed monthly.

The Crisis was designed for adult readers; however, once a year a single special issue intended for children was published. This particular issue outsold all other monthly copies. The popularity of this children's issue encouraged Du Bois to publish a magazine aimed at the interests of black children. He was concerned about the negative effects that popular media had on them. Periodicals available to the general public denigrated blacks through the display of negative images, and few positive black images were presented in storybooks available to black children. On the rare occasions when blacks were depicted in children's literature, they were typed as comical and/or unattractive. Du Bois wrote in the "Opinion" section of *The Crisis* in 1919:

> *The Children's Crisis* has been published annually for nine years and is usually the most popular number of the year—that is, it makes the widest appeal to our readers. This is as it should be. Of course, we are and must be interested in our children above all else, if we love our race and humanity.
>
> But in the problem of our children we black folk are highly puzzled. For example, a little girl writes us—we remember her as red-bronze and black-curled, with dancing eyes—"I want to learn more about my race so I want to begin early. . . . I hate the white man just as much as he hates me and probably more!"
>
> Think of this from twelve little years! And yet, can you blame the child? To the consternation of the Editors of *The Crisis* we have had to record some horror in nearly every Children's number—in 1915, it was Leo Frank; in 1916, the lynching at Gainesville, Fla.; in 1917 and 1918, the riot and court martial at Houston, Tex., etc. (1919, p. 286)

Newspapers and magazines from the early 1900s reported lynchings and public attacks on blacks with surprising frequency. The Hollywood portrayal of racial minorities was especially negative; blacks were cast as comics and buffoons. These media portrayals presented false images to many unsuspecting whites and were effective in creating a chasm between light-skinned and dark-skinned blacks in their families and neighborhoods. Du Bois was disturbed by what had become a tragic American tradition. As a countermeasure, Du Bois teamed with the literary editor of *The Crisis*, Redmon Fauset, and its business manager, Augustus Dill. Together they published *The Brownies' Book* for 2 years (Figures 1.4, 1.5, and 1.6).

The Brownies' Book appeared between 1920 and 1921, and was designed for black children ("children of the sun") in early grades. This monthly contained poetry, stories, news events, puzzles, and games. Black families waited with great anticipation each month for their copy to arrive. It brought parents and children together for reading, discussions of news

Figure 1.4
The Brownies' Book, June 1920

THE BROWNIES' BOOK

*Published Monthly and Copyrighted by DuBois and Dill, Publishers, at 2 West 13th
Street, New York, N. Y. Conducted by W. E. Burghardt DuBois; Jessie Redmon Fauset,
Literary Editor; Augustus Granville Dill, Business Manager*

VOL. 1.   JUNE, 1920   No. 6

CONTENTS

FIFTEEN CENTS A COPY; ONE DOLLAR AND A HALF A YEAR
FOREIGN SUBSCRIPTIONS TWENTY-FIVE CENTS EXTRA

RENEWALS: The date of expiration of each subscription is printed on the wrapper. When the subscription is due; a yellow renewal blank is enclosed.

CHANGE OF ADDRESS: The address of a subscriber can be changed as often as desired. In ordering a change of address, both the old and the new address must be given. Two weeks' notice is required.

MANUSCRIPTS and drawings relating to colored children are desired. They must be accompanied by return postage. If found unavailable they will be returned.

Entered as second class matter January 20, 1920, at the Post Office at New York, N. Y., under the Act of March 3, 1879.

Source: *The Brownies' Book* (New York: Du Bois and Dill, Publishers, 1920).

Figure 1.5
The Brownies' Book, June 1920

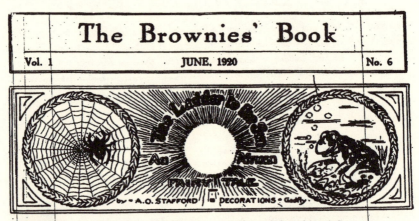

The Brownies' Book

| Vol. 1 | JUNE, 1920 | No. 6 |

IN the olden times, long before the white man came to Africa, there was a great chief whose oldest son Kee'mäh was regarded as u youth of rare promise.

In the arts of war as practised by his people Kee'mäh took a leading part and in the assemblies of his tribe where questions of interest were discussed or laws enacted, he became a speaker of force and skill.

In form he was tall, his carriage free and graceful, his eyes dark and full of fire and his color that of old bronze. No father or mother passed him without a feeling of admiration and no maiden saw him without a look of interest. But to Kee'mäh the emotions which his appearance and fine character aroused in others meant nothing, so intent was he in preparing for the day when he would take up the rule of his father.

Like all fathers, Kee'mäh's wished before he died to see his son happily married. So on several occasions the old chief had hinted to Kee'mäh that the time had come for Him to select a wife but to these hints the son had turned a deaf ear.

Finally Kee'mäh said to his father: "I will not marry any girl on earth, but for bride I must have a daughter of the Sun and Moon."

The astonishing wish of his son seemed to the old chief a very foolish one—one that could not be realized—one that he dared not discuss with the elders of his tribe, as it would indicate to them that his eldest son, regarded so highly as a youth of courage and wisdom, was somewhat unbalanced in mind.

But no argument changed this strange wish of Kee'mäh. At last, more to humor his son, the chief called one of his men, famed for his writings on pieces of bark, and told him to write a letter to King Sun and ask for one of his daughters to be the bride of Kee'mäh.

To his son the chief then gave the letter, believing that would be the end of this fanciful wish—but Kee'mäh felt that some way would be found to deliver the letter to King Sun.

As no man of the tribe could make the journey it was suggested that some animal or bird would undertake the unheard of trip. At that time man could converse with the creatures of the jungle and the birds of the air. So the deer was called and asked to deliver the letter.

"On earth I can run with the wind, but without wings I cannot go to the land of the Sun," returned the deer when he heard of the wish of Kee'mäh.

"Call the hawk," replied the anxious youth. But when the hawk heard the message that bird answered, "I fly above trees and rivers, but the land of the Sun is beyond me."

Then the eagle was given the task but his reply was:—

"Though I fly above the clouds on mountain peaks, the home of the Sun is farther than the dwelling place of the thunder and lightning; there I cannot fly."

Now the sorrow of Kee'mäh was great when he heard these answers. He felt that his letter would never be delivered and he brooded much alone, far away from the home of his father, in

Source: The Brownies' Book (New York: Du Bois and Dill, Publishers, 1920).

Figure 1.6
The Brownies' Book, June 1920

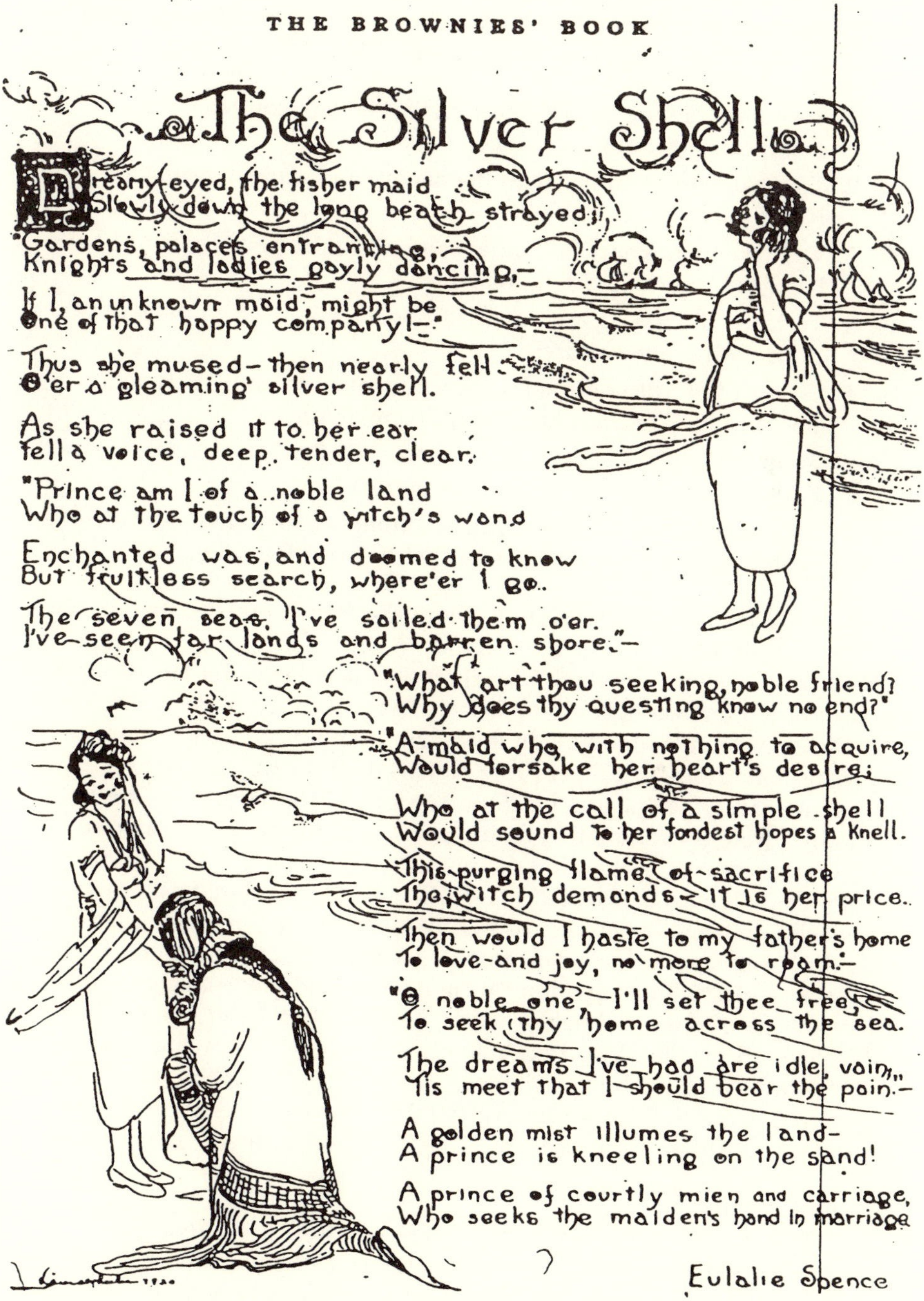

The Silver Shell

Dreamy-eyed, the fisher maid
Slowly down the long beach strayed;

Gardens, palaces entrancing,
Knights and ladies gayly dancing,—

"If I, an unknown maid, might be
One of that happy company!—"

Thus she mused—then nearly fell
O'er a gleaming silver shell.

As she raised it to her ear
Fell a voice, deep, tender, clear.

"Prince am I of a noble land
Who at the touch of a witch's wand

Enchanted was, and doomed to know
But fruitless search, where'er I go.

The seven seas, I've sailed them o'er,
I've seen far lands and barren shore.—

"What art thou seeking, noble friend?
Why does thy questing know no end?"

"A maid who with nothing to acquire,
Would forsake her heart's desire;

Who at the call of a simple shell
Would sound to her fondest hopes a knell.

This purging flame of sacrifice
The witch demands—it is her price.

Then would I haste to my father's home
To love and joy, no more to roam.—

"O noble one, I'll set thee free
To seek thy home across the sea.

The dreams I've had are idle, vain,
'Tis meet that I should bear the pain.—

A golden mist illumes the land,
A prince is kneeling on the sand!

A prince of courtly mien and carriage,
Who seeks the maiden's hand in marriage.

Eulalie Spence

events, and recreational interaction created by games, poetry, and puzzles for children (Sinnette 1965; Harris 1989). For Du Bois, *The Brownies' Book* satisfied an important ambition—to enable black children to value their natural characteristics positively. He detailed this mission in 1919:

1. To make colored children realize that being "colored" is a normal, beautiful thing.
2. To make them familiar with the history and achievements of the Negro race.
3. To make them know that other colored children have grown into beautiful, useful and famous persons.
4. To teach them a delicate code of honor and action in their relations with white children.
5. To turn their little hurts and resentments into emulation, ambition and love of their homes and companions.
6. To point out the best amusements and joys and worthwhile things of life.
7. To inspire them to prepare for definite occupations and duties with a broad spirit of sacrifice. (Du Bois 1919, p. 286)

The philosophies of Washington and Du Bois were debated among blacks at all levels, through the 1950s. Early in the 1960s, Malcolm X became known for revolutionary rhetoric, and Martin Luther King, Jr., was known for reconciliation and consensus through negotiation. Each had a considerable following in the black community. Black writers, politicians, educators, and other professionals used their positions to present a point of view. White and black professionals who served black schoolchildren were concerned that their responses to the flow of events would be constructive.

In 1963, James Baldwin (1924–1987), an African-American essayist, penned a letter to his nephew describing, in part, the prevailing attitude among black intellectuals concerning a celebration of the hundredth anniversary of the Emancipation Proclamation. Baldwin published the letter as a part of the nonfiction work *The Fire Next Time*, "Letter to My Nephew on the One Hundredth Anniversary of the Emancipation" echoed sounds and symbols of thousands of conversations that could have occurred between black adults and children during the civil rights movement of the 1960s. An exerpt from the letter is reprinted below.

Dear James:
I have begun this letter five times and torn it up five times. I keep seeing your face, which is also the face of your father and my brother. Like him, you are tough, dark, vulnerable, moody—with

a very definite tendency to sound truculent because you want no one to think you are soft. You may be like your grandfather in this, I don't know, but certainly both you and your father resemble him very much physically. Well, he is dead, he never saw you, and he had a terrible life; he was defeated long before he died because, at the bottom of his heart, he really believed what white people said about him. This is one of the reasons that he became so holy. I am sure that your father has told you something about all that. Neither you nor your father exhibit any tendency towards holiness: you really *are* of another era, part of what happened when the Negro left the land and came into what the late E. Franklin Frazier called "the cities of destruction." You can only be destroyed by believing that you really are what the white world calls a *nigger*. I tell you this because I love you, and please don't you ever forget it.

I have known both of you all your lives, have carried your Daddy in my arms and on my shoulders, kissed and spanked him and watched him learn to walk. I don't know if you've known anybody from that far back; if you've loved anybody that long, first as an infant, then as a child, then as a man, you gain a strange perspective on time and human pain and effort. Other people cannot see what I see whenever I look into your father's face, for behind your father's face as it is today are all those other faces which were his. Let him laugh and I see a cellar your father does not remember and a house he does not remember and I hear in his present laughter his laughter as a child. Let him curse and I remember him falling down the cellar steps, and howling, and I remember, with pain, his tears, which my hand or your grandmother's so easily wiped away. But no one's hand can wipe away those tears he sheds invisibly today, which one hears in his laughter and in his speech and in his songs. I know what the world has done to my brother and how narrowly he has survived it. And I know, which is much worse, and this is the crime of which I accuse my country and my countrymen, and for which neither I nor time nor history will ever forgive them, that they have destroyed and are destroying hundreds of thousands of lives and do not know it and do not want to know it. One can be, indeed one must strive to become, tough and philosophical concerning destruction and death, for this is what most of mankind has been best at since we have heard of man. (But remember: *most* of mankind is not *all* of mankind.) But it is not permissible that the authors of devastation should also be innocent. It is the innocence which constitutes the crime.

Now, my dear namesake, these innocent and well-meaning people, your countrymen, have caused you to be born under conditions not very far removed from those described for us by Charles Dickens in the London of more than a hundred years ago. (I hear the chorus of the innocents screaming, "No! This is not true! How *bitter* you are!"—but I am writing this letter to *you*, to try to tell you something about how to handle *them*, for most of them do not yet really know that you exist. I *know* the conditions under which you were born, for I was there. Your countrymen were *not* there, and haven't made it yet. Your grandmother was also there, and no one has ever accused her of being bitter. I suggest that the innocents check with her. She isn't hard to find. Your countrymen don't know that *she* exists, either, though she has been working for them all their lives.)

Well, you were born, here you came, something like fifteen years ago; and though your father and mother and grandmother, looking about the streets through which they brought you, had every reason to be heavyhearted, yet they were not. For here you were, Big James, named for me—you were a big baby, I was not—here you were: to be loved. To be loved, baby, hard, at once, and forever, to strengthen you against the loveless world. Remember that: I know how black it looks today, for you. It looked bad that day, too, yes, we were trembling. We have not stopped trembling yet, but if we had not loved each other none of us would have survived. And now you must survive because we love you, and for the sake of your children and your children's children.

This innocent country set you down in a ghetto in which, in fact, it intended that you should perish. Let me spell out precisely what I mean by that, for the heart of the matter is here, and the root of my dispute with my country. You were born where you were born and faced the future that you faced because you were black and *for no other reason*. The limits of your ambition were, thus, expected to be set forever. You were born into a society which spelled out with brutal clarity, and in as many ways as possible, that you were a worthless human being. You were expected to aspire to excellence: you were expected to make peace with mediocrity. Wherever you have turned, James, in your short time on this earth, you have been told where you could go and what you could do (and *how* you could do it) and where you could live and whom you could marry. I know your countrymen do not agree with me about this, and I hear them saying, "You exaggerate." They do not know Harlem, and I do. So do you. Take no one's word for anything, including mine—but trust your experience. Know whence you came. If you know whence you came, there is really no limit to where you can go. The details and symbols of your life have been deliberately constructed to make you believe what white people say about you. Please try to remember that what they believe, as well as what they do and cause you to endure, does not testify to your inferiority but to their inhumanity and fear. Please try to be clear, dear James, through the storm which rages about your youthful head today, about the reality which lies behind the words *acceptance* and *integration*. There is no reason for you to try to become like white people and there is no basis whatever for their impertinent assumption that *they* must accept *you*. The really terrible thing, old buddy, is that *you* must accept *them*. And I mean that very seriously. You must accept them and accept them with love. For these innocent people have no other hope. They are, in effect, still trapped in a history which they do not understand; and until they understand it, they cannot be released from it. They have had to believe for many years, and for innumerable reasons, that black men are inferior to white men. Many of them, indeed, know better, but, as you will discover, people find it very difficult to act on what they know. To act is to be committed, and to be committed is to be in danger. In this case, the danger, in the minds of most white Americans, is the loss of their identity. Try to imagine how you would feel if you woke up one morning to find the sun shining and all the stars aflame. You would be frightened because it is out of the order of nature. Any upheaval in the universe is terrifying because it so profoundly attacks one's sense of one's own reality. Well, the black man has functioned in the white man's world as a fixed star, as an immovable pillar: and as he moves out of his place, heaven and earth are shaken to their foundations. You, don't be afraid. I said that it was intended that you should perish in the ghetto, perish by never being allowed to go behind the white man's definitions, by never being allowed to spell your proper name. You have and many of us have, defeated this intention; and, by a terrible law, a terrible paradox, those innocents who believed that your imprisonment made them safe are losing their grasp of reality. But these men are your brothers—your lost, younger brothers. And if the word *integration* means anything, this is what it means: that we, with love, shall force our brothers to see themselves as they are, to cease fleeing from reality and begin to change it. For this is your home, my friend, do not be driven from it; great men have done great things here, and will again, and we can make America what America must become. It will be hard, James, but you come from sturdy, peasant stock, men who picked cotton and dammed rivers and built railroads, and, in the teeth of the most terrifying odds, achieved an unassailable and monumental dignity. You come from a long line of great poets, some of the greatest poets since Homer. One of them said, *The very time I thought I was lost, My dungeon shook and my chains fell off.*

You know, and I know, that the country is celebrating one hundred years of freedom one hundred years too soon. We cannot be free until they are free. God bless you, James, and Godspeed.

Your uncle,
James

(Baldwin 1963, pp. 3–5)

Educators were impressed with the realism expressed in Baldwin's work, and the extent to which his images matched what they observed in their schools. He was invited to give a talk at an in-service meeting of New York City teachers. The talk was published in the December 21, 1963, issue of the *Saturday Review*.

Early Childhood Education and the Poor

Historically in the United States, children were viewed as a church and/or family responsibility. Children born to poor families could be raised by the family, or abandoned to institutions and government programs for the poor. This was also the fate of many mentally or physically disabled children born to financially stable families. The quality of tax-supported facilities for the disabled and orphans varied from state to state.

For these children, some modest aid was available from philanthropic organizations and churches. Most of this aid came from government grants, portions of which were earmarked for participating agencies' "administrative costs." Occasionally, philanthropic and church funds were supplemented by direct assistance to the organizations, with a percentage to be allocated for the needs of the poor. It was in this context that public schools emerged. It still remains the view of some people that education should be a family responsibility and should not be fully funded by the state.

Individualism was under strong pressure during the Great Depression. To bring financial stability to families, socialistic policies like Social Security were integrated into the U.S. capitalist system. Many families in the country were facing economic ruin. Parents who had followed the American creed of hard work, religious beliefs, moral commitments, and patriotism were unable to provide food and clothing for their families. Industrialists who had reaped profits wanted the federal government to hold fast to the principle of hard work or no pay. There were too few jobs available for those willing to perform hard and unpleasant work.

The 1930s witnessed a period of economic disenchantment with the U.S. economic system, and many people turned to Communist, Socialist, Socialist Labor, and other political parties opposed to capitalism. To blunt the effectiveness of these new parties, President Franklin Delano Roosevelt proposed legislation based on the principle that citizens had a *right* to expect that their government would come to their aid during desperate times.

The association of poor families with early childhood education has prompted initiatives by the federal government to provide facilities and financial support for such programs. The nursery school, working closely with families, was viewed as a critical means of improving education, health, and social services for the poor. The Roosevelt administration established building construction projects and social programs to create employment opportunities and serve the needs of a debilitated citizenry. In 1933, the Works Progress Administration (WPA), among other things, established over 1,700 nursery schools and employed teachers who fostered relationships with parents and their at-home infants. Programs were set up in churches and other neighborhood buildings with suitable space. The program provided jobs for adults willing to work with children, and freed mothers to seek employment. The National Association for Nursery Education recruited and supervised child care personnel. Recruitment and training were organized on a regional basis. The Northeast Region was supported by Abigail Eliot, director of the Ruggles Street School in Boston. She had received her training under the direction of Rachel and Margaret McMillan in England. Schools in her district did not admit children younger than three.

The philosophy that government assistance was a *right*, and not a privilege, led in 1935 to the greatest surge of social legislation in U.S. history. Social Security, the WPA, the Civilian Conservation Corps, and what we call welfare (Aid to Families with Dependent Children; AFDC), and other programs were enacted to provide income for a distressed country. These new programs were in keeping with the major goals of the new political parties. As a result of Roosevelt's innovative legislative initiatives, their effectiveness started to wane and their membership to diminish.

With the coming of World War II, Americans of European descent took jobs in defense plants, leaving behind a racially discriminated-against class of black unemployed. Now, the government assistance viewed as a *right* by recipients who were unemployed became a *privilege* after they were employed in lucrative jobs. By the 1950s, the social classes and racial groups who were discriminated against in hiring were viewed as lazy for not accepting jobs at the lowest levels. These circumstances were described by Stephanie Coontz in 1992.

According to legend, after WW II a new, family oriented generation settled down, saved their pennies, worked hard, and found well-paying jobs that allowed them to purchase homes in the suburbs. In fact, however, the 1950s suburban family was far more dependent on government assistance than any so-called underclass family of today. Federal GI benefits available to 40% of the male population between the ages of twenty and twenty four, permitted a whole generation of men to expand their education and improve their job prospects. . . . Government spending was also largely responsible for the new highways, sewer systems, utility services and traffic-control programs that opened up the suburbs. (p. 13)

By 1965, education for the young was seen as a benefit for poor families. In February of that year, Head Start was announced as a summer program in preparation for a full-year program for preschool children. This represented a resurrection of the philosophy of the free kindergarten movement of the late 1880s: aid to poor families through school services for their preschool children.

The lingering effects of poverty that restricted the ability of some families to provide for the basic needs of their children became the major focus of the president of the 1960s, Lyndon B. Johnson. The improved economic conditions of the 1950s and 1960s, which brought secure jobs and home ownership for many citizens, did not reach all families. Too many families who were poor in the 1940s were still poor; and their children, who had grown up in poverty, were now attempting to raise their own children in a similar environment. This condition was labeled "the cycle of poverty" because for generations, too many of the same families and their children seemed unable to change their economic status. Those families who were able to improve their economic status through their own persistence and government social programs moved away from distressed neighborhoods to a better life. In many communities, federal housing programs provided a way out. Such housing was intended as a short-term solution for low-income families. Thousands of families used it to accumulate enough resources to afford home ownership in a traditional neighborhood. But over the years such housing tended to become a permanent residence for those who, for a variety of reasons, were unable to improve their economic status.

Gradually, these permanent residents—sharing the same debilitating financial condition—created a neighborhood within a neighborhood that became known as "the projects." The large high-rise projects in urban areas housed families eligible for practically every social program available to the poor. It seemed unwise to arrange a system that concentrated large populations of economically disadvantaged people in a "city" of their own. Nevertheless, these massive building programs were welcomed by financially strapped cities; they brought construction jobs, and social service providers saw an advantage to having clients more visible and accessible in one part of the city, rather than scattered over a wide geographic area. In the final analysis, for many cities, housing developments for the poor solved fewer problems than they created.

Many poor rural families moved into cities for the social services, better housing, and employment. They often became the new residents in the projects, and frequently they were no better off than before. Deficiencies in health and education for poor children were being reported by human services providers in both urban and rural communities. By the late 1950s the needs of the poor became too much for communities to sustain, and municipal governments looked to the federal government for help, as they had done in the 1930s.

In response, President Lyndon B. Johnson proposed the Great Society, in which he envisioned a role for the federal government in improving the lives of poor families. He launched the War on Poverty to attack the debilitating conditions of poor families on several fronts. Head Start would focus on their children. It was theorized that poor children needed early intervention programs to ensure a successful academic journey through the grades. Studies had shown that for a variety of complex reasons, school success seemed to correlate positively with family income. Children from low-income families tend to do less well academically than children from upper-income families, and children from nonpoor families were more likely to arrive at school well-fed and healthy. Children from poor families enter school with fewer academically related cultural experiences and less time in an organized nursery school or day care center.

In response to these findings, Head Start provided funds to community agencies and school systems to organize centers that would offer health, social services, and academic programs for children from poor families. The largest program for children ever created by the federal government, it was a part of the 1964 Economic Opportunity Act, along with several programs under the umbrella title Community Action Programs, like VISTA (a domestic Peace Corps) and the Job Corps. By the summer of 1966 there were over 600,000 children in almost 3,000 Head Start centers throughout the nation.

Program planners in Washington, D.C., encouraged community agencies to submit proposals while they were enlisting the help of professionals to find ways to articulate guidelines that would address the medical, dental, nutritional, and academic needs of poor children who would be attending neighborhood-based Head Start programs. Even though school learning was accepted as a major goal by the planners, the chief of Head Start, Sargent Shriver, emphasized mental and physical health in the initial stages.

Robert Cook, a physician, was selected as chairman of the planning committee. Julius Richmond, dean of the Medical School at New York

State Medical College at Syracuse, later became the national director. Among the other professionals brought in late were Mamie Clark, an expert in mental health; and Keith Osborne, Polly Greenberg, James Hymes, and Bettye Caldwell, experts in early childhood education. Hymes and other committee members were known for their innovative ideas concerning child care. Attempts were made to create a balance between academic needs and health needs, with the ultimate goal that Head Start would be a catalyst for social reform.

During World War II, James Hymes (1913–1998) managed the child service division of the Kaiser shipyards in Portland, Oregon. During the war, more than a thousand children of female shipyard workers, between the ages of eighteen months and six years, were cared for in up-to-date Kaiser nursery centers. Excellent early childhood education and care, along with meals, medical, care and counseling, was provided; these centers were viewed as models of ideal work-place child care for its time.

Hymes was a pioneer in televised teaching methods that, in the 1990s, are labeled "distance learning." In 1961, in a series of television broadcasts, he offered a college course, *The Child Under Six*, aired by CBS in Washington, D.C., long before early childhood was embraced by popular media. Hymes became "The Story Man" for a program of stories that aired for young children in the Washington, D.C., area. After World War II, Hymes was selected President of the National Association for Nursery Education, known today as The National Association for the Education of Young Children.

Head Start introduced many innovations. Except for early kindergarten and Maria Montessori, it was the first educational program to emphasize a significant role for parents. Its guidelines mandated a consulting role for parents in program policy, teacher and site selection, and funding at the local level. Parents were also included in the budget process, and their elected president signed the proposals prior to site funding. This was a radical departure from the role of parents in the traditional parent-teacher relationships common to PTAs. Head Start also introduced men as teachers in preschool classrooms and parents as aides to teachers, social workers, and health providers. In many cases this gave an incentive to those parents with the time and inclination to complete their own professional education through funding provided by an affiliated program, New Careers.

Head Start seemed to provide new energy for the thousands of advocates for poor families and their children. There was renewed interest in early education for all children at traditional institutions like Bank Street College, at the many universities where campus laboratory schools had been in operation since the 1920s and 1930s, and in public school systems.

The fact that our federal government was about to launch an early childhood initiative aimed at children of the poor served to focus the attention of parents and professionals on all levels of child care. Affluent families were not excluded, because 15 percent of the enrollment could be children from families with higher incomes. Head Start also created a fervor among child care professionals to make an important difference in the lives of poor families. Head Start appeared to be a natural connection between grass-roots community organizers and their government. There were, however, many skeptics among civil rights groups who feared that this was a government tactic to divert attention from pressing issues of voting rights and empowerment of oppressed Southern blacks.

The professionals from universities and public school systems in the Northeast and the West quickly learned not to expect that all families had the same access to child care services that was available to Northern communities. For instance, not until the mid-1980s did Georgia require all communities to provide kindergartens in public schools. And in 1965, the governor of Mississippi had refused to approve the opening of Head Start programs.

In Mississippi, poor parents and community professionals, with the assistance of the Washington office, founded the Child Development Group of Mississippi (CDGM), and received Head Start funds totaling $1.4 million. The grant came through a college, since Mississippi Governor Paul Johnson had threatened to veto the flow of federal funds to community groups for the program. Many poor Mississippi parents viewed Head Start as a benefit for their children, but equally important, it provided employment for them and hundreds of other poorly paid blacks in the state.

The program was open to all poor children and 15 percent of the nonpoor, but white parents rarely enrolled their children. By 1966 CDGM had received $5.6 million in federal grants to provide Head Start services. The politicians in the state were stunned by the amount of money flowing to black residents and eventually gained control of the major portion of the funds. There was also conflict between the voter registration and civil rights advocates, as well as participants and administrators of antipoverty programs, like Head Start. Both groups defined themselves as being within the "movement" and attempted to resolve their conflicts at the grass-roots level. In some rural communities the first programs were set up in homes because the churches were afraid of being bombed or burned. In the early stages of the program, when local politicians managed to have the funds halted, black parents continued their work without pay. In rural Mississippi one community reported that poor white parents enrolled their children in several Head Start classes in defiance of threats from more affluent whites. As the years passed, Head Start parents made more demands for better-quality schools as they learned their rights through their Head Start experience.

By 1967 funds were provided for research into the positive effects of Head Start. There were many health and nutritional benefits, increased community interest in early education, and a greater willingness among poor parents to support the work of their local grade schools. However, mixed results were reported regarding the academic gains of the children. Despite the short duration of the program prior to the studies and the flawed nature of several of these studies, the belief that gains from the Head Start experience might not last past grade 3 was taken seriously by the executives in Washington.

The national director and staff of Head Start expanded the scope of the original model by adding Follow Through. This gave parents and program directors the opportunity to select either an academic or a child development model for classrooms that would follow Head Start graduates through kindergarten to grade 3.

The "academic models" for Follow Through programs in the grade schools would be provided by current theorists and practitioners whose work was guided by philosophers like Locke, Rousseau, or Dewey, and theorists like Froebel, Piaget, or Skinner. Before the inauguration of Head Start, teachers and administrators in schools throughout the nation created teaching-learning environments in their schools and classrooms that reflected the theories and practices that they had learned during their professional training.

Prior to Follow Through, Head Start programs were staffed by professionals from a variety of teacher training institutions. Some institutions of higher learning grouped grades 1 through 6 in a professional program called elementary education. Other colleges and universities provided a concentration of study in kindergarten through grade 3. The latter was uncommon at colleges and universities in states that did not have mandatory kindergarten programs in public schools.

In most major cities, the college or university whose teacher training program concentrated on the education of young children enrolled students in a program of early childhood education. They usually studied children from birth to age nine (grade 3). Until a decade before Head Start, early education was often a part of a division of child and family studies, home economics, and/or child development departments. These programs were, more often than not, restricted to studies of children from birth through preschool.

Colleges and universities where early childhood education covered up to the third grade, and programs that were in home economics/child development departments, usually had a campus nursery school or similar setting for their students to engage in practice and child study. Such programs were more concerned with *how* children learn. The elementary education program (K–6) was more concerned with *what* children should be taught.

Within the context of these various approaches—sometimes overlapping, sometimes completely different—there were also various theoretical and philosophical perspectives on child development and learning. Teachers recruited during the first days of Head Start could come from any one of these. Their few differences over pedagogy were overshadowed by the rich diversity to which poor children were exposed.

Why has a program for poor families with such a distinguished record faced so many threats of demise? The reasons are both philosophical and political. In capitalist societies such as ours, children are viewed as a *family* responsibility and not a *social* responsibility. Public policy requires most families to meet their child care needs in the private marketplace. The disparity in family income that enables some families to purchase high-quality services, whereas others can afford only poor services, or none at all, is seen as an acceptable condition of capitalism. To change the status of poor children who need the early intervention of preschool services would require local legislatures to lower the age for entry to tax-supported public schools to accommodate children three years of age or younger. Persons who can afford to pay for child care, however, and receive a tax credit for the purchase of such services, are not likely to support a plan that would extend school services to include younger children, thereby increasing their taxes. Some states have found alternative methods that use nontax revenues—such as proceeds from state-sponsored gambling lotteries—to finance preschool services for all children regardless of family income.

The financial commitment to Head Start tends to mirror the policies of the political party of the president. Under the Republican administrations, Head Start has been viewed as a privilege for a group of parents who should be required to pay for child care purchased from private, for-profit providers. Their policy preference was to close the existing Head Start program. During Democratic presidents, Head Start has been accepted as one of several programs that enable poor families to have a better life. The legislative process that sets policy for social programs often results in compromises between the two political camps. For Head Start, it has been a continuous political struggle to avoid complete dismantling. In the 1990s, however, its proven potential is generally agreed among professionals, and funding has been maintained to assure its existence.

REFERENCES

Andrews, C. C. 1830; 1969. *The History of the New York African Free-Schools.* New York: Negro Universities Press.

Aries, P. 1962. *Centuries of Childhood: A Social History of Family Life.* Translated by Robert Baldick. New York: Alfred A. Knopf.

Bailyn, B. 1960. *Education in the Forming of American Society: Needs and Opportunities for Study.* New York: Vintage Books.

Baldwin, J. 1963a. *The Fire Next Time.* New York: Dial Press.

———. 1963b. "A Talk to Teachers." *Saturday Review* (December 21).

Baylor, R. M. 1965. *Elizabeth Peabody: Kindergarten Pioneer.* Philadelphia: University of Pennsylvania Press.

Bernal, M. 1987. *Black Athena: The Afroasiatic Roots of Classical Civilization, Volume 1: The Fabrication of Ancient Greece, 1785–1985.* New Brunswick, NJ: Rutgers University Press.

Biber, B. 1970. "Goals and Methods in a Preschool Program for Disadvantaged Children." *Children* 17(1): 15–20.

Binet, A., & Simon, T. 1916. *The Development of Intelligence in Children.* Baltimore: Williams & Wilkins.

Bowden, A. B. 1935. *Early Schools of Washington Territory.* Seattle: Lowman and Hartford.

Boyd, W., & King, E. J. 1973. *The History of Western Education.* New York: Barnes & Noble.

Bracken, Bruce A. 1987. "Performance of Black and White Children on the Bracken Basic Concept Scale." *Psychology in the Schools* 24(1): 22–27.

Braun, S. J., & Edwards, E. P. 1972. *History and Theory of Early Childhood Education.* Worthington, OH: Charles A. Jones.

Breasted, J. H. 1944. *Ancient Times: A History of the Early World.* New York: Ginn and Company.

Broderick, D. 1973. *Image of the Black in Children's Fiction.* New York: R. R. Bowker.

Burt, C. 1940. *Factors of the Mind.* London: University of London Press.

Bushnell, H. 1864. *Work and Play.* New York: Scribner's.

Cattell, R. B. 1963. "Theory of Fluid and Crystallized Intelligence: A Critical Experiment." *Journal of Educational Psychology* 54(1): 1–22.

Charlesworth, W. 1976. "Human Intelligence as Adaptation: An Ethological Approach." In L. Resnick (ed.), *The Nature of Intelligence.* Hillsdale, NJ: Lawrence Erlbaum.

Child, L. M. 1831. *The Mother's Book.* Baltimore: C. Carter.

Cohen, R. M., & Scheer, S. 1997. *The Work of Teachers in America: A Social History Through Stories.* Mahwah, NJ: Erlbaum Associates.

Cole, L. C. 1950. *A History of Education.* New York: Holt, Rinehart and Winston.

Coontz, S. 1992. "A Nation of Welfare Families." *Harper's Magazine* (October): 13–16.

Cremin, L. A. 1964. *The Transformation of the School: Progressivism in American Education, 1876–1957.* New York: Alfred Knopf.

Cronbach, L. J. 1949. *Essentials of Psychological Testing.* New York: Harper.

Cubberley, E. P. 1948. *The History of Education.* Cambridge, MA: The Riverside Press.

deMause, L. 1974. *The History of Childhood.* New York: The Psychohistory Press.

Detterman, D. K. (Ed.) 1986. *What Is Intelligence?* Norwood, NJ: Ablex.

Dewey, J. 1897. "My Pedagogic Creed." *The School Journal* 54(3) 77–80.

Du Bois, W. E. B. 1919. "The True Brownies." *The Crisis* 18: 285–286.

Dwight, T. 1835. *The Fathers Book: Or Suggestions for the Government and Instruction of Young Children, On Principles Appropriate to a Christian Country*. Springfield, MA: G. and C. Merriam.

Dworkin, M. S. 1959. *Dewey on Education*. New York: Teachers College Bureau of Publications.

Edwards, N., & Richey, H. G. 1947. *The School in the American Social Order: The Dynamics of American Education*. Boston: Houghton Mifflin.

Elkind, D. 1971. "Two Approaches to Intelligence: Piaget and Psychometric." In D. R. Green, M. P. Ford, and G. B. Flamer (eds.), *Measurement and Piaget*. New York: McGraw-Hill.

Ford, E. M., & Tisak, M. S. 1983. "A Further Search for Social Intelligence." *Journal of Educational Psychology* 75(2): 196–206.

Forten, C. 1864. "Life on the Sea Islands, Part I." *Atlantic Monthly* 13(79) (May).

———. 1961, 1967. *The Journal of Charlotte L. Forten*. R. A. Billington (ed.). New York: Collier Books.

Forward, S., & Buck, C. 1978. *Betrayal of Innocence*. New York: Penguin Books.

Frederiksen, N. 1984. "The Place of Social Intelligence in a Taxonomy of Cognitive Abilities." *Intelligence* 8(4): 315–337.

Froebel, F. 1909. *Pedagogics of the Kindergarten*. Boston: D. Appleton.

Funk, A. L. 1966. "The Boatload of Knowledge." *Outdoor Indiana* 32(1): 24–35.

Gage, W. L. 1867. *The Life of Carl Ritter*. New York: Scribner's

Gesell, A. 1949. *Gesell Developmental Schedules*. New York: Psychological Corporation.

Getzels, J. W., & Jackson, P. W. 1962. *Creativity and Intelligence*. New York: Wiley.

Goddard, H. H. 1912. "How Shall We Educate Mental Defectives?" *Training School Bulletin* 9(43).

Gordon, I. 1973. "Early Child Stimulation Through Parent Education." *International Journal of Early Childhood* 3 (1): 26–36.

Gould, S. J. 1981. *The Mismeasurement of Man*. New York: W. W. Norton.

Greenberg, P. 1967. "CDGM, an Experiment in Preschool for the Poor—by the Poor." *Young Children* 22(5): 305–315.

Guilford, J. P. 1967. *The Nature of Intelligence*. New York: McGraw-Hill.

Harris, V. J. 1989. "Race Consciousness, Refinement, and Radicalism: Socialization in *The Brownies Book*." *Children's Literature Association Quarterly* 14(3): 192–196.

Hatch, T. C., & Gardner, H. 1986. "From Testing Intelligence to Assessing Competencies: A Pluralistic View of Intellect." *Roeper Review* 8 (3): 147–150.

Horn, J. L., and Cattell, R. B. 1967. "Age Differences in Fluid and Crystallized Intelligence." *Acta Psychologica* 26(2): 107–129.

Hunt, J. 1961. *Intelligence and Experience*. New York: Ronald Press.

International Kindergarten Union. 1924. *Pioneers of the Kindergarten in America*. New York: Century.

Jackson, J. G. 1939. *Ethiopia and the Origins of Civilization*. New York: Blyden Society.

Kamin, L. J. 1974. *The Science and Politics of IQ*. Potomac, MD: Lawrence Erlbaum Associates.

Kaufman, A. S. 1992. "Evaluation of the WISC-III and WIPPSI-R for Gifted Children." *Roeper Review* 14 (3): 154–158.

Lancaster, J. 1821. *The Lancasterian System of Education Improvements*. Baltimore, MD: Joseph Lancaster.

Laughlin, H. H. 1922. *Eugenical Sterilization in the United States*. Chicago, IL: Psychopathic Laboratory of the Municipal Court of Chicago.

Leakey, L. S. B. 1969. *The Progress and Evolution of Man in Africa*. London: Oxford University Press.

Lee, V. E., Brooks-Gunn, J., & Schnur, E. 1988. "Does Head Start Work? A One-Year Follow-up Comparison of Disadvantaged Children Attending Head Start, No-Preschool, and Other Preschool Programs." *Developmental Psychology* 24 (2): 210–222.

Martin, F. G. 1982. "The Egyptian Ethnicity Controversy and the Sociology of Knowledge." *Black Economics Review* 10(3): 35–40.

McCelland, D. C. 1973. "Testing for Competence Rather Than for Intelligence." *American Psychologist* 28: 1–14.

McMillan, M. 1904. *Education Through the Imagination*. London: J. M. Dent & Sons.

Monroe, P. 1970. *A Textbook in the History of Education*. New York: AMS.

Nettleship, R. L. 1968. *The Theory of Education in the Republic of Plato*. New York: Teachers College Press.

Parker, C. S., & Temple, A. 1925. *Unified Kindergarten and First-Grade Teaching*. Boston: Ginn and Company.

Paulsen, F. 1908. *German Education. Past and Present*. New York: Scribner's.

Peabody, E. 1873. "Our Reason for Being." *Kindergarten Messenger* 1(1): 1.

Peabody, E., & Mann, M. 1864. *Moral Culture in Infancy and Kindergarten Guide*. Boston: Burnham

Piaget, J. 1951. *Play, Dreams, and Imitation in Childhood*. London: Routledge & Kegan Paul.

Quick, P. H. 1890. *Educational Reformers*. New York: Appleton.

Rice, J. M. 1893. *The Public-School System of the United States*. New York: Century.

Scarr, S. 1981. "Testing for Children." *American Psychologist* 36: 1159–1166.

Sinette, E. 1965. "*The Brownies' Book*: A Pioneer Publication for Children." *Freedomways* 5: 133–142.

Snowden, F. M. 1970. *Blacks in Antiquity*. Cambridge, MA: Harvard University Press.

Snyder, A. 1972. *Dauntless Women in Childhood Education 1856–1931*. Washington, DC: Association for Childhood Education International.

Spearman, C. 1904. "General Intelligence Objectively Determined and Measured." *American Journal of Psychology* 15(1): 201–293.

Sternberg, R. 1985. *Beyond IQ: A Triarchic Theory of Intelligence*. New York: Cambridge University Press.

Temple, A. 1920. "The Kindergarten Primary Unit." *Elementary School Journal* 20 (April): 498–502.

Terman, L. M., 1916. *The Measurement of Intelligence*. Boston: Houghton Mifflin.

———. 1919. *The Intelligence of School Children*. Boston: Houghton Mifflin.

Terman, L. M., & Merrill, M. A. 1937a. *Measuring Intelligence*. Boston: Houghton-Mifflin.

———. 1937b. *Stanford-Binet Intellectual Scale: Manual for Third Revision from L-M*. Boston: Houghton-Mifflin.

Thorndike, E. 1936. "Factor Analyses of Social and Abstract Intelligence." *Journal of Education Philosophy* 27: 231–233.

Thurstone, L. L. 1938. *Primary Mental Abilities*. Chicago: University of Chicago Press.

Thurstone, L. L., & Thurstone, T. G. 1946. *Tests of Primary Mental Abilities for Ages Five and Six*. Chicago: Science Research Associates.

Ulich, R. 1945. *History of Educational Thought*. New York: American Book Company.

Vandewalker, N. C. 1907. "The History of Kindergarten Influences in Elementary Education." In *Sixth Yearbook of the National Society for the Scientific Study of Education*, pt. 2. Chicago: Public School Publishing Company.

Wechsler, D. 1974. *Manual for the Wechsler Intelligence Scale For Children–Revised*. New York: Psychological Corp.

Zigler, E. 1970. "The Environmental Mystique: Training the Intellect Versus Developing the Child." *Childhood Education* (May): 402–412.

Zigler, E., & Trickett, P. K. 1978. "IQ, Social Competence and Evaluation of Early Childhood Intervention Programs." *American Psychologist* 33(9): 789–798.

Zigler, E., & Valentine, J. (eds.). 1979. *Project Head Start: A Legacy of the War on Poverty*. New York: Macmillan.

2

Philosophical Imagination

> The direct contact of teacher with student through persuasion is an exhibition of the universal character of dynamic interrelatedness among actual things. The teacher plants a seed in the soul of the pupil which grows and sustains itself, producing new seeds of its own for new soil. The pupil eventually becomes his own teacher, proceeds on his path unassisted; once mature, he too becomes a teacher of others. Thus, learning is a thing which reproduces itself forever, and sustains itself from generation to generation.
>
> —Plato (*Epistles* 360 B.C.)

Human service fields of study like early childhood can be categorized into three sections; *practice, theory,* and *philosophy.* It is important that specific areas of study receive their appropriate attention at different levels of inquiry. Undergraduate university students are focused primarily on the *practice* of teaching, while fifth year (Masters degree), sixth year (Ed. S.), and doctoral students focus more on *philosophy* and *theory.* And the Ph.D., the doctor of philosophy signifies the study of the philosophy of a particular discipline.

This does not mean that areas of focus are isolated into practice, theory, and philosophy, but the focus occurs at different levels depending upon the academic degree for which one is studying. For example, undergraduates as a group, regardless of their major area of study, concentrate on a core of courses for the first two years. During that time all students, regardless of major areas of study, study English, math, science, political science, history, philosophy, and Western civilization, to name a few. The last two years of academic work for undergraduate education majors are taken up with teaching methods and spending time student teaching in classrooms at the selected level of their major (early childhood, elementary, or secondary).

Early childhood majors, more often than not, do their practice teaching below the fifth grade. Here the concentration is on the practice of teaching, with some connections made to theory presented in their course work. When they take courses at the graduate level, the focus will be more on theory and philosophy because they are now teachers, practicing in their workplace. If they are fortunate, their graduate courses will not repeat the study of the practice taught in their undergraduate work. Sometimes this does occur, and it is time wasted.

ANCIENT GREECE

Philosophical perspectives on education can be traced before the birth of Christ. The earliest children's literature was written by Aesop in approximately 600 B.C. Aesop's fables were not intended for children, but down through the ages they have been adapted for their use. Aesop, a slave from Phrygia, is considered here for his fables and also because their content set the stage for Plato's examinations of ethics, justice, and morality. In this regard, his contributions—like those of Socrates and Aristotle—were philosophical.

Aesop's fables are more fully explored in Chapter 6. They are considered here because persons involved in practice (writing children's stories, teaching, founding schools, etc.) often create a philosophy that will be followed by other scholars. For example, in German schools during the Reformation (mid-1500s), as soon as children had learned to read, they were required to explain certain of Aesop's fables as a morning exercise.

A Greek orator, Demetrius of Phaleron, collected Aesop's fables around 300 B.C. and translated them into Greek as *Aesopic Tales*. By the end of the fifteenth century, twelve-year-old pupils in England were assigned to write Greek verses, short poems, and Latin themes, and to translate Aesop's fables from Greek to Latin.

During the Renaissance, translations of Aesop were required of pupils in Jesuit middle grammar schools. By 1484 Aesop had been translated into English, and illustrated by William Caxton. The fables were also commonly used for language study in European grammar schools.

Socrates (470–399 B.C.) was another major philosophical figure who was both a practitioner (teacher) and a philosopher. He taught Plato, the most prolific writer influencing Western thought, who in turn taught Aristotle. Socrates was not known as a writer, but his ideas were described by Plato, and the world still celebrates the "Socratic method" of discourse: the putting forth of a series of questions in order to reveal the logical conclusion, already known to the questioner.

Plato wrote *The Republic* (ca. 376 B.C.), in which he suggested that after the age of six, children should not be left to the self-serving interests of parents. Children of the well-off, he thought, should be provided free education by the state, with teachers selected for that purpose. This was a radical view for its time because it viewed children as a responsibility of the society and not of the family. Plato thought that the state should educate its military and government leaders from the ranks of children from affluent families. He did not believe that girls and children from poor families had a place in the state educational system.

Teachers in Athens at the time held schools on a fee basis. Elementary schools started with the teaching of the alphabet and spelling, followed by reading. The curriculum also included gymnastics, writing, and singing (accompanied on the lyre, which students learned to play as a part of the regular curriculum). While learning to read and write, children used a wax tablet that folded over so that the wax surface was protected. A stylus, the shape and size of the present-day pencil, recorded letters and numbers in the wax. The rounded end of the stylus was an eraser to remove unwanted indentations.

Socrates did not teach in a school per se, but walked around the marketplace and attracted a band of scholars to other gathering venues. His methods of teaching brought sharp criticism from schoolteachers because his students were their severest critics. These teachers were often no better than his students, and occasionally they were less competent. Some historians have suggested that this situation was part of the reason for the harsh treatment that Socrates received. Although he committed relatively minor infractions of the law, he was charged with rejecting the gods established as sacred by the state, thus corrupting the youth. He had exerted a great deal of influence on the thinking of young men, including Critias and Alcibiades, whom the public came to view as traitors. Eventually, his teachings were seen as responsible for their behavior, and he was sentenced to death.

The Athenian method of education had a long life, and for centuries only boys from well-to-do families attended school. Socrates' tradition of teaching followed a philosophy based on the open academy where teacher and student gathered for an exchange of information. The teacher proposed questions to his audience of learners that encouraged them to ponder their own sense of morality, their ideals, and their sense of right and wrong.

JOHN AMOS COMENIUS

It was not until the the 1500s that any attention was given to education of children from peasant families as a means of improving their condition as adults. This occurred within the concept of education for all children. The philosophy of John Amos Comenius (1592–1670) is credited

Figure 2.1
John Amos Comenius

with significantly influencing the transition from the medieval mistreatment of children to the modern concept of education (Figure 2.1). His insights have led to him being called the "grandfather of modern education." Comenius wanted to enlist the aid of educators and families in developing a universal language that could serve to promote basic knowledge for all. In the 1600s, this philosophical paradigm was intended to bring the education generally available to the clergy and the well-to-do within the reach of common folk. Comenius firmly believed that child rearing should involve both parents, who shared the nurturing of the infant. (More than two centuries later, in the 1990s, the agenda for women's rights includes similar ideas. Comenius' proposal came during a period when parents, and people hired to look after children, maintained an emotional distance. His rejection of practices that espoused social distance between women caring for babies, in one group, and men, in the other, made Comenius one of the earliest proponents of equal treatment for women.)

Comenius was born in Nivince, Moravia, on March 28, 1592, to middle-class parents. Before he was twelve, his parents and two sisters had died in an epidemic. For most of his teen years he lived with an aunt and attended a common grade school. It was common in European schools of that period for teachers to administer harsh punishment and perpetuate a fearful atmosphere. In his writings, Comenius refers to terror and torture as characteristic of his early education. These childhood experiences contributed to his desire to reform common practices in the rearing and education of children. In *The School of Infancy*, he gave this advice to parents: "When we lift them up, put them to rest, show them anything, or smile on them, we aim that they in turn should look on us, smile, reach out their hands to take what we give" (p. 98).

After Comenius completed grade school, he enrolled at the school run by Unitas Fratrum (United Brethren) at Prerov, a school started by a nonviolent Protestant group in the early 1500s. The Brethren saw religion and education as essential for male and female members. At the time of Comenius' enrollment, the school was over a century old. Under the leadership of Bishop John Lanecius, who recognized his potential, Comenius was encouraged to expand his intellectual horizons.

After graduating from the school at Prerov, Comenius went to Germany for advanced study in theology. While there, he met many scholars—including Johann Alstead, Johann Fisher, and David Pareus—from whom he gained insights into Calvinism and philosophy. He also married and fathered two children.

After teaching for a while, Comenius was finally ordained and became the minister and head of the church school at Fulnek. In an environment where most intellectual thought was based on religious principles, knowledge was imparted through schools and churches within the context of a Christianity where deep differences prevailed. From these deep divisions a war emerged between Catholics and Protestants.

Comenius' Protestant church and school were ransacked by Catholics. Comenius went into hiding, and his wife left with the children to live with relatives in Prerov. Soon thereafter, she, their two older children, and their newborn died of an unnamed illness

The spoils of this religious war went to the Catholics, who confiscated Protestant churches and their property. In describing other consequences of the Thirty Years' War, Ernest M. Eller writes in his introduction to Comenius' *School of Infancy* (1957):

> Catholics alone could be citizens, marry, operate businesses, have valid wills, receive hospital care. Refusal to attend mass brought punishment. Deliberate currency depreciation sank the crucified nation into deeper ruin. Recanting committees and soldiers ranged through the land, torturing and burning. Protestants by the thousands were scourged, burned, hacked to pieces, until the nation became a field of blood. Many thousands migrated to Holland, Hungry, Poland, Germany and Protestant states where they could have some measure of religious freedom, if not peace from war. But large numbers remained to continue to face the horrors under the leadership of men like Comenius who for much of seven years lived a hunted existence. Regardless of personal danger, though, he ministered to the persecuted people and labored against the day when the terror would lift. (p. 15)

War and disease had taken Comenius' parents and siblings, his wife and children, and his religion seemed to be destined for destruction as well. Remarkably, after these personal tragedies, Comenius was able to champion mankind as caring and nurturing. He later wrote eloquently to mothers for the benefit of children. He believed that a caring and nurturing childhood was the means by which mankind could be saved from itself. His philosophy of free access to education emerged from his experiences with religious conflicts, which he perceived as originating in a lack of knowledge within, and between, religious groups.

Comenius' most important work concerning early childhood was *The School of Infancy*, first published in Czechoslovakian, and later in German (1633). Other versions appeared in Polish and Latin. The original Latin text, with facing-page English translation, was edited with an introduction by Ernest Eller in 1956 (Figures 2.2, 2.3, and 2.4). In it, Comenius suggested an age for starting school that would prevail in most of Europe and the United States until the late 1800s.

> I do not advise that children be removed from the mother and delivered to teachers before their sixth year for these reasons: First the infant requires more watchfulness and care than a teacher with a number of children under him can give. It is therefore better for this time that children continue under the mother's care. Then it is safer that the brain be rightly consolidated before it begins to sustain labors. In a child the whole skull is scarcely enclosed and the brain properly formed within the fifth or sixth year. It is enough

Figure 2.2
Page from John Amos Comenius' *School of Infancy*

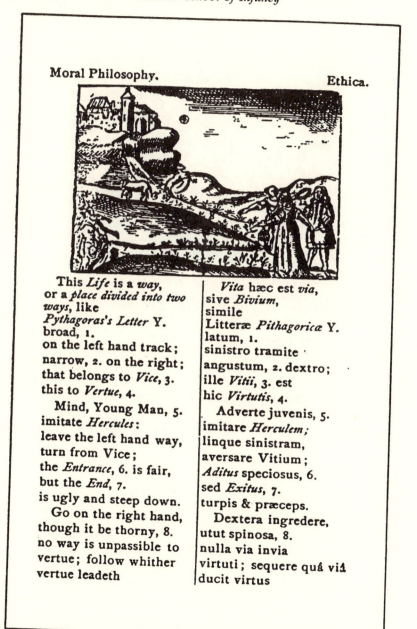

Moral Philosophy.   Ethica.

This *Life* is a *way*, | *Vita* hæc est *via*,
or a *place divided into two* | sive *Bivium*,
ways, like | simile
Pythagoras's Letter Y. | Litteræ *Pithagoricæ* Y.
broad, 1. | latum, 1.
on the left hand track; | sinistro tramite ·
narrow, 2. on the right; | angustum, 2. dextro; ·
that belongs to *Vice*, 3. | ille *Vitii*, 3. est
this to *Vertue*, 4. | hic *Virtutis*, 4.

Mind, Young Man, 5. | Adverte juvenis, 5.
imitate *Hercules*: | imitare *Herculem;*
leave the left hand way, | linque sinistram,
turn from Vice; | aversare Vitium;
the *Entrance*, 6. is fair, | *Aditus* speciosus, 6.
but the *End*, 7. | sed *Exitus*, 7.
is ugly and steep down. | turpis & præceps.

Go on the right hand, | Dextera ingredere,
though it be thorny, 8. | utut spinosa, 8.
no way is unpassible to | nulla via invia
vertue; follow whither | virtuti; sequere quâ viâ
vertue leadeth | ducit virtus

Figure 2.3
Page from John Amos Comenius' *School of Infancy*

Humanity.   Humanitas.

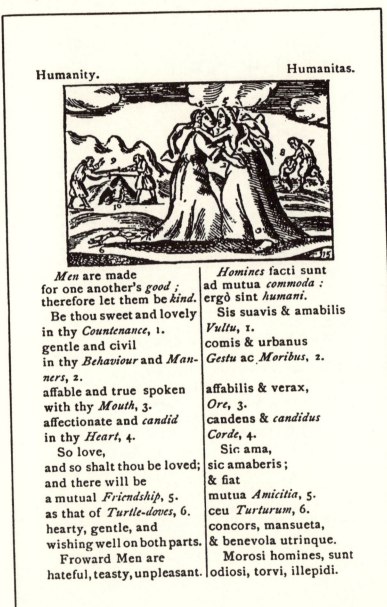

Men are made	*Homines* facti sunt
for one another's *good* ;	ad mutua *commoda* :
therefore let them be *kind*.	ergò sint *humani*.
Be thou sweet and lovely	Sis suavis & amabilis
in thy *Countenance*, 1.	*Vultu*, 1.
gentle and civil	comis & urbanus
in thy *Behaviour* and *Man-*	*Gestu* ac *Moribus*, 2.
ners, 2.	
affable and true spoken	affabilis & verax,
with thy *Mouth*, 3.	*Ore*, 3.
affectionate and *candid*	candens & *candidus*
in thy *Heart*, 4.	*Corde*, 4.
So love,	Sic ama,
and so shalt thou be loved;	sic amaberis ;
and there will be	& fiat
a mutual *Friendship*, 5.	mutua *Amicitia*, 5.
as that of *Turtle-doves*, 6.	ceu *Turturum*, 6.
hearty, gentle, and	concors, mansueta,
wishing well on both parts.	& benevola utrinque.
Froward Men are	Morosi homines, sunt
hateful, teasty, unpleasant.	odiosi, torvi, illepidi.

Source: From *The School of Infancy* by John Amos Comenius. Edited with an introduction by Ernest M. Eller. Copyright © 1956 by the University of North Carolina Press, renewed 1984 by Ernest M. Eller. Used by permission of the publisher.

Figure 2.4
Page from John Amos Comenius' *School of Infancy*

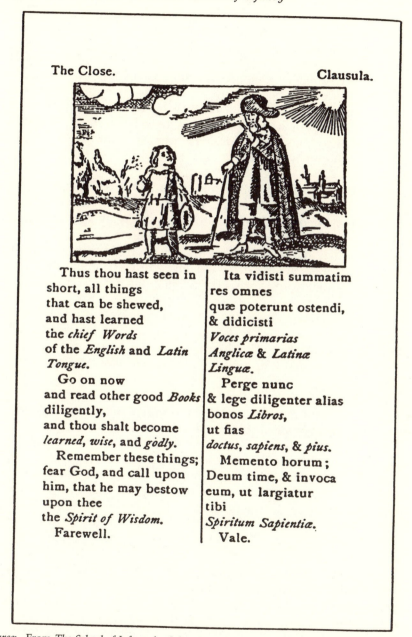

The Close.　　　　　　　　　　　　　　　Clausula.

Thus thou hast seen in short, all things that can be shewed, and hast learned the *chief Words* of the *English* and *Latin Tongue.*	Ita vidisti summatim res omnes quæ poterunt ostendi, & didicisti *Voces primarias Anglicæ* & *Latinæ Linguæ.*
Go on now and read other good *Books* diligently, and thou shalt become *learned, wise*, and *godly.*	Perge nunc & lege diligenter alias bonos *Libros*, ut fias *doctus, sapiens,* & *pius.*
Remember these things; fear God, and call upon him, that he may bestow upon thee the *Spirit of Wisdom.* Farewell.	Memento horum; Deum time, & invoca eum, ut largiatur tibi *Spiritum Sapientiæ.* Vale.

Source: From *The School of Infancy* by John Amos Comenius. Edited with an introduction by Ernest M. Eller. Copyright © 1956 by the University of North Carolina Press, renewed 1984 by Ernest M. Eller. Used by permission of the publisher.

therefore for this age that they learn spontaneously, imperceptibly, and, as it were, in play what ever may be learned at home. (p. 116)

The age of six for the start of formal schooling had been suggested by Plato under state sponsorship and was the practice in the private schools of Athens. As a religious intellectual of his time, it is likely that Comenius had read the writings of Plato. In addition, Comenius was the first to express the relationship between the needs of healthy young plants and growing young children. Over a century later, Friedrich Froebel, the founder of the kindergarten in Germany, repeated Comenius' analogy between growing plants and children. He went so far as to call his school *kindergarten* (children's garden).

Little plants after they shoot up from the seed are transplanted into orchards that they may better grow and bear fruit. In just the same way children cherished in the mother's care, having now acquired strength in mind and body, should be delivered to the care of teachers so that they may better grow up. For young trees when transplanted elsewhere always grow tall, and garden fruit has always a richer flavor than forest fruit. (*The School of Infancy*, p. 116)

The School of Infancy also contains Comenius' advice to mothers concerning education and family living in general. In the chapter titled "Learning by Doing: How Children Ought to be Accustomed to an Active Life and Perpetual Employment," he places before mothers the following:

Boys ever delight in being employed in something, for their youthful blood does not allow them to rest. Now as this is very useful it ought not to be restrained, but provision made that they always have something to do . . . continually occupied in doing something, carrying, constructing, and conveying, provided always that whatever they do be done prudently. Elders ought to assist by showing them the forms of all things, even of playthings (for they cannot yet be occupied in real works) and by playing with them. . . . Infants try to imitate what they see others do. Let them therefore have all things except those that might cause injury to themselves or anything, such an knives, hatchets, glass. When it is not convenient to give them real instruments, let them have toys like leaden knives, wooden swords, ploughs, little carriages, sledges, mills, buildings. With these they may always amuse themselves and thus exercise their bodies to health, their minds to vigor, their bodily members to agility. In a word, whatever children delight to play with, provided it not be hurtful, they ought rather to be gratified than restrained from it, for inactivity is more injurious both to mind and body than anything in which they can be occupied. (pp. 91–92)

In making early childhood curriculum recommendations, Comenius combined his philosophy of education with suggested practices for classroom teachers and/or mothers:

Children also in their fourth and fifth years to be exercised in *Drawing* and *Writing*, according as their inclination may be noticed or excited. Supply them with chalk (poorer persons may use a piece of charcoal) with which they make at their will, dots lines, hooks, or round O's either as an exercise or amusement. In this way they will accustom the hand of the chalk hereafter. They will learn to form letters, will understand what a dot is, and what a little line. All this will afterwards greatly abridge the labors of teachers. . . . The elements of *Arithmetic* can begin to be propounded to children in the third year as soon as they begin to count upward to five, or at least to pronounce the numbers correctly. Although they may not at first understand what these numbers really are, they will soon observe the use to which they are put. In the next three years it will be sufficient if they number up to twenty in succession, and be able to clearly distinguish that seven is more than five, and fifteen more than thirteen; what is an even and what an odd number, which they may easily learn from the play which we call *par impar*, odds and evens. . . . About the second year the principles of *Geometry* may be perceived. When we say of anything that is large or small: They will afterwards easily know what is short or long, wide or narrow. In the fourth year they may learn the differences of forms; for example, what is a circle, what lines, what a square. . . . And if anything more comes spontaneous to their knowledge, they should be shown how to try to measure, to weigh it, thus comparing one with the other and increasing their knowledge. Music is especially natural to us, for as soon as we see the light we immediately sing the song of paradise, thus recalling to our memory our fall: A, a! E, e! I maintain that complaint and wailing are our first music from which it is impossible to restrain infants. And if it were possible, it would be inexpedient, since it contributes to our health. As long as other exercises and excitements are wanting, by this very means their chests and other internal parts relieve themselves of their superfluities. (pp. 93–95)

A major area of study for early childhood scholars today is language acquisition. There are theorists, among them behaviorists, who suggest that the child's knowledge of language is primarily a proposition of memory. Through observations of adults using language, and their own trial and error, children ultimately find out what works as they attempt to satisfy their needs. According to some language theorists, experiences in the environment, accompanied by reinforcements, form the basic pattern for language acquisition. Behaviorists hold the view that young children have a general learning potential, but not a specific one for language.

Other theorists, including those who support the theory of a language acquisition device, suggest that humans are born with an innate capacity to acquire language. The rapid rate at which children seem to solve many intricate problems posed by language indicates that infants must have a head start. It appears that children in all cultures demonstrate similar patterns in mastering complex patterns to achieve a workable vocabulary and syntax, usually within twelve to twenty-four months after birth. Any adult trying to learn a new language will attest to the short time this represents in acquiring an additional language.

Remarkably, one can find aspects of these theories, as well as references to whole language, represented in Comenius' recommended approaches to teaching. His perception of the relationship between language and thought was that they were associated with speech, grammar, and poetry (required areas of study for youth), and should involve both parents and teachers. He also was aware that children enter the learning environment at various levels of development—some are more advanced than others.

> *Grammar*'s beginnings appear in some children as early as their first half-year—in general, however, it is towards the end of the year when they begin to form certain letters such as a, e, i, or even syllables like ba, ma, ta. The following year brings more syllables as they try to pronounce whole words. Then it is the custom to propose to them the easiest words such as tata, mama, papa, and nana. And this baby talk is proper. Nature itself impels them to begin with these easier words since the way adopted by us grown-ups of pronouncing father, mother, and the like is too difficult for babies' tongues. . . . Why shouldn't mother, sister or nurse as a game with infants teach them to pronounce distinctly first of all letters and syllables, and then entire words, starting with the shortest? This exercise gives sufficient grammar for the second year, and for some children who are slower than others it will need to continue into the third year. Thereafter their language will increase with increase in knowledge of things, provided the exercise is continued so that children make it a habit to name what ever they see or do. . . . *Rhetoric*'s principles also arise in the first year, in great part instinctively through gestures. As long as the mind and the

power of speech in this early age remain in their deep roots, we by custom draw babies to knowledge of ourselves and things by gestures and external actions ... I maintain that a baby immediately in its first and second year is able to learn to understand what a wrinkled and what an unwrinkled forehead means, what a threat with a finger means, what a rod, what a repeated rod. All of this is in truth the foundation of rhetorical action.... The principles of *Poetry*, which binds and as it were entwines language in rhythm and measure, likewise arise with the beginning of speech. As soon as a baby begins to understand words it begins to love melody and rhythm. Therefore when an injured baby wails, nurse by custom solace it with ... rhymes. (*The School of Infancy*, pp. 97–99)

Another Comenius work, *The Visible World* (1659), was an illustrated book for children that was hailed as a milestone in literature for young people because it matched illustrations and text. His theory of education, which survived for many years, was described in *The Great Didactic* (1632). Comenius' concern for the education of young children led many to seek his advice. In England, Comenius was commissioned to work with a parliamentary committee to reform education, and this work led to the formation of the British Royal Society. He later worked with a commission that reformed the Swedish educational system.

JOHN LOCKE

The framers of the U.S. Constitution were well-read and well-informed men with various experiences. Thomas Jefferson and others had attended institutions of learning that provided a classical education, probably patterned after a European model. They likely studied European philosophers and theorists. Not surprisingly, the U.S. Constitution appears to reflect the philosophy of John Locke. Locke was not a teacher; he was a philosopher who wrote extensively, usually in support of the wealthy and of governmental policy. Only his thoughts on education will be examined here.

John Locke (1632–1704), born the year Comenius' *The Great Didactic* was published, exerted tremendous influence on emerging education policy and on the writers of the U.S. Constitution. On education theory he wrote *Some Thoughts Concerning Education* (1693), which concerned the instilling of morality and virtue in children. His writings on government included *Two Treatises of Government* (1690), in which he expressed the need for man to subsume his needs within the context of society's needs.

Comenius' ideas concerning the transmission of knowledge through a universal language leading to an informed public was later proposed by Locke and other philosophers of his time. Unlike Comenius, Locke did not espouse an environment of freedom in child rearing and in the class-room. He believed that the teacher should be in charge beyond doubt; one way to do so was to place classroom furniture in fixed places in order to symbolize the strict discipline required.

Locke was among the first to propose the concept of tabula rasa, the idea that learners approach their teacher as a blank slate. This assumes that teachers alone possess the knowledge that needs to be known, and that their role is to impart this knowledge to students, who have little to contribute to this process outside of attention. Locke and his followers were focusing on language and experience as a means of advancing sci-entific knowledge. His empirical view of the dissemination and acqui-sition of information later served to reinforce behaviorist theory.

The behaviorist pattern of didactic teaching is a model for the practice of teaching that flows from the theory of behaviorism, which is sup-ported by the tabula rasa philosophy. These ideas are common to the work of B. F. Skinner and John B. Watson. This example can be used to explain the relationship among philosophy, theory, and practice. By con-trast, those who espoused the romantic views of Comenius, Rousseau, Oberlin, and Pestalozzi treated children as learners in their teaching en-counters, which occurred in an environment where the children were encouraged to interact with people and objects under the careful obser-vation of their teachers. Here, the experience was viewed as important for both child development and knowledge acquisition.

In the classroom, the interaction/observation revealed to the teacher the knowledge that learners brought to the experience. This knowledge could be expanded by the teacher, who through observations could de-termine future teaching/learning plans. These ideas were built upon the concept that learners bring more than a "blank slate" to the experience; they also bring an important knowledgeable person—themselves. These ideas are common to theories of Piaget, Freud, and Erikson, and em-phasize experiences before, during, and after schooling. Their roots are in the philosophy common to Rousseau and other Romantics.

JEAN-JACQUES ROUSSEAU

The French philosopher Jean-Jacques Rousseau (1712–1778) rebelled against the seemingly endless laws and social rules that restricted human experiences. It was his view that individuals are born basically good, and if left alone, they will follow the rules of nature and "everything should be brought into harmony with natural tendencies."

Rousseau's ideas were expressed in his book *Emile*, which described in minute detail a relationship between a tutor and his pupil. It aroused controversy because of its challenge to the stiff, over-regulated, and dis-tant relationships between teachers and their pupils. With his focus on the freedom of experience, the pupil Emile is given great latitude to explore elements in the immediate environment and nature. As the tutor proposes questions to Emile, discussions take place among the elements that called forth the questions. Therefore, natural environments enhance the learner's readiness to acquire knowledge, and responses are appropriate for the pupil's maturational level. "We know nothing of childhood; and with our mistaken notions the further we advance the more we go astray. The wisest writers devote themselves to what a man ought to know, without asking what a child is capable of learning" (Rousseau 1979, p. 1).

When practitioner interest turned to the growth and development of children with special needs, persons with traditional training in education did not focus on children below kindergarten age. The practitioner and theorist Itard, in his carefully documented work on the education of mentally retarded children, provided guidance to theorists and practitioners in the field.

JEAN-MARC-GASPARD ITARD

Jean-Marc-Gaspard Itard (1775–1838), who served as a surgeon during the French Revolution, was also a member of the Academy of Medicine. During the period when psychologists were applying emerging scientific approaches to the study of knowledge acquisition, he applied psychological theories to the study of what is now termed "special education."

Itard's writings on the topic inspired many theorists and practitioners interested in the growth and development of children with special learning needs. In his *Reports on the Savage of Aveyron*, he detailed his educating of an eleven-year-old boy found naked and wild in a forest (1801–1805). This story has been documented in scientific reports and retold in novels and motion pictures. Itard's detailed account has been deemed a milestone by many educational historians. His teaching of his patient/student was hailed by the public as a success. Itard, however, was aware of the limitations of how much was learned by the "savage"—and in his view he had failed. The French scientific community also saw Itard's work as a success.

(Thirty years later the French physician Jean-Etienne-Dominique Esquirol wrote that mental retardation and mental deficiency were not the same. Prior to that time, they were not viewed as being different. Esquirol suggested that idiocy was not a disease but a condition in which the intellectual facilities never matured to the extent that enabled the idiot to acquire age-appropriate knowledge.)

Itard's interest in children with special needs is thought to have originated during his contact with Sicard, director of a school for deaf-mutes in Paris. It was Sicard who asked Itard to make a scientific study of the physiology of hearing. Itard expanded his contribution to the field when he published *Mutism Produced by Lesions of the Intellectual Faculties* (1824) and *Treatise on the Maladies of the Ear and of Hearing* (1842).

EDUCATION OF THE DEAF AND THE MENTALLY RETARDED

Edouard Séguin, one of Itard's students, opened a school for the mentally retarded in France in 1837. Within certain limitations, Séguin's students learned many necessary skills for living. Following his success, by 1880 there were almost 100 schools in Europe and the United States for education of the mentally retarded. This relatively large number of schools for this special learning group was not supported by reliable methods or empirical studies. Theorists and practitioners were guided primarily by the limited writings of Esquirol and Séguin, and Itard's *Wild Boy of Aveyron*. The publication of a dictionary of signs completed by Sicard contributed to his worldwide reputation. He was a longtime advocate of signing as a means to teach the deaf to communicate, but later in life came to embrace oral methods.

There was little improvement of basic empirical information until 1904, when the French minister of public education appointed a committee to study the possibilities of special education. Alfred Binet, a member of the commission, devised a screening test for children enrolled in Paris public schools. His interest in mental retardation, and a book that he wrote on the subject, probably led to his appointment to the commission.

Roche-Ambroise Cucurron Sicard (1742–1822) succeeded Séguin as director the National Institute for Deaf-Mutes in Paris, and opened another center in Bordeaux (1786–1789). In 1780, he published *Memoir on the Art of Teaching Deaf-mutes from Birth*.

In the United States, educators were aware of French success with deaf learners. Thomas H. Gallaudet, who was planning the first school for the deaf in the United States, was invited to visit with Sicard at the National Institute in Paris in order to study his methods. After becoming proficient in the French methods of teaching the deaf, Gallaudet returned to the United States with Laurent Clerc, who had been recommended by Sicard. Clerc became one of the first teachers hired to teach at Gallaudet's new school (Bender 1970; Lane 1984).

WILHELM WUNDT

Probably no psychologist has written more on topics in experimental psychology, higher mental processes, social behavior, and language systems of various ethnic groups than Wilhelm Wundt (1832–1920). Considered the originator of scientific psychology, Wundt influenced numerous American psychologists through their study at his German laboratory of scientific psychology, founded at Leipzig in 1879. He insisted that his students publish the results of their work and establish laboratories in their own countries. Through these methods, Wundt thought, information concerning scientific psychology would become widespread.

A significant separation occurred between psychology and philosophy when Wundt's students returned to their native lands and founded laboratories in which the new psychology would be treated as a scientific study. A man with tremendous memory for scientific studies, Wundt worked toward an understanding of the basic elements that comprised consciousness, and defined the principles determining how these elements combined to form consciousness.

Wundt's work was especially relevant for child development because of its assessment of children's thinking, the symbolic meaning of childhood play, social interactions, and children making meaning from their experiences. Wundt's idea about perception coincided with the general view of other German psychologists. In general, they conceptualized individual differences in sensation and perception as errors rather than as individual differences. Individual differences posed a problem for German psychologists in the testing movement, because they could not be eliminated, nor could they all be accounted for (Goodenough 1949).

LEV S. VYGOTSKY

Lev S. Vygotsky (1896–1934) was a Russian psychologist who, as a student during the height of Wundt's popularity, theorized unique perspectives regarding children's play. From the beginning of Pestalozzi and Froebel's early childhood curriculum, play had formed the foundation for the conceptualization of early learning. It was their view that play was an unfolding developmental aspect of childhood, and its emergence provided pleasure; but more important, it was a developmental necessity. (Piaget's "developmental" descriptions supported this principle. His qualitative descriptions of his observations of children's logical thinking were in part the results of his observations of children at play.)

Several philosophical and theoretical ideas associated with Vygotsky's interpretation of children's play are at variance with the notions of Froebel, Pestalozzi, and Piaget. Vygotsky interpreted the role of pleasure as an aspect of play that is variable and incidental, but not fundamental.

To define play as an activity that gives pleasure to the child is inaccurate for two reasons. First, many activities give the child much keener experiences of pleasure than play, for example, sucking a pacifier, even though the child is not being satiated. And

second, there are games in which the activity itself is not pleasurable, for example, games predominantly at the end of preschool
and the beginning of school age, that give pleasure only if the child
finds the results interesting. Sporting games (not only athletic
sports, but other games that can be won or lost) are often accompanied by displeasure when the outcome is unfavorable to the
child. But while pleasure cannot be regarded as the defining characteristic of play, it seemed to me that theories which ignore the
fact that play fulfills the children's needs result in the pedantic in-
tellectualization of play. (Vygotsky 1978, p. 92)

Vygotsky approached the study of human behavior through his commitment to the historical materialism of Marxism. In a scientific environment that included John Watson, the "father of behaviorism" in the
United States; Wilhelm Wundt, considered the originator of experimental
psychology; and Gestalt psychologists Wolfgang Köhler, Kurt Koffka,
Kurt Lewin, and Max Wertheimer, Vygotsky's experimentation in Russia
infused sociocultural perspectives into the work of experimental psychology.

Vygotsky proposed that all phenomena are perceived in a fluid state
that is always undergoing change. In this context, it has a past and a
present that can be transformed from elementary patterns into complex
ones. In addition to the stimulus-response behaviorist observation of
Watson and his students, and the part/whole interpretations of experiences by Gestaltists, Vygotsky's theory of human development proposed
that all phenomena have a past, a present, and a proposed future. Past
experiences influence society, and, according to Marx, the circumstances
of the here and now take on patterns that are influenced by history.

Vygotsky's proposals for various phenomena can be viewed within
this sociocultural context. For example, he theorized that child development in general and children's activities in particular are shaped
through sociocultural experiences. The emergence of play as a function
of experience is described thus:

A very young child tends to gratify her desires immediately; normally the interval between a desire and its fulfillment is extremely
short. No one has met a child under three years old who wants to
do something a few days in the future. However, at the preschool
age, a great many unrealizable tendencies and desires emerge. It is
my belief if needs that could not be realized immediately did not
develop during the preschool years, there would be no play, because play seems to be invented at the point when the child begins
to experience unrealizable tendencies. Suppose that a very young
(perhaps a two-and-a-half-year old) child wants something—for ex-

ample to occupy her mother's role. She wants it at once. If she cannot have it, she may throw a temper tantrum, and she can usually be sidetracked and pacified so that she forgets her desire. Toward the beginning of preschool age, when desires that cannot be immediately gratified or forgotten make their appearance and the tendency to immediate fulfillment of desires, characteristic of the preceding stage, is retained, the child's behavior changes. To resolve this tension, the preschool child enters an imaginary, illusory world in which the unrealizable desires can be realized, and this world is what we call play. Imagination is a new psychological process for the child; it is not present in the consciousness, it originally arises from action. The old adage that child's play is imagination in action must be reversed: we can say that imagination in adolescents and school children is play without action. (Vygotsky 1978, p. 93)

Basic to Vygotsky's themes is that children learn through social interactions with older and more knowledgeable persons within their environment. Social interaction and communication between children and more experienced adults assist children in advancing their knowledge. In Vygotsky's view, he makes the use of language within socio/cultural systems central to children's knowledge acquisition. For these reasons, Vygotsky's ideas have been called "sociocultural theory." On the other hand, Piaget focused on children's knowledge emerging from internal age-related developmental cues that unfold in the presence of experiences. Piaget's ideas have been criticized for several reasons, among them, that they are culturally generic. The sociocultural concepts of Vygotsky emphasize social interaction and are therefore sensitive to cultural variations to which children might be exposed. Vygotsky concludes that basic fundamentals of social systems should be known, but knowledge of variations and nuances that defines one's culture is essential. In this regard, one can become intellectually and politically relevant.

THE TRANSCENDENTALISTS

By the 1830s transcendentalists like Bronson Alcott, William Ellery Channing, Ralph Waldo Emerson, Margaret Fuller, Elizabeth Peabody, and Henry David Thoreau had formed ideas, through their speaking engagements, work in schools, and writings, that childhood provided opportunities for the general improvement of humanity. Their ideas called for the public education system to provide kindergartens and early education to inspire youth toward nonmaterialistic "natural" models of life and living.

Through her relationship with Channing and Emerson, Elizabeth Peabody came into direct contact with persons who could assist her in understanding transcendental philosophy. Peabody's ideas about early childhood education were influenced by New England transcendentalism and its belief that children not only were basically good but also were malleable. Transcendental thought concluded that since divine guidance was present in all of nature, individuals could transcend evil. As Comenius had suggested many years earlier, children required nurturing and guidance, not restraint.

Channing who offered his publication *Emancipation* to Peabody so that she could disseminate her views on women's rights and the abolition of slavery. In 1835, in *Record of a School*, she detailed Pestalozzi's methods as employed by Bronson Alcott at the famous Temple School.

Emerson defined transcendentalism for his readers in his 1836 book *Nature*. He explained to his readers that as a philosophy, transcendentalism expressed an idealism of their time.

> Transcendentalism among us, is idealism.... As thinkers, mankind have ever divided into two sects, Materialists and Idealists, the first class founding on experience, the second on consciousness; the first class beginning to think from the data of the senses, the second class perceive that the senses are not final, and say, The senses give us representations of things, but what are the things themselves, they cannot tell. The materialist insists on facts, on history, on the force of circumstances and the animal wants of man; the idealist on the power of Thought and of Will, on inspiration, on miracle, on individual culture. These two modes of thinking are both natural, but the idealist contends that his way of thinking is in higher nature. He concedes all that the other affirms, admits the impressions of sense, admits their coherency, their use and beauty, and then asks the materialist for his grounds of assurance that things are as his senses represent them.... Every materialist will be an idealist; but no idealist can ever go backward to be a materialist. (Bode 1981, p. 92)

Ralph Waldo Emerson (1803–1882) attended the Boston Latin School and graduated from Harvard University in 1821. In the early 1820s he was a schoolteacher, and in 1829 he became the minister of a Unitarian church in Boston. While in Europe in 1832, he met Thomas Carlyle, Samuel Taylor Coleridge, and William Wordsworth. During his lifetime he spoke out against slavery and, along with other members of "the Concord School," condemned the practice in his writings. This group of Emerson's colleagues included Margaret Fuller, Nathaniel Hawthorne, Henry David Thoreau, and Bronson Alcott, the father of Louisa May Alcott.

Amos Bronson Alcott (1799–1888), born near Wolcott, Connecticut, was one of the first American educational innovators to use methods attributed to Pestalozzi. He taught in rural Connecticut schools and, following Pestalozzi's methods, emphasized a child-centered approach that focused on affective aspects of child development rather than the memorization of multiplication tables and historical facts commonly required in the schools.

In the late 1820s Alcott moved to Philadelphia, where one of his daughters was born and where he founded an experimental school. After four years in Philadelphia, he returned to New England and opened the famous Temple School.

A belief in the nurturing of childhood learning through the active engagement of children in their own learning was demonstrated by Alcott through his own teaching at Temple. Elizabeth Peabody worked as Alcott's assistant at the school and recorded detailed descriptions of the school and his methods.

> About twenty children came the first day. They were all under ten years of age, excepting two or three girls. I became his assistant to teach Latin to such as might desire to learn. Mr. Alcott sat behind his table, and the children were placed in chairs so far apart, that they could not easily touch each other. He then asked each one separately, what idea she or he had of the object of coming to school. To learn; was the first answer. To learn what? By pursuing this question, all the common exercises of school were brought up—successively—even philosophy. Still Mr. Alcott intimated that this was not all; and at last someone said, "to behave well," and in pursuing this expression into its meanings, they at last decided that they came to learn to feel rightly, to think rightly, and to act rightly. A boy of seven years old suggested, and all agreed, that rightly actions were the most important of these three. (Cohen & Scheer 1997, p. 73)

Soliciting children's ideas in classrooms of that time was considered a radical endeavor. This approach involved a Socratic interaction between the teacher and children seldom witnessed in schooling previously. Newspaper stories that focused attention on Alcott's innovative methods attracted widespread attention. Alcott's *Conversations with Children on the Gospels* described various teacher-pupil dialogues. These dialogues interpreted Pestalozzi's curriculum as implemented by Alcott, but were denounced by some as obscene and blasphemous.

Alcott spent the final years of his life directing the Concord School of Philosophy, conducted during summers for the study of Hegel's philosophy and transcendentalism. From 1859 to 1865, he was selected as superintendent of schools in Concord, Massachusetts. During his lifetime he was often dismissed as an idealist, and even today he is seldom credited with the philosophical thought later espoused by John Dewey.

Louisa May Alcott (1832–1888), author and transcendentalist, was educated by her father, as well as Ralph Waldo Emerson and Henry David Thoreau. In 1868 she edited *Merry's Museum*, a magazine for young girls. She wrote *Little Women* (1868), long considered a classic, and *Little Men* (1871), which never achieved the popularity of *Little Women*.

Goodwill toward humanity was basic to Immanuel Kant's conceptualization of transcendental philosophy. Through a mixture of friendship and collegiality, speech-making, formal group meetings, and informal gatherings, a group of New England thinkers whose names read like the Who's Who of their times became transcendental activists and scholars. As first defined by Kant, transcendental philosophy suggested that individuals possess a subjective awareness of an experience followed by certain human principles that can enable objective interpretations of that experience.

Elizabeth Peabody disseminated liberal views through the *Dial*, a publication for which Hawthorne wrote, and that was later published by Emerson. Peabody also held regular discussions of the literary scene at a bookstore she owned. Through the relationships formed at these discussions, her sister Sophie married Hawthorne, and her sister Mary married Horace Mann. After the death of her friends William Channing and Margaret Fuller, Peabody closed the bookstore.

Inspired by the German philosophers Immanuel Kant (1724–1804), Johann Friedrich Herbart (1776–1841), and Friedrich Wilhelm Nietzsche (1844–1900), and the English Romantic poet William Wordsworth (1770–1850), American transcendentalists held the period of childhood in high regard because, in their view, this was the purest stage of human development, not yet consumed by self-serving impulses. They also theorized that early education of the proper kind, combined with "naturalistic" child-rearing practices, could influence the retention of the "saintly" spirit of childhood and provide succeeding generations of adults with positive humane values. Wordsworth wrote in "My Heart Leaps Up" (1807):

> My heart leaps up when I behold
> A rainbow in the sky:
> So was it when my life began;
> So is it now I am a man;
> So be it when I shall grow old,
> Or let me die!
> The Child is father of the Man;

And I would wish my days to be
Bound each to each by natural piety.

The rejection of extreme materialistic philosophies designed to direct and control human behavior at the expense of reducing human freedom was a persistent thesis of Rousseau's work. Educators frequently cite *Emile* as an expression of Rousseau's ideas; there exist, however, many volumes of posthumous works and letters containing a broad description of Rousseau—the citizen, the writer, philosopher, and father. Transcendentalism can be compared to ideas found in Rousseau's writings. Of these comparisons, Rousseau's disdain for eighteenth-century-type teacher-controlled learning environments would be supported by nineteenth-century transcendentalists. Both Rousseau and transcendentalists would agree that a primary function of the teacher is to create a learning environment where purity of childhood can be nurtured and sustained.

The transcendental support for kindergarten and early education was encouraged by the belief that guidance and education of the very young offered the best opportunity for infusing in society a counterbalance to materialism. The Ethical Culture philosophical movement also shared these ideals with transcendentalists. Felix Adler, mentioned earlier as an early founder of a free kindergarten in New York City and a leader in the New York Society for Ethical Society, also actively supported the West Coast Free Kindergarten activists.

IMMANUEL KANT AND JOHANN FRIEDRICH HERBART

Immanuel Kant, born of poor parents in Königsberg, Germany, was expected by his mother and a supportive family minister, F. A. Schultz—a recognized philosopher—to follow a career in theology. While at the University of Königsberg, he met Martin Knutzen (1713–1751), a professor of philosophy, and Johann Gottfried Teske (1704–1772), a professor of physics, who had a profound effect upon his thinking. With modest financial aid from an uncle, he completed his university studies in 1746.

His financial condition turned Kant to private tutoring in his hometown, and this contributed greatly to his formation of instructional techniques and a love for teaching. After ten years of tutoring, Kant returned to the university as a lecturer in mathematics. For the next forty years he lectured on philosophy, physics, classroom teaching methods, metaphysics, and logic. He also educated himself in physical geography and anthropology. Kant's interest in pedagogy was supported by his belief in some of the ideas expressed by Rousseau and the German reformer Basedow (see Chapter 1). His concern was whether an education theory should constitute a moral basis for granting children complete independence. He theorized that freedom in the learning environment provided the intellectual basis for scholarship.

Kant's philosophy of education was articulated in four categories: civilization, cultivation, discipline, and moralization. Briefly, civilization implies a need for individual socialization. This suggests the need for one to achieve equilibrium in one's social context. Cultivation encompasses the skills and techniques that are made available to individuals through pedagogy and teacher/learner interactions. Discipline refers to the relationship between the learner and the environment, and a redirection of human inclinations to exploit human and physical nature (which invokes what Sigmund Freud later referred to as the id). Finally, moralization implies that the relationship between child and teacher will lead to the pupil's selection of proper aims for the fulfillment of life.

In his own education, Kant creatively selected a broad range of topics about which to learn. And like Rousseau, he reflected that these four conditions could not exist in an atmosphere that did not afford freedom of exploration. He also believed, however, that experience was essential for the advancement of knowledge. He theorized that knowledge and the reality of natural events were unified by experience. He continued to explore the relationship between reality and idealism in *Critique of Pure Reason* (1781), *Critique of Practical Reason* (1788), and *Critique of Judgment* (1790).

Johann Friedrich Herbart, German philosopher and educator, through the work of an excellent tutor and a devoted mother achieved competence in Greek, mathematics, metaphysics, logic, and music by the age of twelve. His scholarly works included a thorough study of Locke and Rousseau. He placed great emphasis upon thoughtful instruction and the direct teaching of morality. He was a critic of Rousseau's view of the learner's natural inclinations toward education, as well as of Locke's contention that persons should be educated for civic participation and citizenship. The teaching of morality, he thought, was an important task for educators. He interpreted Rousseau as viewing morality as incidental to the teacher/learner relationship, and Locke as viewing morality as secondary to citizenship and the common good.

Herbart completed university studies at Jena under the primary influence of the philosopher Johann Gottlieb Fichte. After leaving Jena, he took an assignment to tutor the children of the governor of Interlaken, Switzerland. During this employment his thoughts about logic and reason came together with his ideas about establishing an ideal relationship between pupils and teachers. To help resolve some of the questions confronting him, he conferred with Pestalozzi. After their meeting, he wrote a criticism of Pestalozzi's ideas, *How Gertrude Teaches Her Children*.

Herbart also believed the learner's free access to information and materials was essential for reforms in education. This free access would bring out the noblest character in pupils and enable them to demonstrate positive regard for all beings. Herbart did not, however, believe that positive regard would flow from the free learners in the absence of the teacher's creating an environment where pupils could become aware of such things as morality.

Morality, he thought, should flow naturally from the role of teachers and the professional lives they led. This created differences between the assumed natural inclinations for goodwill in childhood as espoused by American transcendentalists.

Through the work of American educators who were influenced by his philosophical and psychological insights—including Nina C. Vande-walker, director of kindergarten training at the State Normal School in Milwaukee, Wisconsin, and Frank McMurry, professor of education at Teachers College, Columbia University—Herbart exerted significant influence on methods employed in early education in the United States.

EARLY CHILDHOOD EDUCATION IN THE UNITED STATES

Kindergartens in the United States have a different history than grade school programs. In the earliest traditions, the care and development of children was thought to be the domain of women. Within the tradition of seeing women, children, and families as the domain of female professionals, the study of preschool education did not start in colleges of education, but rather in departments of home economics along with nursing, health studies, nutrition, cooking, and sewing. Most teacher training institutions maintained a department of home economics. By the 1960s, many schools integrated their home economics departments into elementary education or into newly formed early childhood education departments; others renamed "home economics" as "human ecology" or "child and family studies."

In the nineteenth century, kindergartens were not viewed as regular schooling; as late as 1895, they were considered the responsibility of the neighborhood settlement house, church missions, almshouses, and other philanthropic institutions that served poor families. In the late 1800s, large numbers of European immigrants began to land in the United States, many of whom had large families. These immigrants, and African-American migrants from the Southern states, tended to concentrate in cities, seeking employment. Major U.S. cities came to have ghettos, districts characterized by poverty and overcrowding. Both adults and school children were sickly, poorly fed, and poorly clothed. Public school personnel generally treated children from these families with disdain. Under these circumstances, it is not surprising that school authorities ignored the needs of preschool-age children from these neighborhoods.

Philanthropists identified the school as the most reasonable place to provide services for preschool children. Persons interested in what was then a new educational movement developed a strategy for its inclusion in regular public schooling. Philanthropic organizations asked school authorities to allow the use of empty classrooms for kindergartens, and agreed to pay the teachers and the cost of materials—and even rent. Larger school systems agreed, offering the most unattractive vacant facilities. Kindergarten advocates were nonetheless pleased, because they saw this as a first step toward encouraging schools to establish kindergartens on their premises. The ultimate plan was to convince schools to pay for kindergarten teachers' salaries and classroom supplies.

By 1900, many cities had incorporated kindergartens in the regular school, and hired a kindergartner to teach (Figure 2.5). As more and more schools, primarily in major cities, established kindergartens as a part of their regular services, school systems accepted the costs of preschool teachers and salaries were raised to match those of regular teachers. This transition called for more preschool-trained teachers. (It was not until the 1940s that education beyond the equivalent of high school completion was required by states for preschool teaching.)

An important initiative in early childhood education occurred because of a president's effort to break the cycle of poverty. Project Head Start was established in 1965 as a part of President Lyndon B. Johnson's War on Poverty. The president called on early childhood specialists to establish guidelines for the recruiting and training of teachers, social workers, nutritionists, and a variety of other workers to provide services for thousands of preschool children.

Once again, national early education for children was tied to family services aimed at reducing the debilitating effects of poverty. Professionals could not agree on the amount of direct instruction that should be mixed with activities meant to promote social, emotional, and physical growth of the child. The concerns of some experts centered around the measurement of academic skills gained by Head Start graduates, and the levels of achievement that poor children would carry with them into regular schools.

The federal government's response was to provide an extension of Head Start called Follow-Through, created to follow Head Start graduates through grade 4, with cooperative working relationships established between Head Start personnel and public school teachers. The supervision of these relationships was assigned to traditional early childhood personnel from universities and colleges. Bank Street College, Columbia University, the University of Rhode Island, Tufts University, and the

Figure 2.5
First Public School Kindergartens in the United States

Bisbee, AZ: Central School, 1907

Denver, CO: 41 kindergartens, 1893

New Britain, CT: 1892

New Haven, CT: Zunder School, 1885; Scranton School, 1885; Cedar
Street School, 1885; Winchester School, 1885

Stonington, CT: Grammar School, 1904

Waterbury, CT: Duggan School, 1902; Driggs School, 1902; Margaret
Croft School, 1902

St. Petersburg, FL: 140 First Street North, 1906

Chicago, IL: Altgeld School, 1889; Bradwell School, 1889; Forestville
School, 1889; Hamline School, 1889; Phil Sheridan School, 1889; Ray
School, 1889

Lake Forest, IL: Halsey School, 1895

Moline, IL: Grant School, 1903; Lincoln School, 1903; Willard School, 1903

Fort Wayne, IN: James M. Smith School, 1899; Hanna School, 1899;
Washington and Jefferson Schools, 1899; Harner and Bloomingdale
Schools, 1899; Nebraska School, 1899

Madison, IN: Eggleston School, 1907

Des Moines, IA: Brooks School, 1884; Bird School, 1884; Elmwood School,
1884; Garfield School, 1884; Grant School, 1884; Henry Sabin School,
1884; Cattel School, 1884; Webster School, 1884

Grinnell, IA: Cooper School, 1890; Parker School, 1890; South School,
1890

Atchison KS: Ingalls School, 1910

Calumet, MI: Public Schools, 1885; Garfield School, 1885; Holmes School,
1885

Flint, MI: Doyle School, 1902

Kalamazoo, MI: Vine Street School, 1898

Duluth, MN: Washington School, 1896

Winona, MN: Kosciusko School, 1892; Madison and Jefferson Schools,
1891

St. Louis, MO: Dozier School, 1873; Marquette School, 1873; Wyman
School, 1873

Walpole, NH: North Walpole School, 1904

Atlantic City, NJ: Brighton Avenue School, 1904; Illinois Avenue School,
1904

Figure 2.5 (continued)

East Orange, NJ: Colombian School, 1895; Franklin School, 1895

Trenton, NJ: Carroll Robbins Training School, 1903; Girard School, 1903; Parker School, 1903; Washington School, 1903

Buffalo, NY: Annex No. 1, 1897; Annex No. 7, 1897; School No. 16, 1897; School No. 20, 1897; School No. 51, 1897

Gloversville, NY: Public Schools, 1888

Jamestown, NY: District No. 4, 1893; District No. 7, 1893; District No. 10, 1893

Lockport, NY: Public Schools, 1899

New York, NY: The Bronx, No. 23, 1893; Manhattan, No. 12, 1893

Rochester, NY: School No. 9, 1887; School No. 10, 1887; School No. 12, 1887; School No. 16, 1887; School No. 19, 1887

Syracuse, NY: Clinton School, 1895; Grace School, 1895; Putnam School, 1895; Sumner School, 1895

Utica, NY: Faxton School, 1890; Blucker School, 1890

Yonkers, NY: School No. 7, 1895; School No. 12, 1895; School No. 18, 1895

Cleveland, OH: Boulevard School, 1894; Lincoln School, 1897; Quincy School, 1897; Tod School, 1896

Dayton, OH: Allen School, 1896; Franklin School, 1896; McKinley School, 1896; Webster School, 1896

Newport, RI: Public Schools, 1882

Salt Lake City, UT: Franklin School, 1906; Wasatch School, 1906

Seattle, WA: Public Schools, 1898

Appleton, WI: Lincoln School, 1897

Eau Claire, WI: Tenth Ward School, 1904

Fond du Lac, WI: McKinley School, 1894; Union School, 1894

Kenosha, WI: 1905

Milwaukee, WI: Thirty-seventh St. School, 1881; Dover St. School, 1881; Twentieth St. School, 1881; Scott St. School, 1881; Forest Home Avenue School, 1881; Clark St. School, 1881

Sheboygan, WI: Franklin School, 1886; Jefferson School, 1886; U.S. Grant School, 1886

National Association for the Education of Young Children were major players.

In the late 1960s after studies reported poor IQ gains among Head Start graduates, community groups and parents associated with Head Start were invited to a conference at which they could select from among various models of early childhood education. The best-known early childhood program directors and college/university professors were invited to make presentations. After communities had chosen their models, personnel who spoke on behalf of the various models were contracted by community representatives to train their Head Start staffs. Follow-Through was funded for several years, but today Head Start stands alone and many of its teachers do not have minimum public school teaching credentials.

REFERENCES

Aries, P. 1962. *Centuries of Childhood: A History of Family Life.* Translated by Robert Baldick. New York: Alfred A. Knopf.

Bender, R. E. 1970. *The Conquest of Deafness.* Cleveland, OH: Case Western Reserve University Press.

Bernal, M. 1987. *Black Athena: The Afroasiatic Roots of Classical Civilization.* New Brunswick, NJ: Rutgers University Press.

Binet, A., & Simon, T. 1907, 1914. *Mentally Defective Children.* Translated by W. B. Drummond, London: Edward Arnold.

Bode, C. 1981. *The Portable Emerson.* New York: Penguin Books.

Botsford, G. W., & Robinson, C. A. 1939. *Hellenic History.* New York: Macmillan.

Braun, S. J., & Edwards, E. P. 1972. *History and Theory of Early Childhood Education.* Belmont, CA: Wadsworth.

Caldwell, W. E. 1937. *The Ancient World.* New York: Rinehart & Company.

Celarier, J. L. 1966. *Plato's Republic: Analytic Notes and Review.* New York: American R.D.M. Corporation.

Cohen, M. R., & Scheer, S. 1997. *The Work of Teachers in America: A Social History Through Stories.* Mahwah, NJ: Erlbaum Associates.

Cole, P. R. 1931. *History of Educational Thought.* New York: Oxford University Press.

Comenius, J. A. 1633; 1957. *The School of Infancy.* Edited by E. M. Eller. Chapel Hill: University of North Carolina Press.

Cremin, L. A. 1965. *The Genius of American Education.* New York: Random House/ Vintage Books.

Cross, R. C., & Woozley, A. D. 1964. *Plato's Republic: A Philosophical Commentary.* New York: Macmillan.

Dahlstrand, F. C. 1982. *Amos Bronson Alcott.* New York: Fairleigh Dickinson Press.

Demos, R. 1966. *The Philosophy of Plato.* New York: Octagon Books.

Douglas, A. 1977. *The Feminization of American Culture.* New York: Avon Books.

Frank, L. 1938. "The Beginnings of Child Development and Family Life Education in the Twentieth Century." *Merrill-Palmer Quarterly* 8 (4): 7–28.

Goodenough, F. L. 1949. *Mental Testing.* New York: Rinehart.

Greenberg, P. 1967. "CDGM . . . An Experiment in Preschool for the Poor—by the Poor." *Young Children* 22 (5): 307–315.

International Kindergarten Union. 1924. *Pioneers of the Kindergarten in America.* New York: Century.

Jacobs, J., & Heighway, J. 1966. *The Fables of Aesop*. Ann Arbor, MI: University Microfilms.

Kaestle, C. F., & Vinovskis, M. 1980. *Education and Social Change in the Nineteenth Century*. Cambridge: Cambridge University Press.

Lane, H. 1984. *When the Mind Hears*. New York: Random House.

Nietzsche, F. 1886; 1990. *Twilight of the Idols*. Translated by H. Henry. New York: Penguin Books.

Peterson, J. 1925. *Early Conceptions of Tests of Intelligence*. New York: World Book.

Plato. 360 B.C.; 1976. "The Seventh Letter." In J. Harward, *The Platonic Epistles*. Translated by J. Harward. New York: Amo Press.

Prentice, W. K. 1940. *The Ancient Greeks*. Princeton, NJ: Princeton University Press.

Rostovtzeff, M. L. 1927. *History of the Ancient World*. New York: Oxford University Press.

Rousseau, J. J. 1762; 1979. *Emile*. Translated by A. Bloom. New York: Basic Books.

Séguin, E. 1886; 1907. *Idiocy: Its Treatment by the Physiological Method*. New York: Teachers College, Bureau of Publications.

Trevor, A. A. 1939. *History of Ancient Civilization*. New York: Harcourt, Brace.

Tucker, T. G. 1922. *Life in Ancient Greece*. New York: Macmillan.

van Hook, L. R. 1923. *Greek Life and Thought*. New York: Columbia University Press.

Vygotsky, L. S. 1978. *Mind in Society: The Development of Higher Psychological Processes*, edited by M. Cole, V. John-Steiner, S. Scribner, and E. Souberman. Cambridge, MA: Harvard University Press.

———. 1934; 1986. *Thought and Language*. Translated by A. Kozulin. Cambridge, MA: MIT Press.

White, R. W. 1963. *Ego and Reality in Psychoanalytic Theory*. New York: International Universities Press.

3

Theoretical Imagination

We know nothing of childhood; and with our mistaken notions the further we advance the further we go astray. The wisest writers devote themselves to what a man ought to know, without asking what a child is capable of learning. They are always looking for the man in the child, without considering what he is before he became a man.
—Jean-Jacques Rousseau

Erik Erikson, Sigmund Freud, Jean Piaget, and B. F. Skinner have been the most influential theorists in early education. Though Skinner was the best-known behaviorist, Edward Lee Thorndike and G. Stanley Hall worked closely with classroom teachers and children in implementing behaviorist objectives.

In the absence of a unified theory of child development, practitioners must choose from a variety of theories that appear to be appropriate for particular teaching and learning situations. The theories of Piaget, Freud, and Erikson can be grouped as stage theories. These theories work within the context of formulating steps and stages in the human life cycle. These three theorists have established stages of early childhood that appear to occur within roughly the same age ranges. For example, Freud's oral stage covers the same age range as Erikson's basic trust vs. mistrust. And Freud's latency period has the same age span as Erikson's industry vs. inferiority and Piaget's concrete operations. Skinner's work lies outside of this group. The models of Piaget, Freud, and Erikson are compared in Table 3.1.

JEAN PIAGET

Prior to 1960, psychologists denounced Piaget's methods because they employed observational techniques rather than the statistical treatments commonly associated with the scientific method. By the mid-1960s, such criticism had waned in light of changing attitudes about what constituted acceptable research methodology. By the 1990s, psychologists view the work of Piaget as an essential contribution to child study, cognitive psychology, and developmental psychology.

Born in Neuchâtel, Switzerland, Jean Piaget (1896–1980) published his first academic paper at the age of ten. It consisted of a single page concerning an albino sparrow. The academic community was slow to accept his work as clearly scientific because a great deal of it was recorded observations. As the research community became more accepting of qualitative work, Piaget's studies came into favor.

A biologist, he had received his Ph.D. at the age of twenty-two. Before the age of thirty-two, Piaget had published more than twenty papers on biological subjects. During this early period he worked in several psychoanalytic clinics and laboratories in Europe with Eugen Bleuler and Théodore Simon, among others.

While employed in Simon's laboratory, Piaget was assigned to scale Sir Cyril Burt's tests of reasoning for young children. This period is thought to mark the beginning of Piaget's interest in children; it was also during this time that his wife gave birth to their first child.

> Piaget's conception of infancy, like Freud's, was influenced by debates on the mechanisms of evolutionary change. Piaget sided with those who wanted to award most of the power for change to the organism's commerce with the environment rather than to genetic mutation. Piaget likened the development of cognitive function to the evolution of organs and bodily processes because, in his conception, the infant's cognitive abilities derive from active interaction with objects in the world and from successive accommodations to new challenges. When Piaget looked at the infant, he saw a baby playing with the mother's face and fingers. Nursing, being nurtured, and exploring the caregiver's fingers are all characteristics of infancy. It is not obvious that one of these functions is more central; theory awards one of them greater status than others. (Kagan 1984, p. 29)

Probably the most difficult to understand aspect of Piaget's theory is created by his terms. Once these are understood, his fundamental theory becomes less complex. First, Piaget proposes that the human organism develops in steps and stages. This development is expressed in terms of

Table 3.1
Models of Early Human Relationships

Age	Object Relationships	Mother-Child Issues	Psychosexual Stages	Psychosocial Stages	
			Freud	Erickson	Piaget
0–3 mo.	none to reflex 3 mo. smile	initial adaptation	oral stage	basic trust vs. mistrust	sensorimotor stage
3–6 mo.	mother preferred	reciprocal interaction			
6–9 mo.	stranger anxiety	early directed activity			
9–15 mo.	exploration and differentiation	focalization	anal stage	autonomy vs. shame and doubt	
12–18 mo.	beginnings of self-awareness	self-awareness			
1 yr.–2 yr.	exploration and differentiation of relationships	initial testing of destructive aggression	phallic stage		pre-operational stage
2–3 yr.	between self and others	modification of aggression			
1–3 yr.	consolidation of body image and beginnings of sex identity	extension of secondary process functions in interaction	oedipal stage	initiative vs. guilt	
3–6 yr.	consolidation of sex identity; genuine concern for others; self-control	development of concern for parents first as extension of self, then as separate people. Differs as to sex			
6–9 yr.	competition and achievement differentiated manner according to sex and age of object	concern turns outward, to school, community, peers	latency	industry vs. inferiority	concrete operations

Source: Compiled by the author.

months and years of age, but there is considerable overlap. For example, Piaget suggests that before the age of three, children do not fully understand how to play according to rules. In reality, however, some children may start to understand rules by the age of thirty months, while others may not gain this understanding until forty months, four months beyond Piaget's cutoff age. However, if one had a large sample, say, 500 children, the average would be thirty-six months for beginning to comprehend the rules of a given game. Age ranges for other stages are equally flexible.

The terms "adaptation" and "assimilation" must be understood in order for Piaget's theory to be fully appreciated. As Piaget conceptualizes adaptation, the theoretical basis borrows from Darwin the idea that in an interaction between the human and the environment, survival requires that the individual adapt to requirements established by the environment. This is true for all living things. Organisms that cannot or will not adapt will not thrive long enough to reproduce themselves, and eventually disappear from our world.

Assimilation and accommodation are ways in which children make meaning from experiences. Our environment creates certain demands that we must accommodate. We will then react to the environment in terms of what we have assimilated (learned). Each of the four major stages—sensorimotor, preoperational, concrete operations, and formal operations—interplays with accommodation and assimilation.

The sensorimotor stage lasts from birth to twenty-four months of age. Some very important experiences occur during this period, including an introduction to the outer world, feeding for survival, and toilet training. Toilet training is often underestimated in relation to human growth and development. Freud and Erikson also theorize the importance of this stage of life. Infants, yet to be toilet trained, recognize the great joy that occurs in the family the day they first use the toilet, and probably will not need diapers any longer. We are also aware of the devastation to the self-concept that occurs among the elderly during the final stages of life, when they fear the loss of control of excretory function. This means that toilet training is an important life factor at the beginning and the end of life.

Piaget suggests that the first stage can be divided into six substages. At birth, infants display reflexes like sucking and grasping, and some visual competence; this is the first substage. In the absence of internal representation, objects that are beyond view do not exist for the infant. A sense of object permanence is an important factor in Piaget's theory. This concept has been examined in infants by placing an object in their view and then moving it out of view. To the infant, the object has disappeared from existence. After the age of twenty-four months, the child will search for the object on the floor, under the bedclothes, or other places common in the environment.

In the next substage, sensorimotor activity becomes more important, in that "motor" implies movement and "sense" implies the use of senses like touch. Infants are busy examining their environment, and things that they are able to grasp will likely end up in their mouth. This involves a complete sensorimotor experience. As the infant's motor skills increase (creeping, crawling, standing, etc.), more advanced sensorimotor experiences present themselves for accommodation and assimilation. To Piaget this is a period when children form the foundations for mathematical concepts and a general notion of how things work. Experience must be considered at this stage because the opportunities available to children allowed a free run about the house involve a variety of experiences that are much richer than experiences of children who are confined to a crib or playpen, to play with whatever the adult provides.

The third substage involves an expansive, coordinated use of the modest drives with which the infant is born. These include the sucking and grasping reflexes, what Piaget refers to as "primary circular reactions." The final substages are taken up with coordination of the various reflexes within a dominant pattern of egocentrism. Egocentrism implies that up to the age of twenty-four months, the sensorimotor period, children are unable to appreciate the perceptions of others. Children of that age express awareness from their perspective, as if it is the only one that exists. Piaget explains it this way:

> We have endeavored to show in an earlier work that thought in the child is egocentric, i.e. that the child thinks for himself without troubling to make himself understood nor to place himself at the other person's point of view. We tried, above all, to show that these egocentric habits have a considerable effect upon the structure of thought itself. Thus it is chiefly because he feels no need to socialize his thought that the child is so little concerned, or at any rate so very much less concerned than we are, to convince his hearers or to prove his points. (1964, p. 1)

The preoperational stage spans from twenty-four months to six years of age. In this subperiod the child appears to center on a single aspect of an object's property. If a ball of clay, after being shown to the child, is rolled into an elongated form of clay in the child's presence, the preoperational child will conclude that the elongated version contains more clay than the round form. It is only after the preoperational period that the child is able to decenter, that is, to conceptualize self from not self. At the concrete operations stage of conceptualization, the child is able to mentally reverse actions and visualize the clay in the previous form of a ball while viewing it in its reshaped, elongated form.

Another interesting aspect of Piaget's theory involves the role of play during the preoperational period. Piaget suggested that preoperational children will interact with objects in a symbolic manner and become engrossed within self and the activity. Some writers have referred to this activity as solitary play.

In terms of children's thinking during this period, Piaget suggests that their reasoning is more transductive than deductive or inductive. In transductive thought, the child may recognize that birds in his backyard have feathers, so when he sees a chicken, he will assume that the chicken is also a bird. Deductive reasoning starts with a generalization and proceeds to the specific. Inductive reasoning starts with specifics and moves to a generalization.

After the age of seven, children are generally able to conserve and thoughtfully pursue various operations. They are able to deal with numbers, classes, and seriations. It is important that children are provided numerous opportunities for experiences in preschool programs or at home. Experiences with objects and individuals in real-life situations expand their ability to fully understand number, seriation, and classes, which are important perceptual factors in early grades.

The concept of number is rather complex for young learners. Parents enjoy seeing their three-year-old children hold up three fingers when asked their age. If one asks the child how many fingers are showing by pointing to the second or third finger, the child will not identify this as "one" finger, but as the number place among other fingers. The number 3, for example, represents an ordinal position between 1 and 4, implying a seriation as well as a collective designation of how many objects are under discussion. Children at the age of three, for example, learn to name each finger, but have not yet learned seriation or ordinal position.

Prior to concrete operations, children have little difficulty putting wood blocks in one pile, and cuddly toys in the other. Piaget found that children are able to classify objects along a single dimension; after the age of six children are usually able to classify objects according to shape, color, and size. Experiences that enable children to manipulate and interact with a variety of objects and individuals lead to a developing awareness of their world.

Through curiosity, children begin to discover their own meanings in the structures of classifications: sorting, comparison, and seriation. The concrete operations stage ushers in the child's ability to conceptualize self from the empirical perception of an action, and the skill to reason on the basis of hypothesizing.

Finally, according to Piaget, preschool children do not think logically, but comprehend the world from their own personal perspective. They are likely to misinterpret or misunderstand reality as often as they make an accurate assumption. These assumptions may be different at different times. Symbolic action, implications of unfulfilled promises, the true meaning of number, and concepts associated with classification and seriation are not understood until the concrete operations stage.

SIGMUND FREUD

Sigmund Freud (1856–1939) dominated the field of psychoanalytic thought from the early 1900s to the 1960s. As a medical practitioner in Vienna, he discovered that certain symptoms occurring among his patients could not be resolved by identifying physical causes. He attributed the causes of these symptoms to what he labeled the "unconscious." He probably meant the subconscious, but the epistemology of the times left few choices as to what this entity should be labeled. (I make this suggestion because for one to be unconscious, one would be in a deep sleep. To be subconscious, one could be active, wide awake, or hypnotized on Freud's therapy couch.)

Freud never treated children as patients, but he learned about childhood from remembrances of his own early experiences and information gathered from his adult patients as they recalled events from their childhood. These childhood remembrances were viewed by Freud as essential to unraveling psychological problems encountered by adults. The stages of childhood, as theorized by Freud, were dynamic and differentiated.

The stages were not conceived as completely distinct and ages of transition varied, but the dynamics grew out of Freud's position on infantile sexuality. Responses to the child's behavior in these stages were alleged to be decisive in the development of personality; this was considered particularly true during the first three stages, which covered the first four or five years of life. The oral stage, with the libido localized in the mouth and oral regions, dominated the first months when the infant was dependent upon the mother. Proper oral gratification became linked to the manner of feeding and weaning. Around the age of two the second stage began when libidinal pressures moved to the anal region, thus making the process of toilet training significant for personality development. A repressive regimen produced far reaching effects, according to Freud, as responses gained at this time were generalized in later behavior. The important aspect of the phallic stage (3–6 years) was the resolution of the Oedipus complex. The strength of the super-ego came into play to form a bulwark against incest. These three significant stages of early childhood were to be further resolved in the subsequent latency and genital periods in which socialization grew and interest became focused on others. (Weber 1984, pp. 110–111)

It was Freud's adult patients discussing their childhood that enabled Freud to hypothesize child development. In response to a patient's symptoms, he examined their feelings, thoughts, and actions, about which they were aware as conscious individuals, and their unconscious (subconscious) mental processes, which influence feelings, thoughts, and actions. Freud theorized that critical childhood experiences that might be responsible for adult symptoms were possibly blocked from the conscious awareness by psychological barriers. In this regard, he was the first to identify childhood experiences as essential for understanding adulthood.

Central to Freud's theory is his identification of the id, ego, and superego as basic human structures. The id involves needs with which we are born and includes aggression, hunger, love, sex, and sleep. Humans are driven to meet these needs by the pleasure principle. Without any concern about the interests of others, the hungry infant will cry as loud as it is necessary for it to be fed. Later in life, individuals learn to moderate their demands for attention, and acquire the mentally processes to be more patient. The device that regulates this process is labeled the ego, and it is modulated by the reality principle.

When sitting at the dinner table with other family members, the child with an active id may demand to be fed first by screaming. At a later age, after the id is modulated by the ego, this same child may be willing to wait and observe the goings-on as family members include the child in taking turns and satisfying family rituals. Reality eventually emerges.

The superego is concerned about the standards and regulations of society. There are rules of behavior that are established by the culture—at school, on playground, in the military, in the marketplace—and those set by the subculture—within family and friendship groups. There are roles that are assigned and roles that are assumed. Assigned roles of son, daughter, pupil, mother, father, and so on have rules of behavior that were established long before the present generation was born. There may be modest variations in role expectations, which in general are set and understood by participants. For those who are uncooperative, negative responses from family, friends, or police will attempt to modify their behavior. The function of the superego encourages the individual to modulate these behaviors for social acceptance.

At birth the human organism has a bundle of uncontrolled desires, and hunger is chief among them. For this reason, the mouth is extremely sensitive and will start a sucking reflex if it is touched. When the nipple or bottle is put into place, the infant will grasp, grip, suck, and protest if interrupted. This behavior is most persistent with new babies. Feeding becomes more relaxed as the infant develops an emotional relationship with the caregiver. The emotional attachment gradually relaxes the infant's id drive, and ego controls become a part of the developing relationship between the child and the family.

Oral gratification through feeding in infancy was considered a critical period by Freud. If the feeding procedures are incomplete, or the child is left to cry hungry for long periods of time, a sense of insecurity may be associated with this period of childhood when the infant becomes an adult. This unresolved period of insecurity can bring on severe symptoms that require psychoanalysis for the adult, and/or lead to excessive oral activity: overeating, smoking, or alcoholism. (Erikson, a student of Freud, identified this period as one during which the infant develops trust or mistrust of the environment. In this regard, his assessment is compatible with Freud's.)

The next stage identified by Freud is the anal stage. Sometime between eighteen and twenty-four months, children become interested in the waste materials that they observe adults discarding. They may be more interested in walking around with their waste in their diapers than in having adults throw it away. This is a period of defiance and possessiveness, when the child expresses a demand for toys and the retention of diaper waste. Freud theorized that preschoolers play with clay and sand, fingerprint, and manipulate other materials as a symbolic means of acting out conflict during the anal stage.

Freud suggests that during the anal stage, the child is seeking value in identity for a sense of self. Harsh and demanding toilet training by adults can undermine the child's quest for a sense of self as an independent member of the family, and lead to rigidity, retention, and selfishness in adulthood.

The phallic stage is the time during which the child becomes aware of the genital area and a sense of gender identity emerges. During this period, according to Freud, the young boy feels a sexual desire for his mother and wants his father excluded from the mother-child relationship. This has been called the Oedipus complex because in ancient Greek mythology, Oedipus unknowingly killed his father and married his mother. Freud goes on to suggest that during the phallic stage, the male child fears that his father will get revenge by cutting off his penis. In a supportive family environment, the male child eventually resolves this conflict by identifying with the father's values, morals, and self-control, which ultimately leads to the full development of the superego. Female children suspect that at some time they had a penis, and they secretly blame their mother for this loss.

Female and male children repress their sexual desires and resolve these conflicts associated with the oedipal stage. During the latency period, there is a natural repression of sexual desires until the onset of the genital stage. During this period, mature relationships are formed after the onset of puberty.

ERIK ERIKSON

The work of Erik Erikson (1902–1990), unlike that of Freud, is based on observations of children in various cultures. Erikson's stages of child development can be set in the context of the works of Piaget and Freud (see Table 3.1). Erikson's cycles presented a challenge and a consequence. For example, during the period that matches Freud's oral stage, Erikson theorizes that positive mother-child experiences can result in the infant's developing a basic trust. If during the oral stage the infant experiences harsh feeding procedures or neglect and hunger, a mistrust of objects and individuals develops and lingers through adult life. Here Erikson was more broad-based than Freud, because he observed and recorded cultural differences, and expanded descriptions of adult and adolescent behaviors.

During Freud's anal stage, Erikson's consequences of harsh toilet training, and the infant's memory of such obstacles to independence, can lead to shame and doubt. When this period presents experiences that are supportive and encouraging, the individual will emerge with a sense of autonomy.

Freud's phallic stage and oedipal stage are grouped together by Erikson because both are associated with the coming of sexual maturation. During these two periods, development can emerge with initiative; the individual can approach life with a positive sense of self, unafraid to assert that feeling, or with a sense of guilt and fear of failure. In the final stage, an individual turns ten years old with a sense of industry that involves purpose and achievement, or demonstrates a feeling of failure. Erikson's dimensions are not to be interpreted as being at either extreme (trust vs. mistrust, for example) but, rather, as continua along which, as the result of childhood experiences, one's personality will fall.

B. F. SKINNER

Burrhus Frederic Skinner (1904–1990) entered graduate school to study biology, but changed his field of study after discovering the work of John Broadus Watson, the celebrated behaviorist. Skinner graduated from Harvard University in 1931 with a degree in psychology. In 1938 he presented the foundation for his theory in *The Behavior of Organisms*.

His description of the management of human behavior through positive control was popularized in his 1948 novel, *Walden Two*. His later writings, of which *Beyond Freedom and Dignity* (1971) is central, clarified his beliefs. Inspired by Pavlov, Watson, and E. R. Guthrie, he separated his theory from theirs in that he was more concerned about the response to a known stimulus beyond the initial response. His experiments went farther, to behaviors paired with other stimuli over a series of trials.

To Skinner, steps and stages of development were less important because he thought learning was primarily determined externally, through paired stimuli. The developmentalists viewed learning as an unfolding internal process that involved readiness. Freud, Erikson, and Piaget examined human behavior as the relationship between the unfolding developmental process and the environment. Skinner theorized that it was the control of the environment that gave teachers a greater access to teaching and learning.

When a selected stimulus elicited a response, Skinner labeled this "respondent behavior." He labeled the response following respondent behavior as "operant behavior." In this regard, the respondent behavior is a reaction *to* the environment, whereas operant behavior acts *on* the environment.

Pavlov's work is termed "classical conditioning." Skinner, by contrast, in addition to operant conditioning describes two types of reinforcement—negative and positive. Skinner explained that the effects of negative and positive reinforcers, and the nature of the reinforcers themselves, determine whether or not they actually reinforce. Most developmentalists respond critically to Skinner's theory concerning punishment, which he believed should be used to extinguish undesirable behavior. The suppression of certain behaviors through punishment may be viewed by some as punishment indeed under certain circumstances, and not as punishment by others, under different circumstances.

Most behaviors in which people engage can be classified as operant. They may include reading a book, driving an automobile, ice skating, preparing a meal, and petting a cat. Certain stimuli lead to each of these behaviors, and in Skinner's view, for any of these behaviors to be repeated, one need only pair a stimulus with the behavior that one wants repeated. The stimulus designed to encourage a repeated behavior is termed the reinforcer. Teachers who give gold stars, high grades, words of encouragement, and other rewards are positively reinforcing behaviors they want pupils to repeat. In Skinner's view, high grades paired with a pupil's work reinforce a repeat of that level of work because the recipient of the high grade wants that experience repeated. After a period of time, the learning experiences will be primarily under the control of the teacher as operant conditioning.

THE USE OF IQ

Performance has been a factor of interest to psychologists since 1905, when Alfred Binet was a member of the commission appointed by the French minister of education to identify pupils in need of special education. Within a few years, psychologists were testing children and expected that schools, on the basis of their reports, would sort children according to their "mental age."

By the 1960s, this practice was called into question, and, following several court cases, the wholesale group testing of schoolchildren for placement was declared illegal. There is still individual testing for the screening of children for special education and gifted programs. The limitations of group IQ tests have been described by Michael Lewis.

> The measurement of IQ is based on a series of assumptions that must be reviewed. First the criterion for intellectual behavior is school performance. Thus the tasks and materials are designed around the tasks and materials used in school. This design would be of little concern if all that was of interest was, in fact, school performance. Unfortunately, the discussion has not been stopped at this point, but theorists have chosen instead to generalize test performance to all mental activity, not just school performance. (Lewis 1983, p. 10)

It became important to several investigators that if IQ scores were to have meaning in other parts of the life of the individual, performance in environments not associated with school must also be examined. Psychologists began to take an expanded view of intellectual performance, and included social competence, motivation, and cognitive style in these new conceptualizations.

COGNITIVE STYLE

Cognitive style should be of particular interest to early childhood educators because it suggests that schools should expand the number of ways in which experience can be enhanced for knowledge acquisition. Cognitive style investigations can be traced to the 1930s, when Gordon Allport was among the first psychologists to use the term "style" in reference to individual personality variations. At various stages in the study of cognitive style, psychologists have often referred to the concept as psychological differentiation (Dyk & Witkin 1965). Howard Gardner in his work renamed cognitive styles "intelligences."

Cognitive style theory suggests that individuals utilize different patterns in acquiring knowledge. Cognitive refers to the processes involved in the overall act of getting to know something. It includes perception, judgment, values, and memory. Style is used here in very much the same manner as in everyday speaking terms, in that we often do things in a different manner than someone else might in carrying out the same act. As a part of the term cognitive style, "style" implies that as individuals, we employ personal characteristics in the acquisition of knowledge and, more often than not, approach a learning experience in ways that differ from other individuals.

Cognitive style is not an indication of one's level of intelligence, but a description of the unique ways that learners employ in acquiring new information. Information is presented to us in various ways, sometimes through experiences that we initiate, as when we select a hobby or read a book; through experiences provided by significant adults during child rearing; or by other persons, as during classroom activities when we are students. A complete elaboration can be found in Harry Morgan's *Cognitive Styles and Classroom Learning* (1997).

Classroom experiences are intended to increase the knowledge of learners, and successful teachers vary the ways in which information is presented. Sometimes teachers are lecturing to the entire class, and learners are expected to remain quiet and relatively inactive. Other times children are engaged in group activities or individual assignments, where they are expected to be actively engaged. We now know that some children demonstrate a greater potential for processing information in an active setting rather than in a quiet one. Other learners prefer to work alone, privately.

Classroom teaching sessions are sometimes followed by written/oral responses to questions or problems posed by the teacher. This enables children to demonstrate what new information they have acquired. The teacher will evaluate the pupil's response and then imply from the student's performance that a certain amount of learning has taken place. The word "imply" is important here because the teacher does not know for certain how much the student has learned from a particular lesson merely by how well the student performs on the oral or written test; we do not know the extent to which performance matches capacity. It is also true that tests are written in various styles, and some styles are more complex for some children to fully decipher than others. So instead of measuring the knowledge that the tests purport to measure, in reality the teacher might be measuring how well particular students perform on different types of tests.

Research in psychology has informed us that our various styles of processing information have been influenced by the environment in which we spent our childhood. For example, there are differences, between the way children process information who were confined to a playpen and those who were allowed to crawl about the entire house and learn to walk by climbing stairs and holding onto furniture during these critical years of early development. The time during which children are learning to use their muscles for sitting up, crawling, standing, and walking is a period that researchers are giving a great deal of thought to understanding how these skills are accomplished. Studies have also shown that often African-American children accomplish these early skills sooner than white children of the same age (Pasamanick 1946; Williams & Scott 1953; Bayley 1965; Ainsworth 1967; Morgan 1990).

Child development experts have also suggested that this important learning period from birth to twenty-four months is the timeframe within which we develop foundations for a later understanding of how things work in logical and mathematical terms. The different experiences that children are encouraged to have during this early period of growth will influence how they process information later in life.

In various cities where major sports teams occasionally go through final playoff games, many children who are not particularly successful in school mathematics, or classroom reading assignments, seem to have little trouble figuring out the meaning of batting averages, or how to spell the names of their favorite athletes. It is also true that many children who do not read well in school have almost no trouble understanding and writing the words of songs that have swept their neighborhood in popularity. Knowledge acquired by these children through out-of-school experiences has been self-selected by their own style of solving the problems of difficult word sounds and arithmetic skills that they have acquired, sometimes on their own.

Because of various individual cognitive styles, learners appear to have skills available to them under some circumstances, and in some situations, that are not necessarily available to them at other times. And some skills seem available to children during out-of-school experiences (that are more under their control) than might be available to them in the quiet settings of the classroom.

The two most common cognitive styles that have been defined and tested by psychologists are *field dependent* and *field independent*. These two styles are linked together in descriptions because they have somewhat opposite meanings. Persons who are more field independent are able to pick out objects that have surroundings which might hide them from view. For example, they can easily see fruit on a vine or tree even though the colors might not be very different from the leaves and branches. In other words, field independent persons are able to view objects in a manner in which such objects are independent from other parts of the scene. On the other hand, field dependent learners are less able to view things separate from the overall environment; they would have greater difficulty viewing fruit as standing apart from the tree or surrounding foliage. Therefore, field dependent learners prefer that things remain in their total context to enable them to better understand the meaning of their individual parts. In social settings, the field dependent style person prefers group interaction, while the *field independent* style person would prefer to interact with individuals or alone.

From various studies, there are reports that black children as a group tend to prefer learning environments that encourage social interaction among pupils and teachers. During neonatal growth periods, and the sensorimotor stage as identified in the theory of Piaget, it appears that black infants are more advanced in motor performance than their white peers. In this regard, the work of neonatal and child development specialists have highlighted some important findings relevant to socialization and child-rearing practices in black families.

In 1946, Benjamin Pasamanick conducted a study in New Haven, Connecticut, on fifty-three black infants, who were compared to three different groups of white babies from foster homes (57), institutions (22), and from two-parent households of well-educated parents (20). Pasamanick reported that female babies—black and white—were more accelerated in development than males. The institutionalized white group was negatively affected by their impoverished environment. Babies living in poor housing conditions did not do as well as those in better housing. On "fine motor, adaptive, language, and personal social behavior black babies did as well as white ones. In other areas investigated, black infants showed a definite acceleration in gross motor behavior" (42).

Pasamanick used well-chosen words and descriptors to avoid identifying differences between groups as racial. This was a period of great debate in the literature, in university seminars, and in conferences of learned organizations regarding "Negro" and white intelligence comparisons. Numerous studies were published from southern environments comparing black children whose families were living in poverty with white children growing up under completely different, affluent circumstances. These poorly balanced studies reached such an absurd level that one of the most respected scholars in the North suggested that "it is safe to say that as the environment of the Negro approximates . . . more closely that of the white . . . inferiority tends to disappear" (189). He went on to suggest that "the real test of Negro-white equality . . . can be met only by a study in a region in which Negroes suffer no discrimination whatsoever and enjoy exactly the same educational and economic opportunities. . . . The direct comparisons between Negroes and whites will always remain a doubtful procedure because of the impossibility of controlling the various factors which may influence the results" (Klineberg 1935, p. 189).

In 1953, Judith R. Williams and Roland B. Scott reported on a study of over 100 black infants to determine if the advanced motor development of black infants reported in Pasamanick's New Haven Study was innately racial. Their study involved infants from three different income groups. They reported that babies raised by low-income parents showed superior motor development when compared to babies from higher-income families. They concluded that differences in motor development were linked to childrearing practices and the way the infants were handled by their parents. For Williams and Scott, this ruled out any genetic explanation for the behavioral differences.

In 1965, a larger study was conducted by Nancy Bayley of the Institute for Human Development at the University of California. Her investigation involved over 1,400 babies from one to fifteen months in age. She reported that all babies scored equally on mental measurement, but black babies scored higher on motor scales when compared with white and Puerto Rican infants.

Mary Salter Ainsworth, in *Infancy in Uganda* (1967), described in great detail the childrearing practices of parents in an African community. Families were observed raising their children from birth, and careful records were maintained to chronicle and interpret these observations. The study focused upon infant development in the context of family and village. Observations were made in Buganda, a province in Uganda on the African continent. Data were derived from conversations, questioning, and other techniques in various settings between 1954 and 1955. Among the many important differences between African children raised in this community and those raised in European-oriented environments were the experiences provided infants by parents and significant others. Using a scale developed by Arnold Gesell to describe normal levels of development for European infants, Ainsworth reported that African infants reached their sensorimotor milestones earlier than European infants.

The sensorimotor milestones included sitting with support, sitting alone, crawling, creeping, standing with support, standing alone, walking, and trotting. Ainsworth sought confirmation from Marcelle Geber (1957), a researcher who had previous experience with testing infants. Geber examined over 200 infants. Her reports confirmed the findings of Ainsworth.

News regarding advanced sensorimotor development among African infants appeared when the U.S. Congress was in the midst of hearing testimony from leading psychologists regarding black inferiority as an argument against school integration. Ainsworth was aware of the volatile nature of her report and chose not to become embroiled in the political implications of her findings. But it did not end there. Researchers in the United States wanted to investigate the extent to which this phenomenon might be true for African-American children. Several studies were conducted in the United States, but they had been confined to scholarly journals, often away from the general public.

Classroom teachers introduce the curriculum, set the rules for learning experiences, and conduct academic activities. These activities are designed to enable learners to maximize their knowledge acquisition. Cognitive style researchers have reported that learners bring a variety of personality and information-processing differences to the classroom, and this information can be useful to teachers. It has been common practice, however, for grade-school teachers not to value racial and cultural differences when they are incompatible with mainstream culture. This is reinforced when the teachers' own childhood and education training has followed a sociocultural pattern similar to the one embraced by the school system where they are employed. For example, some black teachers are among the severest critics of children who use black English ("Ebonics"), and they join some white teachers in lamenting that this neighborhood practice stands in the way of children learning "good" English.

At the same time, socially active African-American pupils are more likely than white males to be suspended because of their activeness. At one extreme, some of the more active students are medicated with Ritalin or similar substances, and many other socially active students are among those in trouble for expanding the expectations of the system. In 1975 the Washington Research Project reported that African-American boys are four times more likely to be suspended from school than their white peers for similar infractions of the rules.

The teacher's knowledge of cognitive style theory provides a theoretical basis for modifying the classroom environment for the purpose of expanding the number of ways that children can process each learning experience. Variations in the way that all children process information in school settings have been reported by several researchers.

A study by Zachary Dershowitz in 1971 reported that fathers in Orthodox Jewish families seldom participate in the daily childrearing practices of their sons. Dershowitz suggested that mothers in these families assume the more dominant disciplinary role. Dershowitz compared a group of Jewish Orthodox boys with a comparable group of white Protestant boys. As he had hypothesized, the Jewish boys were characterized as more field dependent.

In 1974, Manuel Ramirez III and Douglas R. Price-Williams conducted a study of cognitive styles that included Mexican-Americans, African-Americans, and Anglo-Americans in Houston, Texas. They reported that children from families that emphasize conformity to authority with a strong religious affiliation and group identity more often than not tend to be field dependent. Those families that support the child's freedom to question authority and have ties to friendship groups outside of the family tend to be field independent.

Differentiations in cognitive styles call for teachers to use varied ways to enable students to process information. From time to time, schools do experiment with teaching/learning designs in creative and innovative teaching methods. Too often this creativity and innovation is exhausted in the pedagogical process, where the teacher's expectations for the student's displays of learning tend to repeat old comfortable methods. In other words, materials might be presented in a manner that acknowledges various styles of processing information, but too often classroom practice will ultimately demand traditional pupil performances like recitations, paper-and-pencil tasks, or similar displays of classroom etiquette upon which to base pupil achievement and provide proof to teachers that learning has taken place.

The subject of in-school pressures on black males has attracted the interest of the general population—especially the interest of black mothers and fathers. Recognizing this as an increasing concern, *Parenting* magazine (April 1977) published a special report entitled "Are Schools Failing Black Boys?" This extensive report included a special section on "Why White Parents Should Care."

REFERENCES

Ainsworth, M. D. S. 1967. *Infancy in Uganda: Infant Care and the Growth of Love*. Baltimore, MD: Johns Hopkins University Press.

Allport, G. 1937. *Personality: A Psychological Interpretation*. New York: Henry Holt.

Bayley, N. 1965. "Comparison of Mental and Motor Test Scores for Ages 1–15 Months by Sex, Gender, Birth Order, Geographic Location and Education of Parents." *Child Development* 36: 379–411.

Boykin, W. E. 1978. "Psychological/Behavioral Verve in Academic/Task Performance: Pretheoretical Considerations." *Journal of Negro Education* 47: 343–354.

Bracken, B. A., Sabers, D., & Insko, W. 1987. "Performance of Black and White Children on the Braken Basic Concept Scale." *Psychology in the Schools* 24: 22–27.

Brill, A. A. 1938. *The Basic Writings of Sigmund Freud*. New York: Random House.

Coles, R. 1978. "Reconsideration: Jean Piaget." *The New Republic* (March 18): 36.

Cratty, B. 1986. *Perceptual and Motor Development in Infants and Preschool Children*. 4th ed. Englewood Cliffs, NJ: Prentice-Hall.

Curti, M. W., Marshal, F. B., & Steggerda, M. 1935. "The Gesell Schedules Applied to 1, 2, and 3 Year Old Negro Children of British West Indies." *Journal of Comparative Neurology* 20: 125.

Damon, W. 1977. *The Social World of the Child*. San Francisco: Jossey-Bass.

Dershowitz, Z. 1971. "Jewish Subcultural Patterns and Psychological Differentiation." *International Journal of Psychology* 6(3): 223–231.

Dyk, R. B., & Witkin, H. A. 1965. "Family Experiences as Related to the Development of Differentiation in Children." *Child Development* 30: 21–55.

Einstein, E. 1979. "Classroom Dynamos." *Human Behavior* 8: 58–59.

Elkind, D. 1987. *Miseducation: Preschoolers at Risk*. New York: Knopf.

Elkind, D., & Weiner, I. 1978. *Development of the Child*. New York: Wiley.

Erikson, E. 1963. *Childhood and Society*. New York: Norton.

———. 1968. *Identity: Youth and Crisis*. New York: Norton.

Flavell, J. H. 1963. *The Developmental Psychology of Jean Piaget*. Princeton: Van Nostrand.

———. 1985. *Cognitive Development*. Englewood Cliffs, NJ: Prentice-Hall.

Flavell, J. H., & Elkind, D. 1969. *Studies in Cognitive Development*. New York: Oxford University Press.

Freedman, D. 1979. "Ethnic Differences in Babies." *Human Nature* 2(2): 36–43.

Freud, S. 1965. *New Introductory Lectures in Psychoanalysis*. New York: Norton.

———. 1983. *A General Introduction to Psychoanalysis*, rev. ed. New York: Washington Square Press.

Geber, M., & Dean, R. F. A. 1957. "The State of Development of Newborn African Infants." *Lancet* 1: 1216–1219.

Gesell, A. 1949. *Gesell Developmental Schedules*. New York: Psychological Corporation.

Ginsberg, H., & Opper, S. 1978. *Piaget's Theory of Intellectual Development*. Englewood Cliffs, NJ: Prentice-Hall.

Guthrie, E. R. 1952. *The Psychology of Learning*. New York: Harper & Row.

Hymes, J. L., Jr. 1955. *A Child Development Point of View*. Englewood Cliffs, NJ: Prentice-Hall.

Kagan, J. 1984. *The Nature of the Child*. New York: Basic Books.

Lewis, M. (ed). 1983. *Origins of Intelligence: Infancy and Early Childhood*. New York: Plenum.

Morgan, H. 1990. "Assessment of Student Behavioral Interactions During On-Task Classroom Activities." *Perceptual and Motor Skills* 70: 563–569.

Pasamanick, B. A. 1946. "A Comparative Study of the Behavioral Development of Negro Infants." *Journal of Genetic Psychology* 69: 3–44.

Piaget, J. 1962. *The Language and Thought of the Child*. London: Routledge & Kegan Paul.

——— 1963. *The Origins of Intelligence in Children*. New York: Norton.

———. 1964. *Judgment and Reasoning in the Child*. Paterson, NJ: Littlefield, Adams.

Piaget, J., & Inhelder, B. 1967. *The Child's Conception of Space*. New York: Norton.

———. 1969. *The Psychology of the Child*. New York: Basic Books.

Ramirez, M., & Casteneda, A. 1974. *Cultural Democracy, Bicognitive Development, and Education*. New York: Academic Press.

Rousseau, J-J. 1762; 1979. *Emile*. Translated by A. Bloom. New York: Basic Books.

Russell, D. 1956. *Children's Thinking*. Boston: Ginn and Company.

Skinner, B. F. 1938. *The Behavior of Organisms: An Experimental Analysis*. New York: Appleton-Century-Crofts.

———. 1948. *Walden Two*. New York: Macmillan.

———. 1953. *Science and Human Behavior*. New York: Macmillan.

———. 1971. *Beyond Freedom and Dignity*. New York: Knopf.

Staats, A. W. 1964. *Human Learning*. New York: Holt, Rinehart & Winston.

Thomas, R. M. 1979. *Comparing Theories of Child Development*. Belmont, CA: Wadsworth.

Weber, E. 1984. *Ideas Influencing Early Childhood Education: A Theoretical Analysis*. New York: Teachers College Press.

Williams, J. R., & Scott, R. B. 1953 "Growth and Development of Negro Infants: Motor Development and Its Relationship to Child Rearing Practices in Two Groups of Negro Infants." *Child Development* 24: 103–121.

4

Curriculum Imagination

Here is Teresa in dress-up clothes—long skirt, flowery hat, and high heels—talking into the toy telephone. I have already given several notices of clean-up time, and she is the only child left in the house corner. I try to signal her to stop talking, but she pretends not to see me, pointedly turning her back as she continues her conversation. Finally, rather irritated, I reach my arm around her and hang up the phone, telling her it is time to end. She flounces out of the house corner to the furthest ends of the room, where she finds an empty spot. There she reaches for an imaginary wall phone, dials into the air, and speaks into her cupped hand. Then she hangs up with an expression of relief and comes back into the group.

—Anne Martin

THE RISE OF BEHAVIORISM

In 1923, when John Dewey, William Kilpatrick, and Edward Thorndike were members of the faculty at Teachers' College, Columbia University, an important book about early childhood education was published with an introduction by Patty Smith Hill. This book, *A Conduct Curriculum for Kindergarten and First Grade*, described a new curriculum idea that was the result of an almost twenty-year study started at the Speyer School in New York City in 1905. This approach, considered radical for early childhood, was continued at the Horace Mann School, a laboratory school of Columbia University's Teachers' College. The word "conduct" was used as a substitute label for a behavioral approach to teaching and learning.

Initially early childhood education in general, and especially kindergarten, was immersed in Froebelian theory and practice. This behaviorist experiment was introduced in part to lessen the structured influence of the German model and employ a freedom of experience, Dewey-type curriculum, with specific behavioral objectives in mind. Thorndike's work with Patty Smith Hill focused upon making desirable behaviors in school profitable for pupils, and undesirable behaviors unprofitable. Thorndike emphasized individual differences as fundamental to a working model of this theory.

The role of the psychologists was to identify and explain to teachers specific objectives that should emerge from classroom situations in order to ensure that learning had taken place. The newness of this approach led Patty Smith Hill to advance the understanding of teachers and parents through materials prepared for dissemination to them. This new theoretical approach to early schooling was attempted prior to Skinner and Watson's popularized views of behaviorism in education. Hill, sometimes quoting from Watson, found it necessary to define the approach in terms of adjustments in common vocabulary while educating parents and teachers about behaviorism's benefits.

> While improvement in conduct leading to habit is our fundamental aim in making this curriculum, changes in thought and freedom, changes in appreciation, ideals, and attitudes, have not been omitted. Though the knowledge and ideals involved are not listed separately, it should be noted that they usually appear under the headings of activities or outcomes. . . . Since the technical meaning of conduct is better understood by the classroom teacher than that of behavior, we are venturing to call this a "Conduct Curriculum" though a "Curriculum of Behavior" might be technically more correct. Psychologists will pardon this verbal change, if by use of the term we get over to the public the idea that education must set as its objective the *changed child*—the child in which desirable changes in thought, feeling, and conduct are sought and achieved day by day, until habit and character have been established. (Hill 1923, p. xviii)

In 1915, the Horace Mann School had initiated this approach, though it was more in keeping with the psychology of Edward L. Thorndike. The school started out as a Dewey-type democratic classroom system of social interaction and freedom, but after ten years it bore the influence of Thorndike's more conservative concept of "habits."

Familiarity of the teaching staff, parents, and other professionals at Horace Mann with Dewey required that Hill explain why this transition (which was a diversion from Dewey's philosophy), was taking place.

In previous experiments we have attempted to apply the principles of education set forth by Doctor John Dewey, especially in his theory of the socialization of the school, the relation of interest to effort, and the conditions of moral training and of thinking. In this experiment we have endeavored to conserve these brilliant contributions. An effort has, however, been made to analyze these into more definite and measurable form, in closer accord with the standards of present-day psychology. (1923, p. xviii)

The idea of a "more measurable form" indicated an infusion of psychological objectivity into the curriculum. The Thorndike-influenced curriculum was modified to enable empirical psychological observations. The concept of "habit" formation as basic to learning was transported to observation sheets on which behaviors could be observed and recorded for identification. The focus soon was more on quantifiable behaviors than on levels of development.

Teachers as observers and recorders were able to detect behavior changes. It was concluded that the changes in conduct, thinking skills, attitudes, and feelings could be attributed to changes in the central nervous system. This was quite a leap in logic, but Thorndike was pleased with the new objective data-collection techniques. Teachers who were accustomed to Froebel's introspection and symbolic interactions among children were now involved in Thorndike's behaviorist assessments. A model was devised to guide teacher observations (Hill 1923, p. 23):

Typical Activities	Desirable Changes in Thought, Feeling, and Conduct
Taking out blocks and putting them away	Handling blocks with safety for self and others
Building alone or in gregarious groupings	Growing interest in the work of other children
Experimenting with blocks (piling or placing lengthwise, sometimes naming product)	Pleasure in activity; pleasure in using blocks; satisfaction in vigorous use of whole body
Constructing with more definite idea in mind—using more blocks	Getting ideas through imitation
Constructing something, calling it "train," "house," etc., and playing with it	Ability to plan out of experimentation

Because of recorded observations, Thorndike labeled this approach the "science of education." In this approach, the preschooler was deemed a collection of original tendencies without specific direction. The teacher's role, he theorized, was to give these tendencies positive direction through a behavioral, introspective classroom system. In a variety of ways, this approach can be found in what students were taught in the German laboratory of Wundt, and in the philosophy of William T. Harris. (The work of Wundt and Harris is discussed in Chapter 2.)

Since the introduction of ideas concerning a "science of education" in kindergarten and nursery school, there have been consistent efforts to merge the teaching of preschool children with the curriculum of primary grades. This work usually starts with the desire to teach mathematics and reading to preschoolers in the same manner that one would teach these subjects in grades 1 and 2. This approach has been attractive to many parents and teachers. Parents are encouraged because they believe that an early start means their children are better prepared for the university; and teachers who have been trained in elementary education believe that offering preschoolers the curriculum of grades 1 and 2 is merely an early start to achieve the teacher's goals. This latter perspective would replace the scene described by Anne Martin at the beginning of this chapter with instructional procedures commonly found in primary grades.

The persistence of these two views has made it difficult for early childhood education to maintain the flowering of knowledge among young children. The approach to curriculum development in early childhood education should embody a voice for children. It is the articulation of this voice that guides the teacher in the introduction of projects and ideas from which children can make choices. Froebel developed "gifts and occupations"; Montessori designed wood blocks and related materials; and William Kilpatrick, along with John Dewey, introduced the project method that utilizes these items.

THE FROEBELIAN KINDERGARTEN

Activities promoted in U.S. kindergartens during the early 1900s were influenced primarily by the work of Froebel. It was common to find the following activities in these programs:

> Block building. Borrowed from Froebel's gifts, blocks were introduced to enable children to develop a sense of size, number, and form. The teacher would commonly use the child's building structures as a foundation for teacher/child discussions, with the intent of advancing the child's conceptualization and learning about the child's developmental level. The latter was important for future planning and the individualization of programming. (See Figure 4.1.)

Figure 4.1
Building with Large Blocks in a Froebelian Kindergarten. The Chicago Faulkner School Kindergarten, 1910

Source: The Volume Library (New York: Educators Association, 1934), 32.

Bead stringing. This activity was a takeoff from the baby rattle, which usually is a rubber, wooden, or plastic ball containing beads that is attached to a short handle, so as to rattle when shaken. When the child receives the ball without the handle or beads later in development, it is easily recognized as a shape common to the rattle and the beads. The child is given a string and brightly colored beads of various shapes, and asked to string all the yellow ones, then the red ones, followed by the blue ones. The child is then encouraged to experiment with colors of his own choice for play and learning. This can involve placement according to color or shape (cylinder, cube, sphere). These exercises are not isolated, as in Montessori, but integrated with other activities according to the child's preferences. Again, the teacher may engage the child in a conversation about choices.

Paper chains. Children cut colored paper into strips approximately one inch wide and six inches long. The teacher performs this task for children who do not have the small-muscle control to use scissors. The chains are formed by gluing the ends of the paper after looping the strips through the previously glued loop. Children select various color patterns in their construction, and this forms a basis for teacher/child discussion.

Sand and water tables. It was common for school supply houses to sell metal-lined water tables and sand tables. Cups, scoops, and pails were used by the children for measuring, examining textures, and general play. Sometimes a load of sand would be poured within enclosed boards on the playground area.

Clay modeling. A piece of potter's clay about the size of a brick was portioned out to children for construction purposes. They were encouraged to construct forms that they normally handled in the program—cube, cylinder, sphere, and so on. This activity encouraged an appreciation for the aesthetic and also reinforced other concepts. Occasionally children would construct representations of items found in their home and neighborhood.

Painting. Individual children and groups of children were encouraged to paint scenes and objects with their choice of colors. This activity also provided a source of rich language interaction between children and adults.

Music. A study of rhythms and beats was common in programs found in laboratory schools on college campuses and in major city public school systems. Many of these programs had a good supply of child-sized furniture, rhythm instruments, and a piano in kindergarten classrooms. (Note the piano in Figure 4.1.)

The kindergarten and nursery school curriculum, from the beginning of each day, encourages pupil expression. In kindergarten, teacher and children meet to establish some factual information concerning the date, the name of the day and the month, and the weather. The teacher writes this information on a large piece of paper, or places it with items that will be displayed in the room for the rest of the day. In some classrooms, children keep diaries or journals for their writing and drawings.

Occasionally teachers will sit with children individually or in small groups to discuss their journal entries. Some pupil journals are a personalized copy of what has been recorded by the teacher, others may be partly the pupil's own contribution, and others may be solely the work of the child in pictures and narratives. This approach could be observed in the kindergartens of the early 1900s. Starting in the early 1960s, some models, notably High/Scope, did not suggest writing or drawing by the teacher. Here, it was thought important that children be given opportunities to value their own work and not attempt to match the teacher's work, or view it as the model.

Typically in a free kindergarten of the 1880s and 1890s, the American Froebel system was detailed. Children were greeted by the teacher and/or assistants. They were usually from poor homes, so teachers were instructed to engage in morning singing to change the mood from that of their deprived home life to that of the aesthetic qualities of the kindergarten environment. Songs were followed by games that paired participants in such a way that the interests of others were considered. Next came activities promoting cooperation and courtesy. The teacher read a story with an element of morality, honesty, cooperation, or a similar concept. This was concluded with a "thought for the day."

After lunch, children retired to their tables to work with gifts and occupations. This involved the child in craft work with tin, wire, drawing materials, wood, or clay that was used to demonstrate, in some permanent manner, the thought for the day. It was assumed that the thought for the day, and other enjoyable learning activities, would be taken into the home by the child and somehow would reduce the debilitating effects of poverty for the entire family. With some families sending more than one child, the joy of kindergarten could be multiplied for that family and neighborhood.

This was seen as the cornerstone for reducing the negativism of poverty and life in the urban slums by transmitting, in the minds of children, a social uplift. An essential part of the curriculum was the kindergarten teacher's visitation to the homes of her pupils. These visits were designed to include an explanation of Froebel's methods and elements of the curriculum, and later were expanded to include health issues, nutrition, and activities that parents could participate in with their children. This led to meetings of teachers and mothers in the kindergarten setting for open discussions concerning family problems, rent, child care, and public services. These discussions were seen as a part of the curriculum on an extended basis and called for special skills in dealing with ethnic and economic differences between families. Kindergartners thought they were up to the task since their approach to children, unlike that in common schools, was "scientific" because their training involved psychological principles.

FREEDOM OF EXPERIENCE

In the 1930s, Georges Cuisenaire, a Belgian math teacher, introduced materials for use in primary schools that would enable children to visualize basic math concepts. He devised brightly colored rods of wood measuring one to ten centimeters, each being a different color. These became known as Cuisenaire rods. The children's first encounter with the rods is during free play. They are then asked to associate color with length rather than a number, and are encouraged to place rods end to end, and to find the rod(s) that match that length. Children will then identify the rods in terms of their color and length, and describe how many of which color will match the number of a different color. They are guided by visual imagery and perception by associating color with length in the beginning and not by the number of rods.

The conceptual framework for the use of the rods is described by Cuisenaire and Caleb Gattegno in their book *Numbers in Colour*. Gattegno wrote additional books to enable teachers to use the rods so that children could understand the principles of math.

More recently, models have emerged that recommend the child's work as a basis for language and social interaction without the teacher imposing a pattern to be followed. In other words, because of adults' position of power in the classroom, the mere presence of their writing and artwork provides examples that children wish to emulate. The inability to match the teacher's work, according to High/Scope theorists, can cause pupils to hesitate, or to withdraw their work from the teacher's view.

In programs where freedom of experience is encouraged, there usually is seldom direct instruction or memorization of words in the text, nor is there a "times table" to be memorized. And when reading and/or writing are the subjects at hand, "invented spelling" is encouraged. The elements of literature awareness, reading, and/or math are included in all class projects (planting a garden; constructing, serving customers, or making a purchase in a post office; constructing, serving customers, or making a purchase in a grocery store, etc.).

This type of approach was promoted in nursery schools and kindergartens of the early 1890s, and similar patterns are visible today. Early childhood teachers of the late 1990s follow a consistent version of this general approach to curriculum. As children advance to grades 2 and 3, the curriculum becomes more advanced in content. This occurs in subject areas that have been in the curriculum since preschool, but now the children advance along the lines indicated by their age, maturity, and readiness for more specific content. Specified areas of reading, writing, mathematics, music, art, and oral and written language are usually integrated.

For example, a four-year-old will have a large assortment of watercolors and a large piece of plain paper from which to develop an art project. After its completion, the teacher will discuss the project with the child and write on it the identifying features that are designated during the discussion and perhaps the child's name. On the other hand, a seven-year-old might be capable of writing his own description and having a discussion with the teacher concerning lines, patterns, shapes, forms, and subtle variations, and whether he discovered any new colors through mixing paints. Each is learning, at his own developmental stage, aspects of pattern, design, geometry, reading, and writing.

The art experience enables children to mix and match colors as they see them in their environment, or in contrast to what they see. It is the understanding of this integrative process and the ability to carry it through that is central to the differences between early childhood and elementary teaching and learning. In many schools, by the time children reach grades 4, 5, or 6, they have different teachers for different subjects, and integrated teaching is done in a completely different way.

The difference between how elementary school teachers and early childhood teachers are trained can also be explored in terms of art activities. The elementary school teacher might put out one color a day for students' use in their art activity. On Monday the children might be provided, and learn about, red, and paint everything on their art paper red. On Tuesday the color might be yellow, and they experience the use of yellow. Wednesday the color might be blue and on succeeding days the use and memory of the secondary colors might be the subjects. Following their painting project with a single color each day, pupils are assigned to practice writing the word "red" on the same day as their red painting—yellow and blue follow in the same manner—and are drilled to check their memory of the words and colors. The elementary teacher will end the week with a spelling test that will include the colors studied that week.

When teachers trained in elementary or middle school education are assigned to teach in an early childhood setting (grade 3 and below), there is considerable direct instruction of "academics" and rote performance by pupils, followed by testing to assure that some learning has taken place. There also may be worksheets with predrawn scenes or animals for pupil completion in social studies, science, language arts, and math.

The result of such an approach is that a period of growth that should

be devoted to imaginative and aesthetic exploration of content is sometimes absent when curriculum approaches that are intended for elementary grades are used in early childhood education. In language
development, for example, time spent in dramatic play and the housekeeping area cannot be simulated through the use of elementary school
worksheets that children complete in silence. Pupils in the elementary
education context also are given less time for thoughtful adventure, reflection, or social interaction; and opportunities to self-discover important aspects of their world are absent. In response to the back-to-basics
movement in the mid-1980s, Anne Martin, a teacher at Lawrence School
in Brookline, Massachusetts, described current influences on kindergarten curriculum.

> Kindergarten used to mean brightly colored paintings, music, clay,
> block building, bursting curiosity, and intensive exploration. Now
> the kindergarten's exuberance is being muted, its color drained . . .
> and spirit flattened, leaving us with stacks of paperwork and
> teacher manuals. No longer even designated "preschool," kinder-
> garten is becoming an adjunct to first grade, with workbooks re-
> placing art materials and formal instruction replacing activities that
> follow the children's interest. One rationale for this change is that
> because children grow up more rapidly in the age of TV and com-
> puters, they are ready for "skill work" earlier than they used to be.
> Consequently, much of the day is taken up by whole-class drill in
> numbers, letters, and phonics, mostly through coloring and filling
> in commercial workbook pages. . . . This trend toward a formalized
> kindergarten curriculum appears to me not only mistaken—a
> misunderstanding of the way young children learn—but actually
> counterproductive. . . . If we want to engage our gregarious five-
> year-olds to develop language skills, the last thing we should do is
> to consign the children to their chairs to work in silent isolation.
> They should be talking informally and in groups, looking at books
> and reading together, helping each other write signs and messages,
> playing out dramatic scenarios, telling stories and listening to oth-
> ers read and tell them. (1985, p. 318)

After World War II, a group living near the village of Reggio Emilia,
Italy, started the long and difficult task of developing schools for young
children. Their work captured the imagination of Loris Malaguzzi, who
had studied in Geneva at Piaget's School for Young Children; he worked
with teachers to establish a school in the philosophical traditions of Rousseau and Vygotsky. Fortunate to have the combination of enthusiastic
teachers, supportive parents, an encouraging local government, and mo-
tivated learners, the Reggio Emilia experiment has become an exemplary

program. The teachers practice their craft in an environment that provides vast freedom of exploration and expression. As discussed in Chapter 5, the Reggio Emilia schools provide excellent examples of freedom of experience.

Teacher-encouraged, extensive exploration by learners is among the many characteristics that distinguish early childhood and infant schools in Reggio Emilia. Teachers seldom need to intervene in children's conflicts because their peer relationship skills are encouraged throughout the curriculum. Pupil interactions are provided their greatest opportunity for development in the use by teachers of the project method. As pupils work on projects, they are encouraged to view writing, reading, craft activities, and art as symbolic languages of expression. At a time when schools in the United States are moving away from encouraging pupil's spontaneous play and pupil-initiated activities, Reggio Emilia is gaining world recognition by supporting this approach.

Important differences between early childhood education in the United States and in Reggio Emilia can be found in their knowledge of child development. While many U.S. early childhood teachers consider the developmental stages of Piaget, Erikson, and Freud essential, Reggio Emilia educational planners do not see this as a cornerstone of their work. There are, however, similarities between the approach of these Italian educators and that of constructivists in the United States; they have structured the school in a way that classrooms and community are integrated physically as a part of the learning design. And the project approach, as described by Robinson (1921) and Katz and Chard (1989), has been given new meaning in the Reggio Emilia approach. There are, however, some distinctive variations.

> The projects that teachers engage in are distinct in a number of ways from those that characterize American teachers' conceptions of unit or thematic studies. The topic of investigation may derive directly from teachers' observations of children's spontaneous play and exploration. Project topics are also selected on the basis of an academic curiosity or social concern on the part of teachers or parents, or a serendipitous event that directs the attention of children and teachers. Reggio teachers place a high value on their ability to improvise and respond to children's predisposition to enjoy the unexpected. Regardless of their origins, successful projects are those that generate a sufficient amount of interest and uncertainty to provoke children's creative thinking and problem-solving and are open to different avenues of exploration. (New 1993, p. 3)

During the 1920s and 1930s, early childhood education models sought ways of incorporating aesthetics and nature throughout the curriculum.

The Dalcroze method, based on music, body movement, and rhythmic studies, was presented by the teacher, or sometimes a specially trained professional was brought in on a scheduled basis. Universities and normal schools included Dalcroze training in their kindergarten and early childhood education curricula.

Developed by the Swiss music teacher/composer Emile-Jacques Dalcroze (1865–1950), Dalcroze eurythmics involved children in movement activities while listening to rhythmical beats produced by a pupil and their teacher trained in the Dalcroze method, at the piano. The curriculum attempted to connect the body's biological rhythms, nervous system, and muscle functions to a musical experience. Children were encouraged to emulate fluttering butterflies, growing flowers, or prancing ponies as they responded freely to music being played (see Figure 4.2).

THE PROJECT METHOD

Another major focus of the early childhood curriculum was the project method. This curriculum approach was devised by theorists in the early 1900s and adopted by elementary and early childhood educators. J. A. Randall published the first article describing project teaching in 1915, and David Snedden brought out a report on the project method in 1916. In 1916, George D. von Hofe, Jr., an elementary science teacher at the Horace Mann School at Columbia University's Teachers College, supported the usefulness of the method for teaching science and mathematics, and in 1918, John F. Woodhull detailed how the project method could be used in teaching science. William Heard Kilpatrick, one of John Dewey's colleagues, described this curriculum approach in 1918. Mendel E. Branom's book, *The Project Method in Education* (1919), was designed to provide a philosophical framework for project teaching.

The project method was revived in the early 1990s by Lillian Katz and Sylvia Chard (their work will be discussed later). The following description, written in 1921 by Robinson, captures the thought and practice of that decade.

> A project of great interest to the children of the kindergarten of the University Elementary School was one developed during the winter which they called "Our City." During the autumn quarter the children had engaged in housekeeping plays and had built and equipped a grocery and a toy store. As a result they had acquired a background of interesting experiences connected with home and community life.
>
> *The project suggested by the children*—One morning early in January the teacher had all the building-blocks within easy access and said to the children, "What would you like to build with the blocks

Figure 4.2
Children Demonstrate Dalcroze Eurythmics, The Faulkner School, Chicago

THE YOUNG DIRECTOR

The girl in the center is changing the beat from 2 to 3, 4, 5 or 6. The others must watch and accent strongly the first beat. The young director changes the beat at her pleasure and the children get the cue from the movement of the baton. This develops spontaneity and concentration. First and second grade children.

THE UNFOLDING FLOWERS

These little students of the Dalcroze method are listening to improvized music, coming up from the floor as the music rises. This is a combination musical and physical exercise and teaches relaxation and control and trains the ear in graduations of pitch. This is a kindergarten group in the Faulkner School, Chicago.

Source: *The Volume Library* (New York: Educators Association, 1934), 26.

today?" One child answered immediately, "Let's build a town." Although the teacher had intended at some time to lead the children to such a project, she had not expected to introduce it so soon. As the psychological moment seemed to have arrived, however, the children were encouraged to begin at once.

Preliminary discussion and free experimentation—There was first a discussion as to what buildings a town should include, and a list of those suggested was written on the blackboard. This list was later printed on a chart. The following buildings were mentioned the first day: (1) station, (2) state bank, (3) "Congress Hotel," (4) church, (5) grocery store, (6) toy store, (7) houses, and (8) garage. Each child began to work on the building of his choice, selecting his own place in the room for its construction. He also chose the blocks he thought were best suited to the requirements of his particular building.

Organization follows free experimentation—The next day the children were eager to start on their buildings. One little girl said, "I am going to build my church across the street from Barbara's house." Another child said, "I am going to move my garage over next to Stephan's store." This spontaneous grouping of buildings suggested the idea of streets to children, and, after a discussion of the different kinds of buildings being erected, they planned for a "business" street and a "residence" street. Two adjacent sides of the room were set apart for these streets. (Robinson 1921, pp. 194–195)

In an important publication in 1989, Lillian Katz and Sylvia Chard described a curriculum approach to early childhood that revived the interest in the project approach. Their description of the project approach was remarkably similar to the project method introduced by Robinson in the early 1920s.

Our advocacy of the project approach is rooted in our own ideological commitments and values related to the aims of education. An overall aim of this approach is to cultivate the life of the young child's mind. In its fullest sense, the term mind includes not only knowledge and skills, but also emotional, moral, and aesthetic sensibilities. . . . Let us begin with a quick look at project work in progress in an early childhood classroom:

Several children are collaborating on a painting depicting what they have learned about the driving mechanism of the school bus. Their teacher is helping them label the steering wheel, horn, gearshift, ignition, accelerator, hand brake, brake pedal, turn indicators, windshield wipers, and inside and outside rearview mirrors.

A second small group is working on felt pen drawings of parts of the motor, indicating where oil and water are added. The children make a diagram showing how fuel flows from the gas tank to the motor and how the exhaust makes its way through the tailpipe. As they work, they correct each other and make suggestions about what goes where and what details to include.

A third small group is finishing a display of their paintings showing the different kinds of lights inside and outside the bus. The display notes which lights are for signals and warnings and which serve to light the way ahead as well as inside. Some lights are red, some amber, and some white, some flash on and off, and some are just reflectors. Their work is accompanied by a lively exchange of information and opinion about what they have seen and how to picture it so that other children can see what they mean.

A fourth group has prepared a chart of gauges and dials on the dashboard, giving a basic idea of the information each one yields. Two of the children used a rope to establish the width and length of the bus. They have displayed their rope on a counter in front of a sign the teacher helped them write. (Katz & Chard 1989, pp. 1–3)

Katz and Chard noted that the knowledge gained by participants in this project could not be measured through the utilization of national standardized tests.

Because of these and other fundamental differences, there is occasional tension between professionals in early childhood education and professionals in elementary education. Such tension tends to surface at various times and follow predictable resolutions of agreeing to disagree, but the conflict seldom goes away. It has its origin in the early 1900s, following the recommendation in scholarly publications that kindergarten and primary grades should be merged in public schools. The inclusion of kindergarten in public schools was deemed essential by founders of the kindergarten movement in the United States, as a means to break the generation-to-generation cycle of poverty among urban immigrants and Southern migrants who relocated in cities. In fact, it was the ultimate goal of philanthropists in the movement to transfer nursery schools and kindergartens, along with their costs, to a public-funded status by attaching them to regular schools.

When public schools accepted kindergarten as an integrated part of their systems, grades 1 through 3 came to use theories of both the kindergarten movement and the early grades for curriculum and teacher preparation. Previously, universities with teacher training departments had traditionally graduated elementary teachers (grades 1 through 6), and their home economics departments dealt with preschool and kindergarten. By 1920, Columbia University, Harvard University, John

Hopkins University, the University of Iowa, and Yale University had organized programs for kindergartners, and for nursery school and early education teacher preparation.

By the 1930s, with a new early childhood program identity (birth through grade 3), more confusion occurred because some who wanted to be early childhood teachers trained in departments of education with their elementary grades counterparts, and some in departments of child and family studies, which now had a broader focus than the previous home economics departments. Some early education programs were found in nursing schools, and a few remained identified with home economics departments.

HEAD START AND AFFILIATED PROGRAMS

The mid-1960s witnessed the inauguration of Project Head Start (see Chapter 1). There were also some curriculum innovations important to early childhood education: the Bank Street College model, the Ypsilanti early education program, Montessori, and the University of Chicago Laboratory Nursery School program, to name just a few. Head Start brought our attention to several other programs.

The existence of various programs led to research that sought to determine which were the most successful. Direct instruction curriculum models are generally easier to measure than programs that strive for more developmental or affective results. The first assessments of Head Start programs reported that after three years or so, their graduates lost the gains they had achieved. After several rounds of finger pointing, and identification of test errors, the federal Head Start sponsors decided to address the proposed academic losses among graduates.

By 1970, Head Start sponsors and advocates had organized Project Follow-Through, a program funded by the federal government and designed to follow Head Start graduates through the first three grades of schooling. The original planners of Head Start were pleased, because they had anticipated that early childhood philosophy had a rightful place in public schools. With the inauguration of Project Follow-Through, there came a rearrangement among programs that would decrease the diversity nationally while providing community groups with an opportunity to select the curriculum model that in their view best suited the needs of their children.

Follow-Through provided an extension of parent involvement, as well as opportunities for researchers to assist in identifying the most effective ways to advance the academic interests of children from poor families. Diversity could be assured because sponsors supported community choice of model, even if different models were selected by adjoining communities. For example, in Brooklyn, New York, the Ocean Hill–

Brownsville community school selected the Montessori model, while a Bedford-Stuyvesant school, also in Brooklyn, selected the Bank Street College model.

The selection process started with national Head Start planners organizing a demonstration of the various teaching-learning approaches for parent and staff groups. Representatives from various colleges and universities and academic professionals were invited to a conference in Kansas City, Missouri. Each model was presented by professionals from the institution or university identified with that particular approach to teaching and learning. The following are descriptions of the major models presented.

The Bereiter-Engelmann Model

The Bereiter-Engelmann model, renamed the DISTAR program, was developed by the psychologists Carl Bereiter and Siegfried Engelmann. The program is designed to present carefully prepared lessons in language arts, mathematics, and reading. Teaching is done in small, disciplined, and orderly groups, with the language of the teacher and the expected responses from the children predetermined. Children are praised—and given a reward—when their performance fits the program's expectations. In general, it is based on the philosophy of John Locke and the theories of Pavlov, Watson, and Skinner.

In the early phases of the model, when pupils respond with desired behaviors, they are given a small piece of candy or handshake by the teacher (positive reinforcement). If their behavior is disturbing to the teacher, they are ignored or placed in isolation from their peers (negative reinforcement).

In later years, the program underwent some changes and is now known as DISTAR. The fundamental principles, however, remain the same. In 1988, the following description of DISTAR was published in the journal *Education and Treatment of Children*. It is presented here to show in detail how this direct instruction approach differs from the project method.

—The model uses a teacher and an aide at levels 1 and 2 of the program, usually in kindergarten and first grade. The aides are trained to teach and function fully as teachers, and, thus, increase the amount of teacher-student interaction time.

—Programs are designed to focus on teaching the general use of information/skills where possible, so that though teaching a subset, the whole set is learned. For example, by teaching 40 sounds and skills for hooking them together, students learn a generalized decoding skill that is relevant to one-half of the more common English words.

Control the Details of What Happens

—Daily lesson scripts are provided that tell the teacher exactly what to say and do. All teachers and aides use the DISTAR programs in reading, language, and arithmetic developed by Engelmann and his associates.

—Training is provided so that the staff knows how to execute the details of the program.

—Student progress and, indirectly, teacher implementation are monitored through the use of criterion-referenced "continuous progress tests" on the children every two weeks.

—Supervisors (one for each 10 to 15 classrooms) are trained to spend 75% of their time actually in classrooms working with teachers and aides.

—Procedures for teachers, supervisors, administrators, and parents are detailed in implementation and parent coordination manuals.

Efficiently Teaching

—Behavioral principles and logic for resource utilization have been used to develop a number of methods for increasing teaching efficiency and student-engaged learning time. The methods described here include: scripted presentation of lessons, small-group instruction, reinforcement, corrections, and procedures to teach every child by giving added attention to the lower performers.

Scripted Presentation of Lessons

—The printed instructions in each DISTAR program indicate exactly what that teacher will say and do during classroom instruction. This approach is called a "scripted presentation" and it is recommended for a number of reasons. The scripts provide teachers with directions, sequences of examples, and sequences of subskills and wordings that already have been tested for effectiveness. Teachers can use scripts to improve the quality of their instruction. Scripted programs also make the teacher trainer's job more explicit. The trainer-supervisor knows the performance criteria, pinpoints deficiencies quickly, and provides appropriate remedies.

Reinforcements

—The training procedures for the Direct Instruction Model include specifications for the systematic use of positive consequences to strengthen children's motivation for learning. Knowledge of results, behavior-specific praise, enjoyable games, and point systems leading to special consequences are a few of the recommended techniques. An important rule for applying reinforcers is: Never use a stronger reinforcement system than is necessary to get the job done.

Corrections

—When teachers implement traditional instructional programs in group situations, they frequently have to choose among the following awkward alternatives: (a) spending much of the period working with one student's problems that are of little concern to other members of the group; (b) ignoring many mistakes and "pretending" that they do not occur; and/or (c) keying on several students in the group, usually the highest performers, and attending only to their responses. These problems can be avoided or quickly solved when the program is carefully designed to prevent the occurrence of highly probable mistakes. When mistakes do occur in Direct Instruction, teachers do not merely give the correct answer, but remind a student of the process to follow to determine the correct answer.

Implementation

—One important goal of training in the Direct Instruction model is to provide teachers and aides with the skills they must have to teach students in both small and large groups. Teachers learn how to place and group students to produce the best results for each child, how to present the DISTAR tasks, how to reinforce accurate responses, and how to correct mistakes. Training is necessary to properly implement the model and is usually accomplished through a workshop just before school begins, continuing in-service sessions, and classroom supervision. (Engelmann et al. 1988, pp. 303–306)

At least one study of the effects of the intensive methods of this type of direct instruction found that as children grew older, they were more likely to be involved in delinquent behavior than their age-mates who had been in programs using different models.

The Bank Street Model

The Bank Street Model is named for the college that designed the program. Lucy Sprague Mitchell and Harriet Johnson established the Bureau of Educational Experiments in New York City. To provide an environment for research and child development education, they founded Bank Street College of Education as a graduate school with its own experimental day school. It became one of the best-known early childhood centers. The Bank Street program is based on freedom of experience. Learners are encouraged to initiate their own classroom interactions with materials, the teacher, or other children. Play is seen as children's work, and the use of building blocks and other manipulatives is a part of that work. At other sites in New York City, Bank Street College has conducted programs for children from poor families, using the freedom of experience approach. Its work can be identified with the philosophies of Rousseau and Dewey, and the theories of Freud and Piaget. The Bank Street model views Piaget's stages as essential to an understanding of children's logical thinking and their level of readiness to make sense of their environment in thoughtful ways. Ego development is viewed as fundamental to the learner's perceptual ordering of the world. The project method is often seen as integral to the Bank Street model.

An article by Barbara Biber and other Bank Street affiliates stated:

> The children are perceived and responded to as individuals, not as parts of a conglomerate mass, the "class." The teacher enjoys children—their freshness and ebullience, their capacity for naive wonder and intense involvement, the quick tide of their feelings, and the graceful movement of thought by which young minds weave sparse experience into a coherent and workable design for living in the present. Ability to adjust language usage to their capacity and idiom and to understand them through nonverbal as well as verbal forms of communication meaningfully facilitates relatedness. Genuine interaction between teacher and children depends on how much the teacher not only knows the children but allows herself to be known to them as a feeling, fallible human being.
>
> At this stage of children's development, the teacher needs to be at ease with a measure of natural noise and physical movement, recognizing that control of feeling is in flux and negative behavior will result occasionally. Optimally, the teacher does not equate maturity wholly with reasonableness and appreciates the creative potential inherent in the subjective aspects of phantasm. At the same time, she takes responsibility for leading children toward reference systems of reality and objectivity.
>
> The teacher offers support for positive self-feeling. Recognizing conflict is inevitable in the growth process, she is not surprised that children, in any life circumstance, have to counter with feelings of fear, weakness, guilt, and anxiety. Accordingly, she helps the children feel comfortable in having their troubles and doubts known to her with confidence that they will not thus be downgraded in her eyes. She becomes a source of emotional support even when she can only listen to and understand problems that are outside the scope of solution within the school. (1959, p. 559)

The Tucson Early Education Model

The Tucson early education model was designed by Marie Hughes of the University of Arizona. It is built upon the idea that classroom teachers can enable children to develop positive attitudes toward learning. Small-group interaction is encouraged, and the teacher is often engaged in one-on-one interaction with children. Classrooms are grouped in cross-age patterns to optimize heterogeneous groups for interactions. Materials are in great supply and visible to children, who are encouraged to advance their intellectual skills through group work and the project approach. The Tucson model is based upon the philosophy of Rousseau and the theories of Dewey and Piaget. It accepts the stage theories of Piaget as a means of understanding how to respond to the learner's needs in the classroom's socially interactive process.

The Behavior Analysis Approach

Professor Don Bushnell of the University of Kansas proposed a model of teaching and learning for young children called the behavior analysis approach. Programmed materials are utilized in a planned, individual instruction mode. It is a skills approach to teaching that employs parents as teachers. Parents are taught techniques that use behavior modification through positive reinforcement. This approach is rooted in the philosophy of John Locke and the theories of Skinner and Watson.

The Ypsilanti Program

David Weikart of Ypsilanti, Michigan, proposed an approach in which learning objectives are stated in terms of the planned behavioral goals. Starting in the Ypsilanti public schools in 1962, the Perry preschool project was designed to improve the knowledge acquisition of low-income black children in the specific areas of number concepts, visual motor attributes, and language enrichment. Essential to the Ypsilanti program is the encouragement of a positive self-concept through the achievement of academic skills. The approach has three dimensions: a curriculum that is cognitively based; a classroom teacher who is intimately involved in the planning, strives to interact with children, and participates actively in their learning; and a cooperative effort between the teacher and a parent in the home to support the work of the program. The child's competence at each level is assessed to enable the teacher to guide the child's learning in a sequential manner. Philosophically, the program is Rousseau-oriented, and it follows the theory of Piaget. Currently, the model is being utilized by various districts and is named High/Scope.

Program developers designed a table that placed Piaget's levels of development within the context of "teaching implications" and provided examples of what should be learned. In *The Cognitively Oriented Curriculum: A Framework for Preschool Teachers*, Weikart and others who worked consistently with High/Scope offered the following:

The main premise underlying the Cognitively Oriented Curriculum is that there cannot be a basic understanding of self and the world without the ability to place the self in time and space and to classify and order objects and events. Within the Piagetian framework, this means that two kinds of capabilities have to be developed by the child. First, the child must begin to make connections between objects, between events, and between objects and events; that is, he must construct relationships among the things in his environment and then expand his system of relationships into an organized way of dealing with the world. Second, the child must begin to construct mental representations of himself and of his environment and to deal with these in increasingly complex and abstract ways. The two are complementary: the ability to construct and make use of relationships goes hand in hand with the ability to construct meaningful representations. (1974, p. 6)

The authors later describe how Piaget's theory is represented in their practice.

For the first six weeks of school, the goal is for the children to learn to classify things that are the *same* and things that are *different*. Therefore, all blocks are kept in one cabinet and all cars in another cabinet; all dishes are kept in one cupboard and all utensils in another; all books are shelved together and all puzzles are on a different shelf. We realize that a similar kind of classroom arrangement is often set up in preschools, but this is done to maintain order rather than to differentiate *same* and *different* so that while blocks and cars may belong in specific spaces, they are not necessarily separated. (1974, p. 37)

The Far West Model

The Far West Laboratory educational research and development model, directed by Glen Nimnich, has been referred to as an autotelic approach. The learner's language development, sensory and perceptual acuity, concept formation, abstract thinking, and problem-solving skills are viewed as fundamental to knowledge acquisition. Classrooms and other learning environments are designed to promote a positive self-image through autotelic learning activities that are self-rewarding, that is, detached from teacher reinforcements. The overall environment is designed to be responsive to the learner's cognitive style. The teacher's role is that of guide to help children confront problems and arrive at their own solutions. This approach is based on the philosophy of Dewey and the theory of Piaget.

The Educational Development Center Model

The Educational Development Center of Boston utilized a Piagetian approach that motivates teachers and parents to define their own needs in terms of what they want children to learn. During staff training, professionals will advise how these goals can be achieved. In the Educational Development Center model, classrooms are fashioned to the needs of the learners, and the talents and working styles of the teachers. The classroom activities emerge from staff development and parent-teacher approaches that assess the needs of children, parents, and professionals. Each classroom is expected to undergo change from time to time as the needs of learners change with their growth and development. A teacher having considerable experience with children serves as an on-site adviser to the staff.

The Parent Education Model

The parent education model is similar to programs that have involved parents directly in the education of their infants and toddlers. A primary aim of Head Start was to involve parents as teachers, teacher and social service aides, and nutritionists. Several programs became a part of New Careers, a program that fostered higher education for parents. In accord with the traditional valuing of the potential of parents, Professor Ira Gordon at the University of Florida at Gainesville has been experimenting with the growth and development of infants and toddlers from economically disadvantaged families. The parent education model emphasizes family life as the core of its intervention strategies. Parents are recruited from the economically disadvantaged community and trained to become parent educators. It is theorized that parents from the low-income community have a better chance than an outside professional of being accepted in the homes of their neighbors. The minimum requirement for being a parent educator is completion of high school. Parent educators are trained by Gordon's professional staff to use materials readily available in the home where they are working, and to develop a comfortable, trusting relationship with the mother and child. The theories of Piaget provide the framework for Gordon's assumptions about how children learn. The learning tasks used by the parent educators are designed to be age-appropriate according to Piaget's stages of early child development. In "Parenting, Teaching, and Child Development," Gordon wrote:

What we do as teachers and parents, as adults, makes a difference in what happens to children. The common view now is that development equals learning, not that development and learning are parallel and do not meet, but it wasn't many years ago that parents were told there was very little connection between development and learning. If you were a parent, you were supposed to buy Gesell, which was the standard "bible" and had a maturational orientation. If you had a two-year-old, you turned to the right page in Gesell and checked out your child. If he or she were behaving like a two-year-old, you sighed with relief; if the child was behaving like a one-year-old, you locked the child in the back room. But you did not do anything about it. Today, our view is that the parent is the primary teacher of the child. What we do, both as parents and teachers, makes a considerable difference, not only in children's learning of facts but in their total development, self-concept, intellectual development, in all areas of their life. How do parents as the primary teachers teach their children? They teach essentially the way teachers teach. They provide a learning environment, model behavior, and engage in direct instruction with the child. These three means are common to parents and teachers. (1976, p. 173)

Reading Gordon's ideas, one becomes aware that the parent education model is similar to Maria Montessori's theories. This similarity is not unusual, because both Montessori and Gordon expected the recipients of their endeavors to be from poor families. The foundations for Montessori's work were theorized before Piaget, and came from what she called "sense training" and the theories of Sicard. Fundamental to Gordon's work were Piaget's developmental stages.

Studies of Head Start and Associated Programs

In 1986, Lawrence J. Schweinhart and colleagues published the results of a longitudinal study of three early childhood models that were known to the Head Start and Follow-Through programs. Children from DISTAR, High/Scope, and a traditional nursery school were examined for IQ and social changes until they reached the age of fifteen. The study reported:

Sixty-eight impoverished children in Ypsilanti, Michigan were randomly assigned to three programs, attending them at age 3 and 4. Fifty-four of the youngsters (79% of the original sample) were interviewed at age 15. The mean IQ of the children who had attended these high quality programs rose a dramatic 27 points during the first year of the program, from 78 to 105 (on the Stanford Binet Intelligence Scale) and at age 10 was 92 (on the Wechsler Intelligence Scale for Children, or WISC). The three preschool curriculum groups differed little in their patterns of IQ and school achievement over time. According to self reports at age 15, the group that had attended the DISTAR preschool program engaged in twice as many delinquent acts as did the other two curriculum groups, including five times as many acts of property violence. The DISTAR group also reported relatively poor relations with their families, less participation in sports, fewer school job appointments, and less reaching out to others for help with personal problems. (pp. 15–45)

The same group was examined after they reached age twenty-seven, in terms of their preschool experiences and the costs of society for investing in their early education. A report by Weikart in 1996 revealed that the group attending the High/Scope Perry preschool program will return over $7 in benefits to the public in relation to every $1 spent in original program costs. Specifically, 123 African-American children who were born in poverty and enrolled in a High/Scope model program were compared at age twenty-seven with a matched group who did not have access to the program. At age twenty-seven, 95 percent of the original study participants were interviewed, with additional data gathered from their school, social services, and arrest records.

By age 27, only one fifth as many program group members as no-program group members were arrested five or more times (7 vs. 35%), and only one-third as many were ever arrested for drug dealing (7 vs. 25%). At age 27, four times as many program group members as no-program earned $2000 or more per month (29 vs. 7%). Almost three times as many program group members as no-program group members owned their own home (36 vs. 13%); and over twice as many owned second cars (30 vs. 13%). Three-fourths as many program group members as no-program members received welfare assistance or other social services at some time as adults (59 vs. 80%). . . . One-third again as many group members as no-program group members graduated from regular or adult high school or received a General Educational Development Certificate (71 vs. 54%). . . . Program females had only about two-thirds as many out-of-wedlock births as did no-program females (57% of births vs. 83% of births). . . . A cost-benefit analysis was conducted by estimating the monetary value of the program and its benefits, in constant 1992 dollars discounted annually at 3%. Dividing the $88,433 in benefits per participant by the $12,356 in cost per participant results in a cost-benefit ratio of $7.16 returned to the public for every dollar invested in the High/Scope Perry program, substantially exceeding earlier estimates. (pp. 117–118)

Head Start Today

After the first ten years of Head Start, the government made the decision to support quantity more than quality. During the 1980s, Head Start centers were required to serve more children with fewer resources. This trend continued, and the funding per child kept declining. The quality of any program for children rests upon the training received by the professionals who work with the children and upon the training of those who supervise these practitioners. In 1965, the classroom practitioners were college- and university-trained teachers who chose to work in Head Start centers rather than in regular schools.

Head Start centers and classrooms presented professionals with a new and dynamic challenge to use their skills in a way not available to them in traditional public school settings. The recruitment of males as teachers in early education, the use of poor parents as teacher and social service aides, and close cooperative encounters with medical and nutritional providers in a comprehensive approach to the education of poor children made Head Start an attractive career choice for well-trained teachers. By 1980, most of the well-trained professionals no longer worked directly with children. The few who remained were trainers and/or supervisors for the classroom aides. Poor parents, who were the teacher aides of the 1960s and 1970s, became the classroom teachers by the 1980s.

In the early 1990s, the average Head Start teacher's salary was less than $14,000 a year, and the director's salary was less than what beginning teachers in local public schools were earning. Teachers in Head Start are currently required to have the minimum equivalent of high school completion, with some college desirable but not mandatory. A college- or university-trained person is usually assigned to coordinate training and curriculum for several centers in a designated geographic area.

In 1998, the newsletter of the National Dropout Prevention Center announced its support of a campaign called "I Am Your Child." This campaign is sponsored by children's support groups and is coordinated with the Families and Work Institute. It is aimed at raising public awareness of the importance of the first three years of life. Local efforts are being integrated with early childhood development programs that include health care, parent education, quality child care, and intervention programs for families at risk.

The campaign established coalitions in all fifty states to start a dialogue aimed at forming partnerships to strengthen policies and programs concerned with early childhood. The National Governors' Association has established a task force to study public policy options to strengthen support for families with small children. The National Conference of State Legislatures formed a committee to promote legislation concerned with the health needs of young children. And President Clinton announced in 1998 that additional funds will flow to Head Start programs, especially for three-year-old children. Such funds cannot be diverted to Head Start children of other ages. In the same year, modest salary increases were allocated for teachers and other Head Start staff members.

REFERENCES

Bereiter, C., & Englemann, S. 1966. *Teaching the Disadvantaged Child in the Pre-school*. Englewood Cliffs, NJ: Prentice-Hall.

Berrueta-Clement, J. R., Schweinart, L. J., Barnett, W. S., Epstein, A. S., & Weikart, D. P. 1982. "Changed Lives: The Effects of the Perry Preschool Program on Youths Through Age 19." *Monographs of the High/Scope Educational Research Foundation*, 8. Ypsilanti, MI: High Scope Press.

Biber, B. 1961. "Effective Learning and Healthy Personality." *National Elementary Principal* (September) 41(1): 54–58.

Biber, B., Gilkeson, E., & Winsor, C. 1959. "Basic Approaches to Mental Health: Teacher Education at Bank Street College." *Personnel Guidance Journal* 37 (8): 558–568.

Cartwright, S. 1990. "Learning with Blocks." *Young Children* 45 (3): 38–41.

Charters, W. W. 1918. "The Project in Home Economics Teaching." *Journal of Home Economics* 10 (March): 114–119.

Cuisenaire, G., & Gattegno, C. 1954. *Numbers in Colour*. London: Heinemann.

Driscoll, A. 1995. *Cases in Early Childhood Education: Stories of Programs and Practices*. Needham Heights, MA: Allyn and Bacon.

Edwards, C., Gandini, L., & Forman, G. 1993. *The Hundred Languages of Children: The Reggio Emilia Approach to Early Childhood Education*. Norwood, NJ: Ablex.

Engelmann, S. 1988. "The Logic and Facts of Effective Supervision." *Education and Treatment of Children* 11 (4): 328–340.

———. 1991. "Making Connections in Mathematics." *Journal of Learning Disabilities*. 24 (5): 292–303.

Engelmann, S., Becker, W. C., Douglas, C., & Russell, G. 1988. "The Direct Instruction Follow Through Model: Design and Outcomes." *Education and Treatment of Children* 11 (4): 303–317.

Flavell, J. 1963. *The Developmental Psychology of Jean Piaget*. Princeton, NJ: D. Van Nostrand.

Froebel, F. 1909. *Pedagogics of the Kindergarten*. Boston: D. Appleton.

Frost, J. L. 1992. *Play and Playscapes*. Albany, NY: Delmar.

Gattegno, C. 1958. *Arithmetic: Introductory Stage. Books 1, 2, and 3*. London: Heinemann.

———. 1960. *A Teacher's Introduction to the Cuisenaire-Gattegno Method of Teaching Arithmetic*. Reading, UK: Gattegno-Pollock.

Gehlbach, R. D. 1991. "Play, Piaget, and Creativity: The Promise of Design." *Journal of Creative Behavior* 25 (2): 137–144.

Gelfer, J. L., & Perkins, P. G. 1988. "Using Blocks to Build Art Concepts: A New Look at an Old Friend." *Early Child Development and Care* 30:59–69.

Gilkeson, E. 1962. "Freedom and Control: Components of Learning." *National Elementary Principal* 41(7): 32–37.

Ginsberg, H., & Opper, S. 1979. *Piaget's Theory of Intellectual Development*. Englewood Cliffs, NJ: Prentice-Hall.

Gordon, I. 1969. "Stimulation via Parent Education." *Children* 26(2): 57–59.

———. 1970. "Reaching the Young Child Through Parent Education." *Childhood Education* 46 (5): 247–249.

———. 1976. "Parenting, Teaching, and Child Development." *Young Children* 31 (3): 173–183.

———. 1978. "Nurturing Our Roots." *Childhood Education* 55 (1): 4–13.

———. 1979. "How Has Follow Through Promoted Parent Involvement?" *Young Children* 34 (5): 49–53.

Guthrie, E. R. 1952. *The Psychology of Learning*. New York: Harper.

Hill, P. S. 1923. "Introduction." In A. Burke et al., *A Conduct Curriculum for Kindergarten and First Grade*. New York: Scribners.

Holfe, D. 1916. "Giving the Project Method a Trial." *School Science and Mathematics* 16 (December): 763–767.

Horton, D. 1962. "Educational Goals and the Social System of the School." *The National Elementary School Principal* 41 (5): 43–48.

Isenberg, J. P. & Jalongo, M. R. 1993. *Creative Expression and Play in the Early Childhood Curriculum*. New York: Merrill.

Kami, K. K., & Radin, N. L. 1967. "A Framework for a Preschool Curriculum Based on Some Piagetian Concepts." *The Journal of Creative Behavior* 13: 314–324.

Katz, L. 1990. "Impressions of Reggio Emilia Preschools." *Young Children* 45 (6): 11–12.

Katz, L. G., & Chard, S. C. 1989. *Engaging Children's Minds: The Project Approach*. Greenwich, CT: Ablex Publishing Corp.

Kilpatrick, W. H. 1918. "The Project Method." *Teacher's College Record* 24 (September): 319–325.

Kohn, M. 1962. "The Importance of the Beginning: Kindergarten." *The National Elementary Principal* 41 (6): 18–22.

Martin, A. 1985. "Back to Kindergarten Basics." *Harvard Educational Review* 55 (3): 318–320.

New, R. 1990. "Excellent Early Childhood Education: A City in Italy Has It." *Young Children* 45 (6): 4–10.

———. 1993. Reggio Emilia: Some Lessons for U.S. Educators. *Eric Clearing House*, EDO-PS-93-3.

Nourot, P. M., & Van Hoorn, J. L. 1991. "Symbolic Play in Preschools and Primary Settings." *Young Children* 45 (6): 40–48.

Parker, C. S., & Temple, A. 1925. *Unified Kindergarten and First-Grade Teaching*. Boston: Ginn and Company.

Piaget, J. 1951. *Play, Dreams, and Imitation in Childhood*. London: Routledge & Kegan Paul.

Pratt, C. 1948. *I Learn From Children*. New York: Harper & Row.

Randall, J. A. 1915. "Project Teaching." *National Education Association*, 1009–1012.

Robinson, I. 1921. "A Project in Community Life in the Kindergarten." *Elementary School Journal* 22: 194–203.

Shweinhart, L. J., Weikart, D. P., & Larner, M. B. 1986. "Consequences of Three Preschool Curriculum Models Through Age 15." *Early Childhood Research Quarterly* 1: 15–45.

Snedden, D. 1916. "The Project as a Teaching Unit." *School and Society* 4 (September): 419–423.

Sternberg, R. 1991. "Death, Taxes, and Bad Intelligence Tests." *Intelligence* 15 (3): 257–269.

Stone, S. J. 1995. "Wanted: Advocates for Play in the Primary Grades." *Young Children* 50 (6): (September) 45–54.

Temple, A. 1920. "The Kindergarten Primary Unit." *Elementary School Journal* 20 (April): 498–502.

Terman, L. M. 1919. *The Intelligence of School Children*. Boston: Houghton Mifflin.

Thorndike, E. L. 1913. *The Psychology of Learning*. New York: Teachers' College Press.

———. 1922. *The Psychology of Arithmetic*. New York: Macmillan.

———. 1935. *The Psychology of Wants, Interests, and Attitudes*. New York: Appleton-Century-Crofts.

Thorndike, E. L., & Gates, A. I. 1929. *Elementary Principles of Education*. New York: Macmillan.

Vandewalker, N. C. 1907. "The History of Kindergarten Influences in Elementary Education." In *Sixth Yearbook of the National Society for the Scientific Study of Education, Part 2*. Chicago: Public School Publishing Company.

Van Hoorn, J., Nourot, P., & Scales, B. 1993. *Play at the Center of the Curriculum*. New York: Merrill.

Von Hofe, Jr., G. D. 1916. "Giving the Project Method a Trial." *School Science and Mathematics* 16(9) (December): 763–767.

Wasserman, S, 1992. "Serious Play in the Classroom." *Childhood Education* 68 (3): 133–138.

Weikart, D. 1996. "High-Quality Preschool Programs Found to Improve Adult Status." *Childhood* 3: 117–120.

Weikart, D. P., Rogers, L., & Adcock, C. 1974. *The Cognitively Oriented Curriculum: A Framework for Preschool Teachers*. Washington, DC: National Association for the Education of Young Children.

Winsor, C. B. 1962. "Teaching for Learning and Growth." *National Elementary Principal* 41 (4): 49–53.

———. 1973. *Experimental Schools Revisited: Bulletins of the Bureau of Educational Experiments*. New York: Agathon Press.

Woodhull, J. F. 1918. "The Project Method in the Teaching of Science." *School and Society* 8 (July): 41–44.

Zimiles, H. 1961. "Teacher Selection and Personality Assessment." *National Elementary Principal* 41 (2): 51–55.

5

Montessori Imagination

Ours is a driven culture. It is driven on by its achievement, compet-
itive, profit, and mobility drives, and by the drives for security and
a higher standard of living. Above all it is driven by expansiveness.
Drives like hunger, sex, thirst and rest arise directly out of the chemistry of the body, whereas expansiveness, competitiveness, achievement, and so on are generated by the culture; still we yield to the
latter as we do to hunger and sex. Side by side with these drives is
another group of urges, such as gentleness, kindness, and generosity.
                                                            —Jules Henry

Central to our understanding of Maria Montessori's imagination is her
view of the learner's needs for daily living. Her original work was with
children from impoverished families, and this influenced her ideas about
the need for a basic knowledge of skills necessary for day-to-day living.
   Within this context, it is useful to discuss the child's growth and development in terms of the relationship between learners and their environments. In this discussion, the environment includes objects and events
within the learner's purview—among them, other persons. Environments for schooling can range across various extremes of theories and
philosophies. Out-of-school environments also provide important learning experiences for children. The lives of Montessori's first pupils were
spent primarily without adult supervision and nurturing, often on the
streets.

FREEDOM OF EXPERIENCE AND CONTROL OF EXPERIENCE

Keeping in mind the relationship between the learner and the environment, an understanding of early childhood programs and methods can emerge from viewing teaching and learning along a continuum. At each end of this continuum we will place models that represent the most extreme differences in early childhood teaching and learning.

At one extreme of this continuum, there are teachers who assume an approach that takes into account the developmental levels of children. For these teachers, Freud's work provides information concerning psychosexual stages of development; Erikson's and Piaget's theories explain psychosocial stages. Ways of dealing with children come primarily from observations of their interactions with objects and events in their world. We will call this end of the continuum "freedom of experience." In Piaget's view, children need freedom to construct their own meaning.

Educators using Freud, Erikson, and Piaget's work as a guide select materials and books and provide a classroom atmosphere that encourages teacher-child interaction. Practice is guided by perspectives the teacher learns during her training. Children are usually encouraged to explore classroom facilities and materials, and conversations occur between the teacher and the entire class in which they plan for the day, or with small groups as they work on a project, or occasionally with individuals who are playing and/or working alone. These encounters are helpful for designing future learning activities because teachers can gauge the strengths of various children and plan accordingly.

This approach is labeled "freedom of experience" because children are encouraged to interact rather freely under the guidance of the teacher, who wishes to present information and materials at each child's appropriate developmental level. The relatively free environment provides many opportunities for children to explore, to reproduce, and to explain to adults and to each other meanings drawn from their experiences and perceptions.

Classroom supplies may include crayons, paints, and paper, and the children are encouraged to read, write, draw, color, and/or cut out their interpretation of an event or object from their experience. They are supported in constructing knowledge from their familiar world. Following an art project, the teacher might say to a child, "Tell me about this drawing." During the discussion, the child will be encouraged to write about the experience and his interpretation of it, and to put his name on the paper. If the teacher learns from this experience that the child is not yet able to write, she will use this information as a staging point for teaching writing and reading, utilizing an appropriate theoretical perspective.

Educators who approach their work through the other end of the continuum support the view that children should be *taught* the skills known to be appropriate for their grade level in a didactic manner. This didactic relationship requires an active teacher and a relatively passive learner. Teachers holding this view believe that children have needs according to grade level, and the work of teaching is to bring children to these preset skill levels and to provide advanced work for those who are more gifted. It is expected that skills identified by the teacher are on the same level as skills that are tested by nationally administered instruments.

With this knowledge, the educator—not the child—constructs what is deemed appropriate for the child's grade level. Teachers at this end of the continuum are concerned about grade level achievement, while teachers at the other end are more concerned about developmental levels, possibly those described by Freud, Erikson, and Piaget.

In control of experience classrooms, children are provided with materials like scissors, crayons, paper, and pencils—or they are required to supply their own. Their materials include pictures made by commercial artists for schoolchildren to color and cut out (such materials are distributed according to the lesson for that day). In this environment, children are sometimes admonished if they color "outside the lines." Teachers who employ this approach believe that coloring "inside the lines" enables the child to learn small-muscle control that should be acquired by a specified grade level. Occasionally, the language of the teaching staff is scripted to ensure conformity. Special materials are designed to match the lesson plans. (At the other end of the continuum, the freedom of experience teachers seldom use commercial pictures rather than the children's own drawings. The substitution of commercially prepared materials would mean that children are not constructing their own interpretation of objects or events, but rather are being informed, from images provided by the teacher, how these things *should* appear).

Following the teacher's instructions, children attempt to model someone else's interpretation of their own idea; and if they fail (as they often do), they will likely respond, "I am not good at art" or "I can't draw," whenever asked to do so for the remainder of their school life.

At the control end of the continuum, adults may control the learner by offering rewards (sometimes in the form of praise) when the child's behavior pleases the adult, and punitive responses (sometimes negative remarks or even scolding) when things are not to the adult's liking. Also, when children attempt their own interpretation of out-of-school experiences through their artwork, they may earn praise or admonishment in accordance with how well their work matches the teacher's model or that of the commercial display. Students eventually learn from praise (or rejection) of their work that they should construct images from the adult's perspective and not their own.

With the control of experience–freedom of experience continuum in mind, one can envision a midpoint where the teacher establishes a profile of behaviors she considers children need to know, and designs two roles that employ some of both ends of the continuum—one role for teachers and one for learners. The Bereiter-Englemann DISTAR program is a model approaching the control of experience end of the continuum, and High/Scope is an example of a program at the freedom of experience end. (These programs are fully examined in Chapter 4.)

THE MONTESSORI PROGRAM

Curriculum and classroom practices designed for Montessori programs provide an excellent example of a midpoint between freedom of experience and control of experience. The Montessori model encourages children to manipulate special materials designed for learning after they have been introduced to them by the teacher. This is followed by instructions as to their appropriate use. Their use is intended to increase children's knowledge about objects and events in their environment.

This approach provides the same materials as other programs, including manipulatives, along with some unique articles. As has been mentioned, Froebel first designed special objects for preschool children, labeling them "gifts." In the Montessori program, the learner is informed about behavioral boundaries and then allowed to make choices within these boundaries. Requiring the teacher (directress), rather than the learner, to control the use of materials brought criticism from Dewey and his followers.

Montessori theory and practice resemble the freedom of experience end of the continuum because they encourage the learner's access to materials and activities. On the other hand, they resemble the control of experience in that children are directed by the teacher as to how these materials are to be selected and utilized (Figure 5.1). Montessori had specific goals for learners and designed materials to assure that these goals would be met. In the classroom, children might have child-sized housekeeping items for learning what Montessori called "life skills." Such knowledge was considered essential because her first pupils were from impoverished families or were children of the street.

In the Montessori classroom, children were encouraged to use the child-sized dustpan and broom for cleaning a soiled floor, for example, but were not allowed to use these items to pretend the floor needed attention. The use of objects for symbolic play, as encouraged by Froebel and later Piaget, was not condoned in the original Montessori theory.

Following the theories of Seguin, Itard, and Wundt, and the practices of Pestalozzi and Froebel, Maria Montessori identified experience as essential for child development and growth. However, it was the control of children's experiences that was essential to her approach (and

Figure 5.1
Montessori-style Classroom Settings of the 1920s

THE HOUSE OF CHILDHOOD

Each child chooses the material for its work, but all are under the supervision of the Directress.

The children often play the game blindfolded to test their accuracy of the sense of touch.

Source: *The Home and School Reference Work*, vol. 9 (Chicago, IL: The Home and School Education Society, 1917), following 3234.

that brought criticism from Dewey and Kilpatrick). She also insisted on a role for parents, identifying them as the child's first teachers. In her translation of Piaget into practice, she recognized the importance of developmental stages and utilized them in establishing a foundation for the progressive age-related practice she taught her teachers.

Maria Montessori (1870–1952), the first woman to receive a medical degree in Italy, toured the United States in the winter of 1913–1914 to give lectures on her methods of teaching young children. When Montessori schools officially opened in the United States, the first ones had Montessori-trained teachers and Montessori-recommended materials and supplies. Montessori insisted, however, that her methods could be successfully implemented by any other mother. By 1914, there were approximately 100 Montessori schools in the United States and the state of Rhode Island had adopted the Montessori system for its public schools.

After obtaining her medical degree, Montessori was appointed to the faculty of the University of Rome, and at the same time enrolled as a postgraduate student of psychiatry. She experienced great success as director of the Orthophrenic School in Rome, which educated learning-disabled children. Her success, largely attributed to her methods and materials, gained her an extensive reputation. Children in her school reached an academic level comparable with that of the average public school child in Rome and aroused considerable negative criticism of public schools.

An opportunity to put her theories to work came in 1907 when she opened the Casa dei Bambini, designed especially for children from poor families. Through this school, Montessori's methods gained worldwide attention and brought critical attention to the first six years of life.

The Montessori program fits onto the freedom of experience/control of experience continuum at an approximate midpoint. Montessori theorists perceive that they are promoting freedom of experience. Their philosophical perspectives relate well to those of John Dewey and Jean Piaget in terms of encouraging childhood experiences.

The important difference is that the Montessori model selects and defines the experiences that are ultimately controlled by the teacher. Children are encouraged to participate in learning experiences previously identified by Montessori teachers. Within the framework of freedom of experience, materials and how these materials will be used are predetermined by adult planners and practitioners who have been taught the Montessori method. This is not true of all programs that are labeled Montessori because copyrights to the name are exhausted, and not all programs called Montessori employ Montessori-trained personnel or employ the Montessori curriculum.

Montessori programs in the United States have served children from all income groups. Private programs are usually located in areas accessible to middle- and upper-income families because they depend upon tuition for their existence. During the 1960s, when Head Start communities were encouraged to select their own program models, parents selected the Montessori program as the "follow through" for education of their children through grade 3.

In the late 1960s, when the New York City Board of Education experimented with community control of schools, one neighborhood in the Ocean Hill–Brownsville district in Brooklyn selected the Montessori model and hired a Montessori-trained teacher for one of its classrooms. This community control experiment could not withstand the persistent negative onslaught from the teachers' union. The citywide teachers' union, with representatives in each school district, and the central offices launched a backlash against what they perceived as a possible loss of collective bargaining rights through community control.

After a few years, the community control experiment and the Montessori program were eliminated in New York City. Throughout the United States there are still over 100 Montessori classrooms in the public school sector, and numerous private programs. Some of the latter promote their own interpretation of Montessori's theory, and others make use of the name only.

In the Montessori theory of the early 1900s, the teacher was referred to as the directress and was considered the person in charge. She was in a more controlling position than the kindergarten or primary school teacher in public schools. The Montessori teacher strives to remain in the background while keeping a watchful eye on the happenings in her classroom. This means that if she is conducting an activity, she does not interfere with the work of children unless they interrupt the work of others or use materials for unintended purposes. In this latter regard, the attention of children will be redirected if the directress considers that they should be involved in more meaningful exercise.

In the original Montessori program in Rome, a directress in the Casa dei Bambini spent the entire day with the children, approximately two and half more hours than in an American kindergarten. The children ranged in age from three to six years. Occasionally they were admitted as young as two and one half and were encouraged to follow the behaviors of children at or near their age as long as they did not interfere with the work of others.

During Montessori's visit to the United States, John H. Kilpatrick and John Dewey were interested in associating their theories with those of Montessori, with some modifications in her approach to accommodate their freedom of experience context. They disagreed with Montessori's insistence upon providing "freedom" for children within an environment that emphasized a controlling role for the directress and direct instruction as the act of teaching. Dewey and Kilpatrick wanted children to have opportunities to explore a variety of materials and textures on their own, and to share in determining their own explorations. Montessori espoused the child's right to explore, but the objects and mode of exploration should be determined by adults in the program.

Other major points of disagreement surfaced around child development issues. Montessori, with her medical background for support, suggested that the weakest part of the child's body is the legs. She suggested that children should not be encouraged to walk until age four, claiming that children who are encouraged to walk prior to this age have legs and feet that are not developed sufficiently to support the weight of the torso. This, she suggested, was the cause of bowleggedness. Thus, she insisted on carpeted floors in the classroom to enable children "to throw themselves and lie and kick at will."

The idea of children using the floor for exploration and recreation agreed with Dewey's philosophy. He often encouraged group gatherings on the carpet for reading and reflecting on the day's classroom work. The notion that bowleggedness resulted from premature motor activity, and that the floor should be used to relieve this stress, was dismissed after this condition was found to be a nutritional problem unrelated to early walking.

Basic principles that Montessori articulated in the early 1920s were described in various ways, but the conceptual framework can be stated as follows:

1. Activities are based upon childhood freedom to experience elements in the environment for their intended purposes and not for amusement. For example, traditional kindergartens often have child-sized housekeeping utensils for children's use, as might a Montessori classroom. In the United States, kindergarten children are encouraged to pretend play with a child-sized broom and dustpan, whereas a Montessori directress would discourage using these items for play and redirect the children to use them only to remove dirt from the floor.

2. Activities and materials are designed to enhance the learners' sensory capacities and bring their power of observation to the highest level.

3. Self-education and independence are underlying goals.

4. Discipline is reinforced through activities and materials designed to promote a foundation of active discipline based on the self-knowledge of good and evil. Childhood immobility should not be confused with discipline, as in traditional school programs. Self-knowledge and discipline can be acquired only through childhood freedom.

IN THE MONTESSORI CLASSROOM

A typical day starts with the performance of certain duties by the children. They sweep the room, dust, and arrange the furniture for the day's activities. A small group of children set the table for eating, and serve the lunch. Montessori considered these the basic skills of life, and all children should learn how to perform them well.

Some later Montessori classrooms made the eating activities an individual responsibility. Each child obtains his food from a single source, washes the utensils, and puts them away. Activities that are required in the Montessori classroom are similar to those required at home. Montessori said, "Who does not know that to teach a child to feed himself, to wash and dress himself, is a much more tedious and difficult work, calling for infinitely greater patience, than feeding, washing, and dressing the child oneself?"

The materials and furnishings in Montessori classrooms are a major part of the program, and are designed to further sensory training and knowledge acquisition. They do not include items found in the traditional kindergarten that are designed for amusement. Rather, Montessori materials are intended to keep children occupied in carrying out functional activities that encourage the exercise of the senses and small- and large-muscle use. Usually, each child is provided with a small table and chair of a weight that he can move to other parts of the room. The same ideas are involved in the design and use of washstands, pitchers, and bowls for use at mealtime. There are also rugs, case, and cupboards in which to store materials, and larger tables for group sessions. It is not difficult to associate particular items and materials with the activities they are intended to enhance.

Early Montessori programs focused on the sense of touch in training the sensory aspects of human development. The sense of touch was viewed as more important than others because it is central to taste and sight, and indirectly to the ability to discriminate. Montessori emphasized that the first seven years were a critical period for such training.

During this period, according to Montessori, young learners crave a sensory stimulation of nerves in the fingertips that contributes to the child's need to place his hands on every object he sees. Montessori complained that instead of providing opportunities for children to advance during this period of growth, it is common for adults to admonish children when they touch objects, especially when shopping. In this regard, Montessori emphasized cleanliness. It was her view that children touch better with clean hands, and especially must have clean hands at mealtime, when eating utensils are handled.

It was Montessori's view that the human system is more ready for sense acquisitions during the first seven years than at any other time.

For this and other reasons, she often emphasized the role of the mothers as the child's first teacher.

A typical Montessori lesson is usually objective, simple, and brief. For instance, lesson planning that includes a study of word choice is done by the directress. All words that do not serve an identified purpose are eliminated. Words must be truthful and simple, and should lead to an understanding of some objective element that can be demonstrated. The directress presents the activity in such a manner that the child's attention is focused upon the materials and/or the object of learning and not on her.

In the early 1900s, the first teaching activities started with an exploration of rough and smooth surfaces. The child was given a board with one side highly polished with wood and the other side a fine-grain sandpaper. The teacher started the lesson by gently holding the child's hand so that the fingertips were exposed. In a right-to-left motion, the fingers were encouraged to glide lightly over the surfaces. As this motion was being directed, the directress repeated the words *smooth, rough, smooth, rough, smooth, rough.*

The child was then left alone to practice this exercise as the directress moved to another area of the classroom or to another child. Later, the child touched other things in the classroom, repeating the words *smooth, rough.* The ultimate aim was to enable the child to distinguish the feel of cotton, wool, silk, and other surfaces. Children who had engaged in this activity occasionally were blindfolded and asked to name what they were touching.

Another popular exercise for the young child in the early 1900s Montessori classroom was part of a lesson on form. A set of nested rectangular and pyramid-shaped blocks were available in the classroom (Figure 5.2). The child was encouraged by the directress to move his fingertips along the edges of the blocks while naming the objects. The directress then left the child alone to explore and name the blocks. A short time later, cubes, cylinders, spheres, and pyramids were introduced. A blindfold activity followed this exercise in which the child had to identify what was being touched. When the child could name objects from touch (i.e., rough and smooth, cube and pyramid), he moved on to the next exercise.

The visualization of differences in dimensions was considered important for the development of sight. Activities to further progress in this area were paired. Materials included three blocks. One of them had ten holes drilled into it, the diameter of each differing by half a centimeter from those on either side. A wooden cylinder with a small knob on top fit exactly into each hole. The child was given this block of wood and the cylinders, which were not placed in the holes (Figure 5.3). The child

Figure 5.2
Rectangle and Pyramid Blocks from the Montessori Program

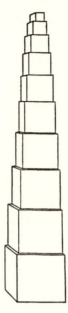

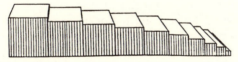

Source: *The Home and School Reference Work*, vol. 9 (Chicago, IL: The Home and School
    Education Society, 1917), 3235, 3236.

was then instructed to place each cylinder in its appropriate hole. After
several tries, the child was expected to become competent at this task.

Parents were encouraged to teach their young by using objects around
the home that had some of these characteristics. In the classroom, beans,
corn kernels, and peas were some of the objects placed in a box for a
blindfolded child to identify. In the early 1900s Montessori classroom,
the child who made the fewest mistakes in identifying objects during a
blindfold test was declared the winner. This was another controlling element over which Dewey and Montessori disagreed. Sensorimotor activities were also emphasized in the early Montessori programs. To satisfy
speech, breathing, standing, and walking needs, children were organized
in group activities consisting of songs and marching games. Montessori's

Figure 5.3
Montessori Cylinders and Holes for Depth Perception

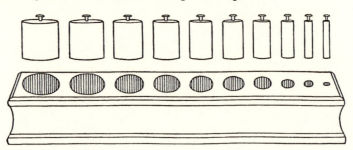

Source: *The Home and School Reference Work*, vol. 9 (Chicago, IL: The Home and School
    Education Society, 1917), 3238.

belief that the lower body of children was weaker than the torso helped
to shape her ideas of the needs of children under the age of seven. Physiological activities that strengthened the lower portions of the body were
essential for the early ages. She assumed that children would walk when
their bodies let them know they were ready for such activities.

In connection with the child's physiological readiness, Montessori exercises included putting on and taking off clothing. For this activity,
teachers and parents were encouraged to make small wooden frames by
nailing together 12-inch lengths of narrow wood, then tack fabric to the
frame. One such frame (Figure 5.4) was covered with colorful fabric on
which large buttons were sewn. (Large buttons were used because small
finger muscle needed to be used.) Working on this board was directly
related to buttoning one's garments. There was also the need to lace
clothing or shoes in real life. To teach the necessary skills, a similar frame
was constructed by the parent for home use and by the teacher for school
use. On it were hooks and eyes, ribbons and bows, and heavy fabric or
leather to match the texture of shoes or coats fastened by buttons requiring a buttonhook.

Initially, these items were shown to the child, then demonstrated and
described by the directress. The child was then asked to try them. If he
was successful, the directress left the child to practice alone. A few buttons, bows, and strings were left undone for the child. The directress
strictly refrained from assisting with the task after the child entered the
practice phase.

Visual perception and the sense of form were introduced with a set of
geometric forms and tablets containing pockets into which these forms
were fitted (Figure 5.5). To encourage the paired development of touch
and sight, children were taught to move their fingertips around the outside edges of the form, then around a similar shape outside the pocket,

Figure 5.4
Montessori Lacing, Ribbons and Bows, Eye Hooks, and Buttoning

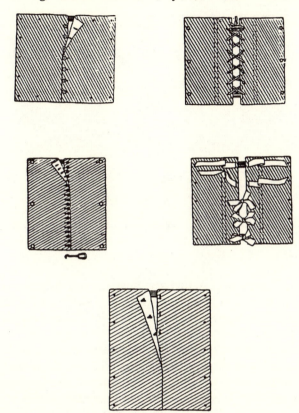

Source: The Home and School Reference Work, vol. 9 (Chicago, IL: The Home and School
Education Society, 1917), 3237, 3238.

until they could fit the proper shape into the appropriate pocket. The
shapes and pockets were cut from cardboard by the teacher for school
use and by the parent for home use. The tablet is of one color and the
shape is of a different color. Color was taught by using a set of cards
that matched and some were wound with one color of silk thread in
gradations from light to dark.

There was an ongoing testing process. For example, after several exercises, when the child was given an object, she was expected to know
its name and function. This type of test was expected to contribute to
language and motor development. Difficulties were often encountered
during the child's attempts at writing. Montessori suggested that this
aspect of skill development is associated with touch training and small-
muscle development. The steps consisted of a series of simple procedu-

Figure 5.5
Montessori Geometric Forms

Source: *The Home and School Reference Work*, vol. 9 (Chicago, IL: The Home and School
  Education Society, 1917), 3244.

res. First, large letters approximately three inches high, made of stiff
cardboard in various colors, were formed in script and placed individually on a piece of cardboard. Along with the letter was a common object
whose name began with the letter. Again, the tips of the fingers were
used to trace the letter outline as the hand would move in writing the
letter. This activity started with the letters that are most easily formed
and was repeated as many times by the learner until the movements
became habituated. While one hand traced the letter, the dominant hand
was positioned to hold a pencil. Sometimes a small stick about the size
of a pencil was used instead to trace the letter. This stick was replaced
with a pencil when the learner had developed the small-muscle controls
for writing.

The various Montessori programs existing today carry on the Montessori tradition in theory and philosophy, but the materials and teaching
approaches have been modernized to bring this popular method in line
with today's needs. There are also programs that go well beyond preschool years, and materials are being developed for them. And, as mentioned previously, there are programs without the sanction of the
international Montessori organization, because copyrights have been allowed to expire.

REFERENCES

Barnett, E. B. 1973. *Montessori and Music; Rhythmic Activities for Young Children.*
  New York: Schocken.

Chattin-McNichols, J. 1992. *The Montessori Controversy*. Albany, NY: Delmar.

Curtis, V. H. 1964. *Our Kindergarten: Experience in Applying Montessori Principles*. New York: Exposition Press.

Elkind, D. 1967. "Piaget and Montessori." *Harvard Educational Review* 37: 535–545.

———. 1983. "Montessori Education: Abiding Contributions and Contemporary Challenges." *Young Children* 38 (2): 3–10.

Fisher, D. F. 1964. *The Montessori Manual for Teachers and Parents*. Cambridge, MA: R. Bentley.

———. 1965. *Montessori for Parents*. Cambridge, MA: R. Bentley.

Gebhardt-Steele, P. A. 1985. *The Computer and the Child: A Montessori Approach*. Rockville, MD: Computer Science Press.

Gitter, L. L. 1969. *Ready Your Child for School the Montessori Way*. St. Meinrad, IN: St. Meinrad Archabbey.

———. 1970. *The Montessori Way*. Seattle, WA: Special Child Publications.

———. 1973. *The Montessori Approach to Art*. Seattle, WA: B. Straub.

Hainstock, E. G. 1968. *Teaching Montessori in the Home*. New York: Random House.

———. 1976. *Teaching Montessori in the Home: The Pre-School Years*. New York: New American Library.

———. 1986. *The Essential Montessori*. New York: New American Library.

Henry, J. 1963. *Culture Against Man*. New York: Alfred A. Knopf.

Kilpatrick, W. 1914. *The Montessori System Examined*. Boston: Houghton Mifflin.

Kohlberg, L. 1968. "Montessori with the Culturally Disadvantaged: A Cognitive Developmental Interpretation and Some Research Findings." In *Early Education: Current Theory, Research and Action*, Robert D. Hess and Roberta M. Bear (eds.), 105–118. Chicago, IL: Aldine.

Kramer, R. 1976. *Maria Montessori: A Biography*. New York: Putnam.

Lillard, P. P. 1972. *Montessori, A Modern Approach*. New York: Schocken.

———. 1996. *Montessori Today: A Comprehensive Approach to Education from Birth to Adulthood*. New York: Schocken.

Montessori, M. 1964a. *The Advanced Montessori Method*. Cambridge, MA: R. Bentley.

———. 1964b. *The Montessori Method*. Translated by Anne E. George. New York: Schocken.

———. 1966. *A Montessori Handbook: Dr. Montessori's Own Handbook*. New York: Putnam.

———. 1976. *Education for Human Development: Understanding Montessori*. New York: Schocken Books.

Orem, R. C. 1969. *Montessori and the Special Child*. New York: Putnam.

———. 1974. *Montessori: Her Method and the Movement: What You Need to Know*. New York: Putnam.

———. 1978. *Montessori: Prescription for Children with Learning Disabilities*. New York: Putnam.

——— (ed.). 1967. *Montessori for the Disadvantaged: An Application of Montessori Educational Principles to the War on Poverty*. New York: Putnam.

Orem, R. C., & Stevens, G. L. 1970. *American Montessori Manual: Principles, Applications, Terms*. Johnstown, PA: Mafex Associates.

Seldin, T. 1981. *Geography and History for the Young Child: The Montessori Approach.* Provo, UT: Brigham Young University Press.

Standing, E. M. 1962a. *Maria Montessori, Her Life and Work.* New York: New American Library.

———. 1962b. *The Montessori Method: A Revolution in Education.* Fresno, CA: Academy Library Guild.

———. 1984. *Maria Montessori, Her Life and Work.* New York: New American Library.

White, J. M., Yussen, R. S., & Docherty, E. M. 1976. "Performance of Montessori and Traditionally Schooled Nursery Children on Tasks of Seriation, Classification, and Conservation." *Contemporary Educational Psychology* 1 (October): 356–368.

6

The Imagination of Literature

I have often reflected upon the new vistas that reading opened to me. I knew right there in prison that reading had changed forever the course of my life. As I see it today, the ability to read awoke inside me some long dormant craving to be mentally alive.

—Malcolm X

Literature for children provides various experiences for which imagination is essential. This literature can be traced to 500 B.C. Stories that stimulate children's interests and imagination started with the fables of Aesop, which date from that time. Designed originally for adults, his fables represent moral philosophy for their time. As societies matured in knowledge and outlook, however, Aesop's stories, which gave a human voice to all living things, were thought of as stories for children. Over the years, they became so widely known that almost any short story ending with a moral was counted among Aesop's fables. Today, Aesop's fables are read to children, and moral descriptions made by adults like "A wolf in sheep's clothing" and "sour grapes" are not uncommon.

FABLES AND MYTHS

From a very early age, children are fascinated with books that are read to them. They will become passionately attached to a few—sometimes a single book will be the one they want adults to read to them, over and over. This is true mostly for books that have strategically placed illustrations representing the text.

Storytelling and fables have been an integral part of information-sharing among individuals and groups, and are as old as civilization. Fables have been traced through the philosophies and folkways of human development. The philosophical pathway for telling and retelling of fables follows a pattern that parallels the growth of politics and religion in communal groups. Traditionally, all living things could be given a voice common to what was believed about the relationship between humans and animals. This practice helped to provide one form of early fables and is still found in *Uncle Remus* and *Aesop's Fables*.

Today, children's books still tell stories about animals that speak like humans and appear in human situations. For example, *Chrysanthemum* is the story of a young mouse who discovers on her first day in school that sometimes classmates—usually with encouragement from a leader—look for ways to demean and tease each other. Chrysanthemum's schoolmates tease her about her name. It is really the name of a flower, and worst of all, it has so many letters it can hardly fit on her name tag. This situation demonstrates for young children their own anxiety about experiences among a group of strangers, away from family. It is an experience common to six-year-old children.

This is not a pleasant experience for Chrysanthemum, and she begins to hate her name. The situation is resolved when the music teacher, whom all the little mice love, tells the class that she thinks Chrysanthemum is a beautiful name and plans to give her expected child that name. Almost immediately, Chrysanthemum's classmates start to praise her name, and Chrysanthemum is delighted.

Chrysanthemum follows a common formula in children's books. The stories start with a problem, resolution is made somewhere along the way, and there is a happy ending that often involves elements of morality and/or broken and resolved friendships.

Readers of and listeners to the story soon forget that *Chrysanthemum* is not a tale about a human family, and they seem to have no trouble transferring the story's events to their own experiences. Making fun of names is common in school, and names are often changed to nicknames. Almost anyone hearing or reading the story could imagine that Chrysanthemum would be changed to "Chris" before long.

Class discussions that follow such stories are important because they afford the teacher an opportunity to use the story to introduce children to related issues, encourage conversation to enhance language development, advance the children's skills for creative thought, and identify children who are reluctant participants.

Children's literature often involves animals that carry on human conversations in a human or animal context. Children's imaginations enable them to internalize very early a separate life for animals that is different from human life. Cognitively, they understand that mice (and other animals) cannot *really* communicate with human language; and even though Chrysanthemum and her parents wear regular clothing, mice do not dress as humans. Children are able to accept these behaviors when they are presented in a fairy tale, and are almost always able to keep these enjoyable stories separate from the fact that adults dislike, and are sometimes fearful of, real mice, and occasionally set traps to kill them.

In early fables and myths, events following such phenomena as earthquakes, disease, floods, and death were imagined as coming from gods with human voices and their own special characteristics. The imagination required for these events and their causes to take on symbolic characteristics did not appear until much later. As human thought started to separate human existence from that of other elements in the environment, fables and myths containing symbolism began to appear. Some of the myths were adopted for religious purposes, while others retained their entertainment value.

Like all of Aesop's fables, other fables and myths, more often than not, have a moral statement at the end of the story. Various stories in the Bible recount myths and parables. Those who interpret the Bible to support their point of view, and reject the views of other religious groups, distinguish between biblical stories and/or parables that are meant to be symbolic and accounts intended to be interpreted literally. In addition, Aesop's fables and myths formed the foundation for Greek drama. In it, symbolism and reality are presented through music, song, scenery, poetry, and dialogue.

Fables were not written for children; they were intended to reflect philosophical thought. More often than not, these early tales depicted adult customs, beliefs, and habits of a particular time. Thus, it is rather remarkable that over the years they have become staples in the lives of young children.

AESOP AND HIS FABLES

Aesop is said to have been a slave from Phrygia, in Asia Minor, who emerged as a literary hero in Greece because his disguised manner of spinning a tale avoided the harsh punishment that was sure to befall the user of unveiled political speech. He was put to death when the authorities finally recognized the full impact of his caustic political wit.

Aesop's fables were turned into Greek verse by Babrius, who incorporated material from an Indian Buddhist collection, and were collected by Demetrius of Phaleron; there was also a Latin version by Phaedrus during the time of Augustus. The Demetrius versions were the most popular for centuries, and that contributed to the myth that Aesop was Greek. Athenian schoolboys were assigned the task of translating Aesop's fables from Phaedrus' Latin versions into Greek.

It is probably not accurate to attribute all fables of this period to Aesop, because storytellers used aspects of Aesop's work to spin off a variety of versions that later became independent tales. As various versions have become parts of different collections, the name of Aesop has remained as a label that identifies fables with too little direct evidence for the attribution.

Aesop's Fables contains 223 Aesop tales illustrated by Arthur Rackham, well known for his illustrations in publications that have become classics, including *The Arthur Rackham Fairy Book, The Wind in the Willows,* and *Peter Pan in Kensington Gardens.* There is also *Aesop's Fables* by A. T. White, which has forty fables selected from the Aesop corpus and is illustrated by Helen Siegel. Another version, *The Fables of Aesop* by R. Springs, contains 143 Aesop fables and is illustrated by Frank Baber.

Aesop's fables are so widely known that images and ideas in them have become almost like clichés. Expressions that have entered common usage can be found in the following fables.

The Wolf in Sheep's Clothing

A wolf had great difficulty in getting at a flock of sheep due to the vigilance of the shepherd and his dogs. One day it found the skin of a sheep that had been flayed and thrown aside, so it put it on over its own pelt and strolled among the sheep. The lamb that belonged to the sheep whose skin the wolf was wearing began to follow the wolf in sheep's clothing; so, leading the lamb a little apart, he soon made a meal of her. For some time he succeeded in deceiving the sheep and enjoying hearty meals.
Moral: Appearances can be deceptive.

The Goose That Laid the Golden Eggs

One day a countryman went to the nest of his goose and found there an egg all yellow and glittering. When he lifted it, it was heavy as lead. He was going to throw it away, because he thought a trick had been played on him. But, on second thought, he took it home and soon found to his delight that it was an egg of pure gold. Every morning the same thing occurred, and he soon became rich by selling his eggs. As he grew rich, he grew greedy; and thinking to get all the gold the goose could give at once, he killed it and opened it, only to find—nothing.
Moral: Greed oft overreaches itself.

Belling the Cat

Long ago, the mice had a general council to consider what meas-ures they could take to outwit their common enemy, the cat. Some said this and some said that; at last a young mouse got up and said he had a proposal to make that he thought would meet the case. "You will all agree," said he, "that our chief danger consists in the sly and treacherous manner in which the enemy approaches us. Now, if we could receive some signal of her approach, we could easily escape from her. I venture, therefore, to propose that a small bell be procured, and attached by a ribbon around the neck of the cat. By this means we could always know when she was about, and could easily retire when she was in the neighborhood." This proposal met with general applause until an old mouse got up and said: "That is very well, but who is to bell the cat?" The mice looked at each other, but nobody spoke. Then the old mouse said (the moral): "It is easy to propose impossible remedies."

COMENIUS AND COTTON

John Comenius (see Chapters 1 and 2) was the first to develop an illustrated book for children. In accord with his views on the role of parents in early childhood, he published a picture book written in Latin to enhance the relationship between children and adults. He proposed that infancy was a special time for nurturing, in which bonding occurs between parents and infants. Children, in his view, became well-adjusted members of society through their early experiences that involved nurturing and caring parents. According to Hunt (1970) and deMause (1974), the idea of childhood as a separate life stage emerged in recent centuries; for most children it consisted of a steady stream of abuse and atrocities committed against them by adults. Comenius was probably responding to childhood practices of that period that included wrapping children in tight swaddling clothes and placing them on convenient hooks placed about the home for that purpose.

His illustrated book for children, *Orbis sensualium pictus* (1658), was intended to bring parents into contact with their children through reading and talking about the words and pictures in the book. His was the first book for children whose story line could be followed by looking at the accompanying pictures. *Orbis sensualium pictus* provided latitude for the imaginations of children and adults, in that it was illustrated to enhance its use with children who could not read, and by parents who did not read well.

In 1646, John Cotton's *Spiritual Milk for Boston*, a children's book, was imported from England. It contained Bible verses and catechism and was generally disliked by children because of its ponderous style. It pleased educators, however, who thought that pleasure should not be a goal of learning. In the late 1690s, *The New England Primer*, also imported from England, was added to the reading material available to children in the New England colonies.

THE BROTHERS GRIMM

Wilhelm Grimm (1786–1859) and Jacob Grimm (1785–1863), brothers who lived in the same house and worked in collaboration, published and revised a collection of stories depicting the German peasant life of their time. The stories they published in the nineteenth century preserved traditional tales told by common folk. The brothers collected stories from peasants living in German provinces including Hanau and Hesse, as well as in Switzerland, Austria, and Prussia. The stories were presented in such a way as to retain their purity by preserving the meanings of the peasant vocabulary and dialect. Between 1823 and 1826, Edgar Taylor translated and popularized the Grimms' tales in a two-volume set especially for children.

The Grimms' books, besides being entertainment for children, were used by scholars to trace mythology. Jacob, a professor at Göttingen and Berlin, also wrote on legends of German heroes. Wilhelm is credited with most of the work on the children's stories. "Rapunzel," presented in its entirety, is one of their best-known works.

Rapunzel

There were once a man and a woman who had long wished in vain for a child. At length the woman hoped that God was about to grant her desire. These people had a little window at the back of their house from which a splendid garden, full of the most beautiful flowers and herbs, could be seen. It was, however, surrounded by a high wall, and no one dared to go into it because it belonged to an enchantress who had great power and was dreaded by all the world. One day, as the woman was standing by this window and looking down into the garden, she saw a bed planted with the most beautiful rampion (Rapunzel). It looked so fresh and green that she longed for it, and had the greatest desire to eat some. This desire increased every day, and as she knew that she could not get any of it, she quite pined away looking pale and miserable. Then her husband was alarmed and asked, "What aileth thee, dear wife?" "Ah," she replied, "if I can't get some of the rampion, which is in the garden behind our house, to eat, I shall die."

The man, who loved her, thought, "Sooner than let thy wife die, bring her some of the rampion thyself, let it cost thee what it will." In the twilight, he clambered over the wall into the garden of the enchantress, hastily clutched a handful of rampion, and took it to his wife. She at once made herself a salad of it, and ate it with much relish. She liked it so much—so very much—that the next day she longed for it three times as much as before. If he was to have any rest, her husband must once more descend into the garden. In the gloom of evening, he let himself down again; but when he had reached the garden, he was terribly afraid, for here was the enchantress standing before him.

"How canst thou dare," said she with an angry look, "to descend into my garden and steal my rampion like a thief? Thou shalt suffer for it!"

"Ah," answered he, "let mercy take place of justice. I only made up my mind to do it out of necessity. My wife saw your rampion from the window, and felt such a longing for it that she would have died if she had not got some to eat."

Then the enchantress allowed her anger to be softened, and said to him, "If the case be as thou sayest, I will allow thee to take away with thee as much rampion as thou wilt. Only I make one condition: thou must give me the child which thy wife will bring into the world. It shall be well treated, and I will care for it like a mother."

The man in his terror consented to everything, and when the woman was brought to bed, the enchantress appeared at once, gave the child the name of Rapunzel, and took it away with her.

Rapunzel grew into the most beautiful child beneath the sun. When she was twelve years old, the enchantress shut her into a tower that lay in a forest. It had neither stairs nor door, but quite at the top was a little window. When the enchantress wanted to go in, she placed herself beneath this window and cried, "Rapunzel, Rapunzel, let down thy hair to me." Rapunzel had magnificent long hair, fine as spun gold, and when she heard the voice of the enchantress, she unfastened her braided tresses and wound them round one of the hooks of the window above. Then the hair fell twenty ells down, and the enchantress climbed up by it.

After a year or two, it came to pass that the king's son rode through the forest and went by the tower. Then he heard a song so charming that he stood still and listened. This was Rapunzel, who in her solitude passed her time in letting her sweet voice resound. The king's son wanted to climb up to her, and looked for the door of the tower, but none was to be found. He rode home, but the singing had so deeply touched his heart that every day he went out into the forest and listened to it. Once, when he was standing behind a tree, he saw the enchantress come there, and he heard her low cry, "Rapunzel, Rapunzel, let down thy hair." Then Rapunzel let down her hair, and the enchantress climbed up to her. "If that is the ladder by which one mounts, I will for once try my fortune," said he. The next day, when it began to grow dark, he went to the tower and cried, "Rapunzel, Rapunzel, let down thy hair." Immediately the hair came down, and the king's son climbed up.

At first, Rapunzel was terribly frightened when a man such as her eyes had never yet beheld came to her; the king's son, however, began to talk to her quite like a friend, telling her that his heart had been so stirred that it had let him have no rest, and he had been forced to see her. Then Rapunzel lost her fear, and when he asked her if she would take him for her husband, and she saw that he was young and handsome, she thought, "He will love me more than old Dame Gothel does." So, she said yes, and laid her hand in his. "I willingly go away with thee, but I do not know how to get down. Bring with thee a skein of silk every time thou comest, and I will weave a ladder with it, and when that is ready, I will descend, and thou wilt take me on thy horse." They agreed that until that time, he should come to her every evening, for the old woman came by day.

The enchantress remarked nothing of this until one day Rapunzel said to her, "Tell me, Dame Gothel, how it happens that you are so much heavier for me to draw up than the young king's son— he is with me in a moment."

"Ah! Thou wicked child," cried the enchantress. "What do I hear thee say! I thought I had separated thee from all the world, and yet thou hast deceived me!" In her anger, she clutched Rapunzel's beautiful tresses, wrapped them twice around her left hand, seized a pair of scissors with the right, and snip, snap, they were cut off. And she was so pitiless that she took poor Rapunzel into a desert, where she had to live in grief and misery.

In the evening of the day that she cast out Rapunzel, the enchantress fastened the braids of hair that she had cut off to the hook of the window, and when the king's son came and cried, "Rapunzel, Rapunzel, let down thy hair," she let the hair down. The king's son ascended, but he did not find his dearest Rapunzel above. The enchantress gazed at him with wicked and venomous looks. "Aha!" she cried mockingly, "Thou wouldst fetch thy dearest, but the beautiful bird sits no longer singing in the nest; the cat has got it, and will scratch out thy eyes as well. Rapunzel is lost to thee; thou wilt never see her more."

The king's son was beside himself with pain, and in his despair he leaped from the tower. He escaped with his life, but the thorns into which he fell pierced his eyes. Then he wandered quite blind about the forest, ate only roots and berries, and did nothing but lament and weep over the loss of his dearest wife. Thus he roamed about in misery for some years, and at length came to the desert where Rapunzel, with the twins to which she had given birth, a boy and a girl, lived in wretchedness. He heard a voice, and it seemed so familiar to him that he went toward it. When he approached, Rapunzel knew him and fell on his neck and wept. Two of her tears wetted his eyes; they grew clear again, and he could see with them as before. He led her to his kingdom, where he was joyfully received, and they lived for a long time afterward, happy and contented.

HANS CHRISTIAN ANDERSEN

Hans Christian Andersen (1805–1875) was born in Odense, Denmark. His father, a cobbler, died when Andersen was eleven years old. By the age of fourteen, he was in Copenhagen, searching for a better life. He was rescued from near poverty by several generous patrons who arranged for his education. By the age of thirty, he had written poetry, plays, and stories. His first novel, *Improvisator* (1835), was an almost immediate success.

Andersen's powerful ability to entertain children led observers to suggest that he write stories for children. His first volume of *Tales Told for Children* seemed to provide his greatest personal gratification and public recognition. The first English translation of Andersen's stories for children appeared in 1846. Andersen's stories were drawn from early folk tales and myths as well as from his own imagination. Regardless of their origin, each reveals the distinct temperament that sets Andersen apart from other storytellers. "The Ugly Duckling," one of Andersen's most popular tales, is presented in its entirety here.

The Ugly Duckling

It was so glorious out in the country. It was summer; the cornfields were yellow, the oats were green, the hay had been put up in stacks in the green meadows, and the stork went about on his long red legs and chattered Egyptian, for this was the language he had learned from his good mother. All around the fields and meadows were great forests, and in the midst of these forests lay deep lakes. Yes, it was right glorious out in the country. In the midst of the sunshine there lay an old farm, with deep canals about it, and from the wall down to the water grew great burdocks so high that little children could stand upright under the loftiest of them. It was just as wild there as in the deepest wood. Here sat a duck upon her nest; she had to hatch her ducklings, but she was almost tired out before the little ones came. And she so seldom had visitors— the other ducks liked better to swim about in the canals than to run up to sit down under a burdock and cackle with her.

At last, one eggshell after another burst open. "Peep! Peep!" In all the eggs there were little creatures that stuck out their heads.

"Quack! Quack!" they said; and they all came quacking out as fast as they could, looking all around them under the green leaves; and the mother let them look as much as they chose, for green is good for the eye.

"How wide the world is!" said all the young ones, for they certainly had much more room now than when they were in the eggs.

"D'ye think this is all the world?" said the mother. "That stretches far across the other side of the garden, quite into the parson's field; but I have never been there yet. I hope you are all together." She stood up. "No, I have not all. The largest egg still lies there. How long is that to last? I am really tired of it." And she sat down again.

"Well, how goes it?" asked an old duck who had come to pay her a visit.

"It lasts a long time with that one egg," said the duck who sat there. "It will not burst. Now, only look at the others; are they not the prettiest little ducks one could possibly see? They are all like their father—the rogue, he never comes to see me."

"Let me see the egg that will not burst," said the old visitor. "You may be sure it is a turkey's egg. I was once cheated in that way, and had much anxiety and trouble with the young ones, for they are afraid of the water. Must I say it to you, I could not get them to venture in. I quacked and I clacked, but it was no use. Let me see the egg. Yes, that's a turkey's egg. Let it lie there, and teach the other children to swim."

"I think I will sit on it a little longer," said the duck. "I've sat so long now that I can sit a few days more."

"Just as you please," said the old duck, and she went away.

At last the great egg burst. "Peep! Peep!" said the little one, and crept forth. It was very large and very ugly. The duck looked at it.

"It's a very large duckling," said she, "None of the others look like that: Can it really be a turkey chick? Well, we shall soon find out. It must go into the water, even if I have to thrust it in myself."

The next day, it was bright, beautiful weather; the sun shone on all the green trees. The mother duck went down to the canal with all her family. Splash! She jumped into the water. "Quack! Quack!" she said, and one duckling after another plunged in. The water closed over their heads, but they came up in an instant, and swam capitally; their legs went of themselves, and they were all in the water. The ugly gray duckling swam with them.

"No, it's not a turkey," said she; "look how well it can use its legs, and how straight it holds itself. It is my own child! On the whole it's quite pretty, if one looks at it rightly. Quack! Quack! Come with me, and I'll lead you out into the great world, and present you in the duck yard; but keep close to me, so that no one may tread on you, and take care of the cats!"

And so they came into the duck yard. There was a terrible riot going on in there, for two families were quarreling about an eel's head, and the cat got it after all.

"See, that's how it goes in the world!" said the mother duck, and she whetted her beak, for she too wanted the eel's head. "Only use your legs," she said. "See that you can bustle about, and bow your heads before the old duck yonder. She's the grandest of all here; she's of Spanish blood—that's why she's so fat. And d'ye see? She has a red rag round her leg; that's something particularly fine, and the greatest distinction a duck can enjoy: it signifies that one does not want to lose her, and that she's to be known by the animals and by men, too. Shake yourselves—don't turn in your toes; a well-brought-up duck turns its toes quite out, just like father and mother,—so! Now bend your necks and say 'Quack!' "

And they did so: but the other ducks round about looked at them, and said quite boldly, "Look there! Now we're to have these hanging on, as if there were not enough of us already! And—fie!—how that duckling yonder looks; we won't stand that!" And one duck flew up at it and bit it in the neck.

"Let it alone," said the mother, "it does no harm to anyone."

"Yes, but it's too large and peculiar," said the duck who had bitten it, "and therefore it must be put down."

"Those are pretty children that the mother has there," said the old duck with the rag round her leg. "They're all pretty but that one; that was rather unlucky. I wish she could bear it over again."

"That cannot be done, my lady," replied the mother duck. "It is not pretty, but it has a really good disposition, and swims as well as any other; yes, I may even say it swims better. I think it will grow up pretty, and become smaller in time; it has lain too long in the egg, and therefore is not properly shaped." And then she pinched it in the neck, and smoothed its feathers. "Moreover, it is a drake," she said, "and therefore it is not of so much consequence. I think he will be very strong: he makes his way already."

"The other ducklings are graceful enough," said the old duck. "Make yourself at home; and if you find an eel's head, you may bring it to me."

And now they were at home. But the poor duckling that had crept last out of the egg and looked so ugly, was bitten and pushed and jeered, as much by the ducks as by the chickens.

"It is too big!" they all said. And the turkey cock, who had been born with the spurs, and therefore thought himself emperor, blew himself up like a ship in full sail, and bore straight down upon it; then he gobbled and grew quite red in the face. The poor duckling did not know where it should stand or walk; it was quite melancholy because it looked ugly and was the butt of the whole duck yard.

So it went on the first day; and afterward it became worse and worse. The poor duckling was shunted about by everyone; even its brothers and sisters were quite angry with it, and said, "If the cat would only catch you, you ugly creature!" And the ducks bit it, and the chickens beat it, and the girl who had to feed the poultry kicked at it with her foot.

Then it ran and flew over the fence, and the little birds in the bushes flew up in fear. "That is because I am so ugly!" thought the duckling; and it shut its eyes, but flew on further. And so it came out into the great moor, where the wild ducks lived. Here it lay the whole night long; and it was weary and downcast.

Toward morning the wild ducks flew up, and looked at their new companion. "What sort of a one are you?" they asked. The duckling turned in every direction, and bowed as well as it could. "You are remarkably ugly!" said the wild ducks. "But that is nothing to us, so long as you do not marry into our family." Poor thing! It certainly did not think of marrying, and only hoped to obtain leave to lie among the reeds and drink some of the swamp water.

Thus it lay two whole days; then came thither two wild geese, or, properly speaking, two wild ganders. It was not long since each had crept out of an egg, and that's why they were so saucy.

"Listen, comrade," said one of them, "you're so ugly that I like you. Will you go with us, and become a bird of passage? Near here, in another moor, there are a few sweet lovely wild geese, all unmarried, and all able to say 'Rap?' You've a chance of making your fortune, ugly as you are."

"Piff! Paff!" resounded through the air; and the two ganders fell down dead in the swamp, and the water became blood red. "Piff! Paff!" it sounded again, and the whole flock of wild geese rose up from the reeds. And then there was another report. A great hunt was going on. The sportsmen were lying in wait all round the moor, and some were even sitting up in the branches of the trees, which spread far over the reeds. The blue smoke rose up like clouds among the dark trees, and was wafted far away across the water; and the hunting dogs came—splash, splash!—on they went, without seizing the duckling.

"O, Heaven be thanked!" sighed the duckling. "I am so ugly that even the dog does not like to bite me!"

And so it lay quite quiet, while the shots rattled through the reeds and gun after gun was fired. At last, late in the day, all was still; but the poor duckling did not dare rise up. It waited several hours before it looked round, and then hastened out of the moor as fast as it could. It ran on over field and meadow; there was such a storm raging that it was difficult to get from one place to another.

Toward evening the duck came to a miserable little peasant's hut. This hut was so dilapidated that it did not know on which side it should fall; that's why it remained standing. The storm whistled round the duckling in such a way that the poor creature was obliged to sit down in order to stand against it; and the wind blew worse and worse. Then the duckling noticed that one of the hinges of the door had given way, and the door hung so slanting that the duckling could slip through the crack into the room; and that is what it did.

Here lived a woman with her cat and her hen. And the cat, whom she called Sonnie, could arch his back and purr; he could even give out sparks; but for that one had to stroke his fur the wrong way. The hen had quite short legs, and therefore she was called Chick-abiddy Shortshanks; she laid good eggs, and the woman loved her as her own child.

In the morning the strange duckling was at once noticed, and the cat began to purr and the hen to cluck.

"What's this?" said the woman, and looked all round; but she could not see well, and therefore she thought the duckling was a fat duck that had strayed. "This is a rare prize!" she said. "Now I shall have duck's eggs. I hope it is not a drake. We must try that."

And so the duckling was admitted on trial for three weeks; but no eggs came. And the cat was master of the house, and the hen was the lady, and always said, "We and the world!" for she thought they were half the world, and by far the better half. The duckling thought one might have a different opinion, but the hen would not allow it.

"Can you lay eggs?" she asked.

"No."

"Then will you hold your tongue!"

And the cat said, "Can you curve your back, and purr, and give out sparks?"

"No."

"Then you will please have no opinion of your own when sensible folks are speaking."

And the duckling sat in a corner and was melancholy; then the fresh air and the sunshine streamed in, and it was seized with such a strange longing to swim on the water that it could not help telling the hen of it.

"What are you thinking of?" cried the hen. "You have nothing to do, that's why you have these fancies. Lay eggs, or purr, and they will pass over."

"But it is so charming to swim on the water," said the duckling, "so refreshing to let it close above one's head, and to dive down to the bottom."

"Yes, that must be a mighty pleasure, truly," quoth the hen. "I fancy you must have gone crazy. Ask the cat about it—he's the cleverest animal I know—ask him if he likes to swim on the water or to dive down: I won't speak about myself. Ask our mistress, the old woman; no one in the world is cleverer than she. Do you think she has any desire to swim, and to let the water close above her head?"

"You don't understand me," said the duckling.

"We don't understand you? Then pray who is to understand you? You surely don't pretend to be cleverer than the cat and the woman—I won't say anything of myself. Don't be conceited, child, and thank your Maker for all the kindness you have received. Did you not get into a warm room, and have you not fallen into company from which you may learn something? But you are a chatterer, and it is not pleasant to associate with you. You may believe me, I speak for your good. I tell you disagreeable things, and by that one may always know one's true friends! Only take care that you learn to lay eggs, or to purr and give out sparks!"

"I think I will go out into the wide world," said the duckling.

"Yes, do go," replied the hen.

And so the duckling went away. It swam on the water, and dived, but it was slighted by every creature because of its ugliness.

Now came the autumn. The leaves in the forest turned yellow and brown; the wind caught them so that they danced about, and up in the air it was very cold. The clouds hung low, heavy with hail and snowflakes, and on the fence stood the raven, crying, "Croak! Croak!" for mere cold. Yes, it was enough to make one feel cold to think of this. The poor little duckling certainly had not a good time. One evening—the sun was just setting in his beauty— there came a whole flock of great, handsome birds out of the bushes. They were dazzlingly white, with long, flexible necks; they were swans. They uttered a very peculiar cry, spread forth their glorious great wings, and flew away from that cold region to warmer lands, to fair open lakes. They mounted so high, so high! And the ugly duckling felt quite strangely as it watched them. It turned round and round in the water like a wheel, stretched out its neck toward them, and uttered such a strange, loud cry as frightened itself. O! It could not forget those beautiful, happy birds; and so soon as it could see them no longer, it dived down to the very bottom, and when it came up again, it was quite beside itself. It knew not the name of those birds, and knew not whither they were flying; but it loved them more than it had ever loved anyone. It was not at all envious of them. How could it think of wishing to possess such loveliness as they had? It would have been glad if only the ducks would have endured its company—the poor, ugly creature!

And the winter grew cold, very cold! The duckling was forced to swim about in the water, to prevent the surface from freezing entirely; but every night the hole in which it swam about became smaller and smaller. It froze so hard that the icy covering crackled again; and the duckling was obliged to use its legs continually to prevent the hold from freezing up. At last it became exhausted, and lay quite still, and thus froze fast into the ice.

Early in the morning a peasant came by, and when he saw what had happened, he took his wooden shoe, broke the ice crust to pieces, and carried the duckling home to his wife. Then it came to itself again. The children wanted to play with it; but the duckling thought they wanted to hurt it, and in its terror fluttered up into the milk pan, so that the milk spurted down into the room. The woman clasped her hands, at which the duckling flew down into the butter tub, and then into the meal barrel and out again. How it looked then! The woman screamed, and struck at it with the fire tongs; the children tumbled over one another in their efforts to catch the duckling; and they laughed and they screamed! Well it was that the door stood open, and the poor creature was able to slip out between the shrubs into the newly fallen snow. There it lay quite exhausted.

But it would be too melancholy if I were to tell all the misery and care that the duckling had to endure in the hard winter. It lay out on the moor among the reeds when the sun began to shine again and the larks to sing: it was a beautiful spring.

Then all at once the duckling could flap its wings: they beat the air more strongly than before, and bore it strongly away; and before it well knew how all this happened, it found itself in a great garden where the elder trees smelled sweet, and bent their long green branches down to the canal that wound through the region. O, here it was so beautiful, such a gladness of spring! And from the thicket came three glorious white swans; they rustled their wings, and swam lightly on the water. The duckling knew the splendid creatures, and felt oppressed by a peculiar sadness. "I will fly away to them, to the royal birds; and they will beat me, because I, that am so ugly, dare to come near them. But it is all the same. Better to be killed by them than to be pursued by ducks, and beaten by fowls, and pushed about by the girl who takes care of the poultry yard, and to suffer hunger in winter!" And it flew out into the water, and swam toward the beautiful swans: these looked at it, and came sailing down upon it with outspread wings. "Kill me!," said the poor creature, and bent its head down upon the water, expecting nothing but death. But what was this that it saw in the clear water? It beheld its own image; and, lo! It was no longer a clumsy dark-gray bird, ugly and hateful to look at, but a—swan!

It felt quite glad at all the need and misfortune it had suffered, now it realized its happiness in all the splendor that surrounded it. And the great swans swam round it, and stroked it with their beaks.

Into the garden came little children, who threw bread and corn into the water; and the youngest cried, "There's a new one!" and the other children shouted joyously, "Yes, a new one has arrived!" And they clapped their hands and danced about, and ran to their father and mother; and bread and cake were thrown into the water. They all said, "The new one is the most beautiful of all! So young and handsome!" And the old swans bowed their heads before him.

Then he felt quite ashamed, and hid his head under his wings, for he did not know what to do; he was so happy, and yet not at all proud. He thought how he had been persecuted and despised; and now he heard them saying that he was the most beautiful of all birds. Even the elder tree bent its branches straight down into the water before him, and the sun shone warm and mild. Then his wings rustled, he lifted his slender neck, and cried rejoicingly from the depths of his heart, "I never dreamed of so much happiness when I was the ugly duckling!"

In various ways, "The Ugly Duckling" has an existential quality because it can be viewed as a description of Andersen's own experiences in seeking meaning for his life. He thought of himself as intellectually superior to others about him. When he failed at a variety of endeavors— acting, dancing, and singing—he blamed society for his lack of achievement. He was not completely satisfied with his recognition as a spinner of excellent tales. It was said that "The Ugly Duckling" was among Andersen's best tales, because of his deeply felt symbolic relationship of this tale to his own life.

CHILDREN'S LITERATURE, 1870s–1950

By the late 1800s, picture books were appearing in great variety, and this enabled the prereading child, after hearing the story told by an adult, to "read" the story from the pictures. Kate Greenaway in 1879 published an illustrated book of verse that became so popular its pictures influenced the design of children's clothing at that time and during certain later periods as well. The stunning reproduction of illustrations in color represented a technical triumph for her time. Her books illustrated children in rather ordinary scenes—mealtime, walking in a garden, and playing with toys—that were attractive to children and adults. This helped to place Greenaway's work among the most popular children's literature during the late 1800s and early 1900s.

Randolph Caldecott in 1878, and Beatrix Potter in 1902, also popularized picture books for children. Potter's detailed illustrations of field animals as pets in *The Tale of Peter Rabbit* and Caldecott's *The House That Jack Built* remain classics in children's literature.

In 1908, Kenneth Grahame published the masterful picture book *The Wind in the Willows*, an enchanting story filled with cheerfulness, warmheartedness, and gentleness. The characters in the story enjoyed a long life and are still produced as toys of various sorts.

In 1922, Margery Williams introduced elements of reality in text. *The Velveteen Rabbit*, the story of a cherished toy received by a child at Christmas, remains popular among children in the 1990s. The happy child plays with the velveteen rabbit for several hours on Christmas Day, but loses interest during the holiday hustle and bustle that includes visits from family and friends.

The rabbit is soon forgotten and lives among other toys on the floor, or in the places where toys are kept. He is not really happy because his velveteen is inexpensive compared with the luxurious coverings of other toys. Skin Horse has lived in the nursery longer than all other animals, and is bruised and battered from the experience. But Skin Horse is old and wise, and one day Velveteen Rabbit asks, "What is REAL?"

Skin Horse replies, "Real isn't how you are made. . . . it's a thing that happens to you. When a child loves you for a long, long time, not just to play with, but REALLY loves you, then you become Real."

"Does it hurt?" asks Velveteen Rabbit.

"Sometimes," says Skin Horse, for he is always truthful. "When you are real, you don't mind being hurt."

The popularity of picture books reached its height in the 1920s. Excellent examples include *Winnie-the-Pooh* by A. A. Milne (1926), a story of the humorous adventures of Christopher Robin and Pooh Bear; *Smokey the Cow Horse* by William James (1926), one of the first stories of animal exploitation by humans; and the classic folk tale *Millions of Cats* (1928), written and illustrated by Wanda Gag.

Other excellent examples of integrating a sense of reality in literature in the lower grades can be found in the Here and Now children's poetry collections of Lucy Sprague Mitchell, written in the 1930s. In her two books, *The Here and Now Story Book* and *Another Here and Now Story Book*,

Mitchell dealt with issues and events of reality that are intimately integrated throughout the experiences of children. The imagination emerges through the placing of oneself in the imaginative possibilities of experience. The intellectual and emotional aspects of the experience are existential in that the "here and now" rests upon the experiencer's interpretation of events, and for a period of time, objectivity is lifted from interpretations. Mitchell has been credited with coining the phrase "here and now."

Margaret Wise Brown, a student of Lucy Sprague Mitchell, writing in the same reality tradition as her teacher, focused on sensory experiences in *The Noisy Book* and *The Quiet Noisy Book*, at a time when children were learning about these experiences at home and in school. The sounds of various environments—city/country, inside/outside—are dealt with in stories. Sensory experiences are emphasized, for instance, when a dog suffers a loss of sight because the doctor has placed a bandage over his eyes. Attention is then focused on the fact that the bandage on his eyes does not prevent him from hearing. How do hearing and seeing work together for people? This is the sort of question that the teacher may put to children after they have heard the story, in order to initiate an exploration of human sensory characteristics.

MULTICULTURAL LITERATURE

Joel Chandler Harris collected oral folk tales from slavery times and early black family life in the United States. He published them in what was considered "Negro dialect" as *Nights with Uncle Remus* (1883) and *Uncle Remus: His Songs and Sayings* (1880), illustrated by Arthur B. Frost. The Uncle Remus stories usually involved the stupid actions of some humans and animals that were taken advantage of by the cunning behavior of others. Similar patterns can be found in Aesop's fables.

Little Black Sambo, published in 1900 by Helen Bannerman, was hailed as the complete picture book because the text and illustrations are presented as a unit. This book is difficult to find in bookstores and schools because of its supposed racism. Actually, Sambo was intended by the author to be a dark-skinned Aryan child from eastern India. (In the United States, blacks were often given the derogatory label "Sambo." In the 1950s and 1960s, readers became sensitive to the situation of blacks and the book was removed from many store and library shelves.)

Beginning with the civil rights movement in the mid-1960s, children's literature has expanded into issues related to the political, economic, and social conditions of family life in the United States. In the 1990s, *African Beginnings*, by James Haskins and Kathleen Benson and illustrated by Floyd Cooper, presents the history of Africa (including Egypt) as that of a glorious civilization. Its style provides good information that is important for all children.

The Leakey Family: Leaders in the Search for Human Origins, by D. Willis, is an excellent description of this famous family's work on humanity's African origins. It is a suitable companion to *African Beginnings*. Primarily for intermediate readers, it can also be read to children in preschool and kindergarten.

Children's books are an important source for curriculum ideas. When slavery is properly discussed with children, the roles of black and white persons are fully described—as perpetrators and as victims. *Nettie's Trip South* by Ann Turner, illustrated by Ronald Himler, is an excellent children's book because it will increase children's knowledge of the slavery period. They will learn how some children like themselves dealt with their knowledge of slavery and about the role of adults like their grandparents.

Ann Turner uses the contents of her great-grandmother's diary to weave a story of a young white girl's visit to the South. She writes to a friend back home in Albany, New York: "Addie, I can't get this out of my thoughts: If we slipped into a black skin like a tight coat, everything would change." The charcoal and pencil drawings enhance the depth of feeling that the words evoke. "There was a fat man in a tight white suit. There was a black woman on the platform. Someone called out a price and she was gone . . . like a sack of flour pushed across a store counter. And two children our age clasped hands but were bought by different men, and the man in the white hat had to tear them apart."

Other important books provide an understandable and accurate view of slavery through biographical stories. *Freedom Train: The Harriet Tubman Story,* by D. Sterling, was written in the 1950s but remains potentially enjoyable and informative reading for any child above the third grade, especially in describing Tubman's childhood. It is a good read-to book for any child above preschool. *The Drinking Gourd,* by F. N. Monjo, is a story about Tommy, a young white boy who comes upon a runaway slave family (mother, father, and a son about his age) in his family's barn. This is an informative book for beginning and intermediate readers, but it can be read to children in any grade. Illustrations by Fred Brenner help to make this an excellent book about the Underground Railroad.

Twelve Years a Slave: Excerpts from the Narrative of Solomon Northrup, edited by Alice Lucas, is available in print and on audiotape. It is the story of a free African American living in New York who was kidnapped and sold into slavery in Louisiana. He regained his freedom in 1853, after twelve years of bondage. African-American actor-singer Wendell Brooks sings work songs and spirituals of the period to add depth to the audio version. This is excellent primary source material for the study of slavery for all grades and even some college courses.

Award-winning authors Patricia McKissack and Floyd McKissack introduced the Great African American series, which includes biographies written for readers in the elementary grades. The series includes Marian

Anderson, the singer; Louis Armstrong, the jazz trumpeter; Mary Mc-Leod Bethune, the teacher and presidential advisor; Ralph Bunche, the peacemaker in the Middle East; George Washington Carver, the scientist who discovered numerous uses for the peanut; Frederick Douglass, abolitionist and activist for women's rights; Martin Luther King, Jr., civil rights leader and man of peace; Mary Church Terrell, leader for equality; Ida B. Wells-Barnett, an activist against the lynching of blacks; and Carter G. Woodson, black history scholar.

Frederick Douglass wrote an autobiographical account, *Escape from Slavery: The Boyhood of Frederick Douglass in His Own Words*. In a more recent edition, editor Michael McCurdy has attempted to make the Douglass story more accessible to young readers. He has skillfully selected eloquent and compelling passages from Douglass's original work, written in 1845. He "kept Douglass' own words, spelling, and distinctive punctuation . . . and rearranged [them] for the sake of clarity." Each chapter is preceded with excellent commentary; however, Douglass's references to the cruelty of the most religious slave owners in the original text are missing from McCurdy's version. This latter point led some reviewers to suggest that Douglass's version is superior because it blends history with social commentary. Reviewers also suggested that Mc-Curdy's version could be considered redeemable if it encouraged young readers to seek out the original.

Paintings by the black artist Jacob Lawrence that date back to the 1940s illustrate *John Brown: One Man Against Slavery*, by Gwen Everett. This book relates the story of the famous abolitionist who organized a group of blacks and whites to attack the U.S. government's arsenal at Harper's Ferry, West Virginia. Some historians have suggested that this event, along with other issues and incidents, precipitated the Civil War. A skillful teacher can use this story to introduce the thought-provoking discussions among young children concerning groups and individuals who have used violent protests in just causes. Jacob Lawrence's work can be seen in various galleries on college and university campuses and in public museums.

From Africa to the Arctic: Five Explorers, by Esther and Donald Mumford and illustrated by Nancy Lee, is a book about early black explorers of North America, including Estebanico, a black Morrocan who explored the American Southwest seeking gold; Jim Beckwourth, who discovered the western river pass that bears his name; Stephen Bishop, explorer and scout who led exploration parties to the Mammoth Cave system in Kentucky; York, the slave who served as interpreter and provisioner for Meriwether Lewis and his master, William Clark; and Matthew Henson, who with Admiral Robert E. Peary reached the North Pole in 1909. This book provides informative and interesting material for advanced readers.

Following a televised series on the Public Broadcasting System (PBS), several books have been written for children describing the Lewis and Clark expedition. The series is also available to schools on videotape from PBS. It would be interesting for children to discuss the fact that after the expedition was over, Native Americans who saved the lives of Lewis and Clark, along with other whites who treated their illnesses and provided vital information for travel, were virtually ignored and not paid as promised. Whites, on the other hand, were rewarded by the public and the U.S. government with gifts, including land. And York, Clark's black slave, asked for his freedom after the long expedition; Clark denied this request.

Another biographical approach to African-American history can be found in *George Washington Carver, Plant Doctor*, by Mirna Benitez and illustrated by Meryl Henderson. This book is easily read and understood by beginning and intermediate readers. Carver is depicted as a scientist and concerned citizen whose work with the peanut plant benefited many people.

Runaway to Freedom, *by* Barbara Smucher, is a story of the Underground Railroad. *Great Women in the Struggle*, edited by Toyomi Igus, provides single-page biographical sketches from the slavery period to today. Included are black women artists, activists, poets, writers, entertainers, athletes, and educators.

I Have a Dream: The Life and Work of Martin Luther King, Jr., written by Jim Haskins, is a photographic chronology that covers King's life from childhood to his murder. Vivid photographs of blacks and whites who were involved in the civil rights movement in the 1960s illustrate the text. *Martin Luther King, Jr., Day* covers King's life and discusses the reason for creating a legal holiday on his birthday. The book has some compelling drawings and photographs, and beginning and intermediate readers will find it both interesting and informative.

Points of Rebellion, by William O. Douglas, associate justice of the Supreme Court, is for intermediate readers. In the text Douglas states that protest against pollution, poverty, segregation, and other social problems is a justifiable activity for citizens.

Langston Hughes, African-American novelist and poet, was a major figure among active black artists during the Harlem Renaissance, a period of artistic proliferation in black communities. It was thought, among black intellectuals, that their artistic endeavors would attract the interests of white society and help ease the way for whites to accept blacks as equals. The Harlem Renaissance extended from the 1920s to 1930s. Arna Bontemps, a major Harlem Renaissance figure, visited Haiti to study their people and collaborated with Langston Hughes in the writing of two children's books—*Children of Haiti* and *Popo and Fifini*. Bontemps also wrote *Sad-faced Boy* and *You Can't Pet A Possum* for children.

Early childhood educators have discovered a children's picture book written by Langston Hughes before his death in 1967. Writings of this type may require some knowledge of African-American childhood experiences and history prior to classroom use. Ilise Benun, writer-in-residence at a Bronx, New York settlement house, discovered that with minor adaptations in wording, *Black Misery* was an excellent means of enabling children to construct their own meaning from personal experiences (see Figure 6.1).

> Though *Black Misery* is a picture book, it is not a straightforward book to teach with. Each page consists of a one-sentence caption and an accompanying black and white illustration that raises complex issues and can inspire engaging discussions. So you need to decide beforehand what to focus on, maybe even choose in advance which captions to read, and anticipate what questions might come up and how you'll respond to them. . . . Beware that some of the captions need some updating, for example, Misery is when your pals see Harry Belafonte walking down the street and they holler, "Look there's Sidney Poitier." Despite the fact that these two actors are alive and well, most children today have never heard of them. I substituted: *Misery is when your pals see Denzel Washington on TV and yell, "Look, there is Martin."* They got that, no problem. (Benun 1998, p. 10)

OTHER TYPES OF CHILDREN'S LITERATURE

Several books in the 1980s and 1990s have attempted to deal with childhood anxiety associated with the arrival of a new brother or sister in the family. Early childhood teachers can recognize changes in children's behavior in school that are created by a new baby in the family. Joanna Cole's book, *The New Baby at Your House* has been revised and has exceptional photographs. *I'm a Big Brother, I'm a Big Sister* and *How I Was Born*, also written by Cole and illustrated by Margaret Miller, can provide a shared experience concerning this issue of concern for parents and children.

Books that may be beyond the skills of some children form a category of "read-to" books that give adults a role in the literary experiences of children. When such books are richly illustrated, children can pick them up and "read" the story from the illustrations. *The Deetkatoo: Native American Stories About Little People*, edited by John Bierhorst and illustrated by Ron Hilbert Coy, can satisfy these needs comfortably.

Some illustrated books provide a level of interest that attracts children who are browsing through their pages. *Where Does It Go?*, by Margaret Miller, about children putting things where they belong, and *Red Dancing Shoes*, a story of a magical gift from grandma that enables its owner to

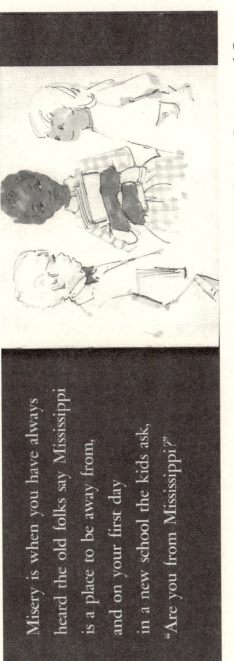

Misery is when you have always heard the old folks say Mississippi is a place to be away from, and on your first day in a new school the kids ask, "Are you from Mississippi?"

Figure 6.1. A page from BLACK MISERY by Langston Hughes. Text copyright 1969 by Arna Bontemps and George Houston Bass as Executors of the Estate of Langston Hughes. Illustration copyright 1969 by Arouni. Used by permission of Oxford University Press.

do all of the dances that are well known in the African-American community, by Denise Lewis Patrick and illustrated by James E. Ransome, are excellent examples of such books.

Picture books experienced a resurgence from the beginning of the 1970s through the early 1990s in a new format called "big books." These large books were designed to be held in the teacher's lap or placed on an easel during the telling (reading) of the story to a group gathered for that purpose. In the first such books, for the most part the story and/or illustrations were undistinguished and the quality of book construction was modest.

CHILDREN AS AUTHORS

Children as authors is an important part of learning to read and write. They can be engaged in projects that produce their own story books; personal writings that resemble a journal, diary, or log; and written assignments that are integrated into other areas of classroom life. Child-developed writings can emerge from a story that the child has read or heard, and the child can be encouraged to describe a similar personal experience. The teacher must have good training, experience with children, and imagination.

The age and developmental stage of the child should dictate the role of the teacher in the child's literary adventures. For children who are at the pre-writing stage, the teacher will perform the task of scribe. During conversation, she will write the child's words, and the child will write the symbols and words within his skills. A continuing discussion between teacher and child will ascertain the accuracy of the child's intentions as written by the teacher. Other children may require less assistance, and the teacher can enable them to expand on some of their ideas through thoughtful questioning and encouragement. Children who have learned to read prior to preschool may ask for the teacher's assistance with spelling or choosing just the right word for a special place in the story. The role of the teacher is not to give the answer but, through discussion, to advance the child's thinking to a higher level of comprehension by asking, "What do you think?" After the child has been made aware of the next step in formulating an idea, she may not be able to fully explore the context without the teacher's asking questions that constructively promote an integrated context.

The *Educational Index* (*EI*) is available online on every university campus with references, periodicals, monographs, and yearbooks. The *EI* indexes have more than 300 educationally related journals for ten months of the year. This service has been provided since 1929.

An example of what can be accessed through the *ERIC* system is the following information on Rosa Parks and the Montgomery bus boycott that many historians cite as the beginning of the 1960s civil rights movement. Herbert Kohl, in the *Journal of Education*'s January 1, 1991, issue, described an appropriate method of integrating the actual history of events into a curriculum that depicts an important period in U.S. history. Kohl provides information of the little-known details that led to the boycott. Among other things, children will learn that black residents of Birmingham, Alabama, had defied the city's segregation ordinance.

Upon entering the first grade, most children have had considerable experience with reading through their observation of signs and symbols often referred to as environmental print. The names of retail chains like Burger King, McDonald's, Walmart, K Mart, and Sears, along with printed matter on boxes, cans, and bottles, are commonly identified by kindergarten children and provide basic literacy experiences that the teacher can use as building blocks for reading.

THE GREAT DEBATE

By 1910, many major U.S. cites had already opened kindergartens in their regular public schools. Gradually, elementary school teachers became colleagues with trained kindergarten teachers (called "kindergartners"), and conceptualizations with various incompatibilities emerged. Kindergartners brought with them a history of Froebel's German early childhood movement, experiences from transcendental activitists like Thoreau, Peabody, Emerson, and Alcott, along with influences from religious groups like Ethical Culture, all assisting in pioneering the U.S. free kindergarten movement.

The preparation of elementary school teachers emerged from some newly founded state teachers colleges and university schools of education. This early childhood mix occasionally included teachers for primary grades who had been educated in university-based departments of home economics.

As early as 1915, Luella Palmer, the assistant director of kindergartens in New York City, authored a very important report for the U.S. Office of Education describing some of the issues in the adjustments of children and teachers to these public school inclusions. Palmer raised questions about when direct instruction of content like reading and mathematics should take place, and which pupil skills are necessary for transition to first grade from kindergarten. The debate concerning reading remains high on the agenda of educators and parents even in the 1990s.

Reading, among other things, is a political issue. The ability to read and comprehend can be a factor that separates income groups. At the end of Fidel Castro's successful revolution in Cuba, he announced a "battle for the sixth grade." Fidel wanted all Cubans—black and white—to achieve reading skills in the language of Cuba. The previous economic system profited from keeping reading instruction away from black and poor white Cubans. This reading campaign involved Cuban citizens—black and white—who were able to read, to travel to the most rural areas to teach. The program was so successful that remnants of military groups left over from the old government killed the most isolated "reading teachers." Today, Cuba has 100 percent literacy and free medical services for all, even visiting tourists. In the United States in the 1990s, many adults who are citizens by birth cannot read, and thousands of children are not covered by health insurance.

Debates about the curriculum for grades K to 3 framed popular discussions among teachers and parents, and reading emerged as a major public topic. The debate about reading raged for some time, and in 1967 Jean Chall's *Learning to Read: The Great Debate* centralized major issues concerning reading programs and their instructional approaches. Since that time this remarkable study has often been the focus of the "reading debate."

When Palmer asked early childhood teachers in 1915 to evaluate the importance of various aspects of their curriculum, kindergarten and primary grade teachers ranked "social habits" and "language usage" as one and two, with "reading and writing" as fifteenth (last). When asked what they thought were the most beneficial skills for children to bring with them to the first grade, "development of the senses" was first, and use of "phonics" was last. This should bring our attention to an issue that is a matter of great debate in the 1990s. That debate concerns the teaching of phonics to beginning readers. Experts in the field tend to agree (there are dissenters) that phonics has an important role in preschool as a part of an overall K–12 or K–3 program, but should not be continued once the child has mastered word sounds. Children are expected to know the sounds of letters by the first grade, and few reading experts suggest the teaching of phonics in isolation.

By the time children enter second grade, they should be able to read written and symbolic materials, designed for their developmental level, that describe events, family life, individual and group adventures, and the roles of neighborhood service providers like postal workers, police, firefighters, and parcel deliverers. They should be encouraged to participate in writing and art projects to advance their understanding in these domains. At this point they should be comfortable with books at their developmental level. These are some of the reasons that the project method has remained popular in early childhood education since the early 1900s.

Third grade is the final level in early childhood education. Developmentally, third graders are sophisticated enough about symbols to recognize most major environmental signs and objects of literacy. They are also knowledgeable about social roles like mother/father, brother/sister, and grandparents, as well as the work of persons who are called teachers, public safety, firefighters, mail handlers, package deliverers, and other neighborhood workers. Literature, writing, and symbolic awareness are all important for the development of successful reading competence and should be utilized in the teaching/learning process.

It is risky to designate a specific age for reading achievement, but, by the age of ten, word recognition, a knowledge of sentence structure, and a comprehension of content should come together for most children. The teaching of reading in the third grade, for example, should include letter sounds, word recognition, an awareness of sentence structure, and the comprehension of text to the extent that children recognize the beginning, middle, and end and can retell the story in their own words. How do teachers enable readers to reach this point?

Controversies abound among teachers as to how children are best taught to read. In the 1990s, the "great debate" has been labeled by some as the "reading wars." In general, all teachers have been educated about various methods to teach reading. Much has been contributed to the field through studies and reports by cognitive psychologists. Among prospective teachers educated in middle grades and/or elementary education, it is likely that their professors emphasized teaching children to "break the code" and stressed a phonics approach. Prospective teachers who are educated in early childhood education are more than likely given a generous treatment of the "whole language" approach. Teachers who have studied early childhood should also know that well-planned preschool activities increase the child's phonics awareness. This early awareness is essential for children from poor and/or immigrant families and can be enhanced by the free flow of early childhood play activities that foster language use and inventive spelling as learners label their projects.

Unfortunately, because of state-by-state certification variations, it is likely that any of these differently educated teachers (early childhood, middle grades, and elementary education) might be assigned to teach grades 1, 2 or 3, a critical period in the lives of pupils learning to read. In a given school with twelve or so early childhood classes (Pre-K–3), prospective teachers from either of these three disciplines might be hired to teach at the same level. Education in these three different disciplines serves to place teachers of the same grades into at least two camps— phonics and whole language—leaving those educated in early childhood the only teachers fully aware of the need to blend early phonological awareness into a philosophically consistent language, writing, and reading program. Such programs can emerge from the traditional project method, which integrates childhood imagination in the development of these skills.

The reading controversies were further fueled by popular media entering the fray at various levels. Magazines, in their quest to increase circulation, have exploited a fad by publishing articles touting phonics. Popular television personalities pitch packaged phonics programs to parents of poor readers and those who want a learn-to-read program for their newborns. This might be parents' first experience with the complexities of teaching a reluctant reader, and these commercial "programs" soon become available at garage-sales.

While *Learning to Read: The Great Debate*, by Jean Chall, informed reading discussions in the 1960s, the most important book in recent times to help inform the "reading wars" is *Beginning to Read: Learning and Thinking about Print*, by Marilyn Jager Adams.

REFERENCES

Adams, M. J. 1990. *Beginning to Read: Thinking and Learning About Print*. Cambridge, MA: MIT Press.

Arbuthnot, M. H. 1961. *The Arbuthnot Anthology of Children's Literature*. Chicago: Scott, Foresman.

Benun, I. 1998. "Misery Is Fun: Using Langston Hughes' *Black Misery*." *Rethinking Schools* 12: 3.

Brown, M. W. 1939. *The Noisey Book*. New York: Harper & Row.

———. 1950. *The Quiet Noisey Book*. New York: Harper & Row.

Chall, J. S. 1967. *Learning to Read: The Great Debate*. New York: McGraw-Hill.

———. 1983a. *Stages of Reading Development*. New York: McGraw-Hill.

———. 1983b. *Learning to Read: The Great Debate*. Updated Edition. New York: McGraw-Hill.

———. 1990. *The Reading Crisis: Why Poor Children Fall Behind*. Cambridge, MA: Harvard University Press.

———. 1991. *Should Textbooks Challenge Students?: The Case for Easier or Harder Textbooks*. New York: Teachers' College Press.

Chomsky, C. 1970. "Reading, Writing, and Phonology." *Harvard Educational Review* 40 (2): 287–309.

Cunningham, P. 1991. *Phonics They Use*. New York; HarperCollins.

de Mause, L. 1974. *The History of Childhood*. New York: Psychohistory Press.

Ehri, L. C. 1987. "Learning to Read and Spell Words." *Journal of Reading Behavior* 19 (1): 5–13.

Eliot, C. W. 1937. *Folk-Lore and Fable: Aesop, Grimm, Andersen*. New York: P. F. Collier & Son.

Freire, P., & Macedo, D. 1987. *Literacy: Reading the Word and the World*. Westport, CT: Bergin & Garvey.

Gates, H. L. 1984. *Black Literature and Literature Theory*. New York: Methuen.

———. 1989. *The Sign and the Signifying Monkey*. New York: Doubleday.

Giroux, H. A. 1983. *Theory and Resistance: A Pedagogy for the Opposition*. New York: Routledge.

———. 1988. *Teachers as Intellectuals: Toward a Pedagogy of Learning*. Westport, CT: Bergin & Garvey.

———. 1992. *Border Crossing*. New York: Routledge.

Goodman, K. S. 1986. *What's Whole in Whole Language?* Portsmouth, NH: Heinemann.

Haley, A. 1992. *Autobiography of Malcolm X*. New York: Ballantine Books.

Hill, L. 1989. *Aesop's Fables* New York: Dilithium Press.

Hudson, D. 1960. *Arthur Rackham, His Life and Work*. New York: Scribner.

Hunt, D. 1970. *Parents and Children in History: The Psychology of Family Life in Early Modern History*. New York: Basic Books.

International Reading Association and National Council of Teachers of English Language Arts. 1996. "Standards for the English Language Arts." Newark, DE: International Reading Association.

Just, M. A., & Carpenter, P. A. 1987. *The Psychology of Reading and Language Comprehension*. Newton, MA: Allyn & Bacon.

Liberman, A. M. 1970. "The Grammars of Speech and Language." *Cognitive Psychology* 1(4): 301–323.

Mitchell, L. S. 1937. *Another Here and Now Story Book*. New York: E. P. Dutton.

Moustafa, M. 1998. *Beyond Traditional Phonics*. Portsmouth, NH: Heinemann.

Palmer, L. A. 1914. "Adjustment Between Kindergarten and First Grade." *United States Bureau of Education Bulletin No. 24*, Whole number 651. Washington, DC: Government Printing Office.

Perfetti, C. A. 1985. *Reading Ability*. New York: Oxford University Press.

Rayner, K., & Pollatsek, A. 1989. *The Psychology of Reading*. Englewood Cliffs, NJ: Prentice-Hall.

Read, C. 1971. "Preschool Children's Knowledge of English Phonology." *Harvard Educational Review* 41 (1): 1–34.

Resnick, L. B., & Weaver, P. A. 1979. *Theory and Practice of Early Reading*. Hillside, NJ: Erlbaum.

Rieben, L., & Perefitti, C. A. 1991. *Learning to Read: Basic Research and Its Implications*. Hillside, NJ: Erlbaum.

Stedman, L. C., & Kaestle, C. E. 1987. "Literacy and Reading Performance in the United States from 1880 to the Present." *Reading Research Quarterly* 22(1): 8–46.

Velutino, F. R. 1979. *Dyslexia: Theory and Research*. Cambridge, MA: MIT Press.

Velutino, F. R., & Scanlon, D. M. 1987. "Phonological Coding, Phonological Awareness, and Reading Ability: Evidence from a Longitudinal and Experimental Study." *Merrill Palmer Quarterly* 33: 321–363.

Vernon-Jones, V. S. 1992. *Aesop's Fables*. New York: Gramercy Books.

Wagner, R. K., & Torgesen, J. K. 1987. "The Nature of Phonological Processing and Its Casual Role in the Acquisition of Reading Skills." *Psychological Bulletin* 101: 192–212.

Walker, A. 1983. *In Search of Our Mothers' Gardens*. San Diego: Harcourt.

Conclusion

I see the mind of a five-year-old as a volcano with two vents; destructiveness and creativeness. And I see that to the extent that we widen the creative channel, we atrophy the destructive one.
—Sylvia Ashton-Warner

At various periods in the United States, early childhood education has been used to aid families of the poor. Central to this aid has been the belief that significant changes can occur for families through improving educational opportunities for their children. A casual examination of the history of education would reveal that early childhood education has emerged from a different historical pathway than elementary education. Concentrated attention from philanthropists, philosophers, psychologists, theorists, and practitioners has influenced present-day early childhood models. The most significant influence on the study of early childhood education and child development has come from the work of Jean Piaget. Rarely will anyone trained in the education or the psychology of childhood today avoid a study of his work.

For several years Piaget's work was rejected by many scholars in education and psychology because his results were drawn from ethnographic and nonparametric observations. Starting in the late 1960s, as behaviorism waned, Piaget's work was more widely accepted. This acceptance brought with it a critical examination of his stages of development. Those who examined Piaget's work (which took place in a scholarly atmosphere of general acceptance) reported that his age-specific stages of cognitive development were not fully explained in adequate detail. While some scholars rejected the tightly structured stages as described by Piaget, others described a more Piaget-related modular concept of mental function. Despite these theoretical differences, Piaget's work has had lasting effects upon education theory and is continually observed in programs of cooperative learning, learning by discovery, the recognition of individual differences, and cognitive styles.

Vygotsky, on the other hand, rejected Piaget's notion that children, through their egocentrism, are the primary agents in enabling themselves to make their own meaning. Vygotysky's theory identified an equally important role for children and their environment. In his view, the environment includes everything in the child's purview, especially other individuals. Vygotsky suggests that mental development emerges for children through interaction with other individuals during social experiences, and this experience is enhanced through collaboration between cultural events and issues. He theorized that collaborative dialogues with more mature individuals stimulated intellectual development. For Vygotsky, this created a central role for language because of its basic function in the transfer of information. This language takes place within a cultural context that Vygotsky calls the "zone of proximal development."

While Piaget suggests that individual children make their own meaning, Vygotsky proposes a similar concept by suggesting that learners acquire a private speech in developing their mental capacities. This private speech takes place during dialogues with more mature individuals in the child's cultural environment.

Critics of Vygotsky's emphasis on language and culture have suggested that his line of reasoning does not capture the primary means through which children acquire knowledge of their own world as it exists for them. In comparison, information-processing theorists have borrowed from Piaget and Vygotsky in delineating categories of knowledge acquisition akin to the functioning of computers.

Among the most well known is the "store model" as described by Atkinson and Shiffrin (1968). They conclude that the storing of information is universal and innate and that the mental system for knowledge acquisition is stored in three parts of a processing system; a sensory register, short-term memory, and long-term memory. Information flows through each store, which has different capacities to transform the information through control processes and/or mental strategies. Information travels through each store and is transformed in the process. The efficiency of thinking and the retention of information are not innate and can vary among individuals as they utilize their control processes and mental strategies. This leads to variations in knowledge acquisition, its utilization, and its integration with previous knowledge.

The essential imagination for early childhood can be traced to the American kindergarten movement, which received its inspiration from

Friedrich Froebel. At the center of this movement was Elizabeth Peabody, a true Renaissance woman who espoused a worldview of Froebel's kindergarten philosophy. To this end, she was one of the planners of the Philadelphia Exposition in 1876, where a model kindergarten on full-time display advanced Froebelian kindergartens in the United States. She was active in antislavery agitation, supported Native American causes, and planned kindergartens for their children. As the owner of a bookstore in Boston, she published works of philosophical writers as well as her own writing. She also provided a forum for discussions among leaders like Horace Mann, educator; William Ellery Channing, Unitarian leader; Bronson Alcott, educator; and Henry David Thoreau, poet. She was a student of Ralph Waldo Emerson, a transcendentalist, and consulted with Friedrich Froebel's wife (who continued his work after his death). She traveled throughout Europe recruiting—with great success—persons trained in Froebel's methods to join kindergartners in America. She encouraged and assisted with the establishment of Froebel kindergartens in England and was instrumental in bringing Margaret McMillan to the United States to educate Boston kindergartners and demonstrate kindergarten practices. Peabody also founded the first kindergarten in the United States to be taught in English. As a philanthropist, she raised funds for the causes she supported, but her primary interest was to improve humanity through kindergarten practice and philosophy.

Her philanthropic mission was concluded with the adoption of kindergarten by regular public schools in the early 1900s. She did not anticipate the conflicts that ultimately emerged from the integration of Froebelian-trained teachers into graded public schools, with teachers trained in elementary education.

Susan Blow, with the aide and support of school superintendent William T. Harris, founded the first kindergarten in a public school in St. Louis. With the support of Peabody, she attracted superior kindergartners to this pioneering Froebelian enterprise, and she subsequently trained others. St. Louis became known as a model center for childhood education.

After Harris' departure, the St. Louis school board appointed an elementary-trained, non-Froebelian grade school teacher, Mary C. McCullough, to supervise kindergarten teachers in the school system. After this appointment, Blow made the accurate prediction that the elementary school's subject-structured forces, under the direction of McCullough, would replace Froebel and Dewey philosophies in St. Louis public school kindergartens.

Kindergartners had envisioned the opposite effects—that the transition would infuse traditional kindergarten philosophy into the early grades—thus creating a primary grade division in public schools with a major focus on how children learn. This was not to be.

Susan Blow resigned and the St. Louis exemplary early education model fell apart as her supporters let it be known that they were also leaving. Various sites around the world sought the services of these highly trained kindergartners. For example, Harriet Niel left to head the Training School Kindergarten in Washington, D.C., Laura Fisher became director of kindergartens in Boston Public Schools, Mary D. Runyan went to Teachers College at Columbia University in New York City to head their kindergarten department, Caroline Hart became director of the Training School of the Kindergarten Association of Baltimore, and Cynthia Dozier became supervisor of the New York Kindergarten Association. Blow moved to Boston, at that time the center of agitation for women's suffrage and antislavery organizing, pressing for Native American rights and the study of transcendental philosophy. She continued her work in the kindergarten movement through lecturing and consulting.

As kindergartens gradually became a part of public schools, universities entered the early childhood teacher training market, each with their own ideas about early childhood philosophy, theory, and practice. Graduates, more often than not, remained to teach within the state where they graduated. State education departments were thus able to groom teachers who fulfilled the state's mission.

For many years, educational planners attempted to fuse the best of early childhood education with the best of elementary education. The poor success of such endeavors is partially tied to the public view that kindergartens devote lots of wasteful time to play. But deeper problems emerge from various models of higher education that prepare teachers for early childhood. These include regional diversity in the valuing of early education, and the presence of a capitalist economic system that is uncomfortable about paying regular salaries to teachers who "look after the little ones." This is coupled with a deeper concern as to whether young children should be a family responsibility or a social responsibility. These matters are made more complex by the shape and the mix of educational imperatives.

Learned societies in early childhood education like NAEYC and ACEI, as well as textbooks, research articles, and other treatises in the field, identify birth through grade 3 as the early childhood domain. This designation begins to break down when state certification agencies start to realign teaching fields to satisfy their need for teachers. The extension of early childhood certification to accommodate grades 4 and 5 will vary throughout the United States, and there are some states where several variations have been tried and abandoned. In the meantime, early childhood materials and learned societies (NAEYC, ACEI) remain a consistent mission.

When statewide realignments take place, it is usually within a short period of time (over several years) and may assume different patterns. These patterns include tampering with early childhood curriculum in state-supported teachers' colleges and universities and introducing new certifying testing procedures. Some states, for example, will use an elementary school test, as opposed to an early childhood test, to certify teachers in early childhood education.

These actions replicate the early 1900s' attempt to sequester the nurturing environments deemed essential for early childhood and enhance the middle-school didactic teacher/learner relationship for all ages. A more reasonable approach, however, would be to infuse the nurturing aspects of early childhood into the middle-school teacher training at the university level. This would make the change more of a long-term goal and provide more than a superficial "back to basics" short-term goal.

Long-term, thoughtful outcomes require long-term study and call for discussions between teachers, state education systems, learned societies, and university personnel. State certifying agencies are unwilling to attempt such a study for change, and for the most part, policy is usually proposed and enacted by political voices in state education agencies. There is still too little respect for the teacher's voice in educational policy matters.

Along with short-term certification changes, there is always a steady stream of entrepreneurs and suppliers of educational materials who promote dubious materials to support theories that tend to recycle over time. For example, we are experiencing a re-awakening of the project method from the 1920s. While this is a tried and reliable teaching approach that works well, its re-entry is accompanied by unnecessary printed matter and testing materials that are promoted for purchase. Shiny, colorful, new materials are not necessary for the project method to be useful.

We have also witnessed a proliferation of "phonics" games and packaged methods for sale on "info-mercial TV," marketed to parents of children who have demonstrated problems in reading. While such materials might enable children to learn letter sounds as a first step (something that can be taught by adults using print in the home and neighborhood), phonics has a role only in the early stages of a coordinated Pre-K–3, or K–12 reading program. (For a more complete discussion, refer to Chapter 6.)

Also, in a research environment where group intelligence testing has been discouraged, entrepreneurs and their enterprises inform us that we now need to be concerned about seven (possibly eight) "intelligences." This notion was introduced by Howard Gardner, who reclassified elements identified for IQ tests in the 1920s that were labeled "factors" contributing to g (general intelligence). There is also a generous mix of cognitive styles in Gardner's speculations.

School districts are encouraged to purchase a wide array of materials for teaching and testing for the presence (or absence) of these intelligences in children, as well as paraphernalia to meet the learning needs that are called for by these "test results." Consumer items deemed necessary for childhood intelligence to emerge are being marketed in a public environment where most states have outlawed the use of group intelligence testing because of wrongful tracking.

The theory that multiple factors contribute to what is generally considered intelligence is not new. Thurstone (1938) identified what he called "primary mental abilities" as essential factors of intelligence, and Guilford (1967) defined intelligence as encompassing five operations. What *is* novel about Gardner's proposal is that each factor (as identified by his work) constitutes a separate construct that qualifies as an intelligence. There is sufficient evidence, however, to suggest that the seven areas (recently extended to eight) of human performance described in the Multiple Intelligence theory are more realistically factors in general intelligence, and/or cognitive styles.

Gardner describes the nature of these intelligences in various way. Two of them, logical mathematical intelligence and linguistic intelligence, are defined as "superior sensitivities." Two others, music intelligence and bodily-kinesthetic intelligence, are defined as "abilities." Another pair, spatial intelligence and interpersonal intelligence, are described as "capabilities," and intrapersonal intelligence is described as "access to one's own feelings." These descriptors can be useful to school personnel who recognize that children frequently demonstrate skills in various school settings that might not be available to them in a test-taking environment. And for the many teachers who believe that all learners are gifted and talented in various ways—and who dread the task of separating children from their classmates because some are labeled "gifted" and some are not—much can be found in Gardner's descriptors. The broad semantic diversity that Gardner employs in this useful service to teachers, however, does not allow for a coherent theory of intelligence to emerge. Sternberg (1991), responding to Gardner's theory of multiple intelligences, suggested:

> Howard Gardner proposed naturalistic assessments, based on his theory of multiple intelligences . . . they are a psychometric nightmare. It is very difficult, if not impossible, to quantify performance on them; assessments take place over long periods of time, and it is questionable whether anything approaching objective scoring is even possible. The tests seem to measure a nondecomposable composite of interest and motivation, initiative, abilities of various kinds, achievement, socialization, and enculturation. The tests are the kind that will generate smiles from teachers, and expressions of horror from those who work in measurement. (p. 266)

What is the professional view of intelligence as a useful concept? There are as many variations in opinions as there are assessment instruments to measure intelligence. Sociologist Jane Mercer stated, "I don't think that intelligence is a useful concept for scientific research or education and should be abolished from our vocabulary" (Stone 1987). Psychologist Arthur Jensen said, "The word intelligence might be useful in popular parlance, but not useful scientifically. I view intelligence as a general factor that runs through all performance" (Stone 1987). Leon Kamin, the first person to turn our attention to the fraudulent IQ reports on twin studies published by psychologist Cyril Burt, wrote: "There exists [sic] no data which should lead a prudent man to accept the hypothesis that IQ test scores are in any degree heritable" (1974, p. 1).

Andrew Hacker, in reviewing the work of Herrnstein and Murray (1994), reminds us that over the past fifty years, white scholars have agreed not to report distinctions between white U.S. residents. African-Americans, however, have been deemed a visible and accessible target; and, according to Hacker, it is "better for white sensibilities, to focus on presumed black deficiencies. But this is neither surprising or new." In the face of such racialist agreements among "scholars" not to report white IQs by ethnic origin, Hacker goes on to cite differences in intellectual performance between white U.S. citizens who have a college degree and whose families have lived for at least three generations in our country.

> Due to our agreement not to sort out white I.Q.s by national origin, I will have to use census information on the number of people who have entered and completed college. . . . Irish 21.3 percent; Italian 21.9 percent; German 22.1 percent; Polish 23.4 percent; Swedish 27.5 percent; English 28.6 percent; and Russian 51 percent. True it takes ambition, discipline and family encouragement to get to and through college. Still a certain kind of mental capacity is minimally necessary. (Hacker 1994, pp. 13–14)

Most educators have recognized the politics embedded in the discussions of intelligence. Historically, intelligence testing has been used to limit immigration of "undesirable" ethnic groups. Schools have used test scores to permanently track individuals from poor families and keep them separated from their affluent peers. Educators, psychologists, and other professionals have continually misinterpreted and misused the information provided by the intelligence testing community. It has become essential that each new generation of teachers must be made aware of information that has been provided by the scholarly work of those who came before them. For example, the fact that the twin studies of Cyril Burt aimed at establishing the heritability of intelligence are now deemed fraudulent has left the pages of our current texts and must be told in lectures to students new to teacher education.

It is important to note that well-planned experiences provided by parents and teachers promote knowledge acquisition for children, and specifically planned lessons can even overcome environmental deprivations (Hunt et al. 1976).

The most recent discussions concerning human knowledge acquisition come from neuroscience. Studies on monkeys and cats have been reported by educators with limited knowledge of neuroscience. This has led to leaps in logic and inappropriate interpretation of the findings. Entrepreneurship and capitalism have led to streams of reports and articles in public media, and self-acclaimed experts and consultants, all selling themselves and their materials to school authorities in the pursuit of "educating the brain." School administrators should know better, but their professors at the university seldom prepare them for the environment of educational commerce. One major reason for this lapse is that even their professors are occasionally not well informed. John T. Breuer (1997) has put the present educational interest in brain studies in this informed perspective:

> Brain science fascinates teachers and educators. . . . When I speak to teachers about applications of cognitive science in the classroom, there is always a question or two about the right brain versus the left brain and the educational promise of brain based curricula. I answer that these ideas have been around for a decade, are often based on misconceptions and generalizations of what we know about the brain, and have little to offer to educators. Educational applications of brain science might come eventually, but as of now neuroscience has little to offer teachers in terms of informing classroom practice. (p. 4)

To be knowledgeable about such things as neuroscience and its contribution to education would require a great deal of reading and a superior level of scholarship. School administrators and university professors should carefully examine every new idea before investing in paraphernalia and proliferating the field of education with more inaccuracies. The commerce-driven consultants and their accompanied materials for "brain-compatible learning" cannot advance teachers' practical knowledge. The most useful information, however, comes from cognitive psychology and cognitive neuroscience.

> We can't choose preschools based on neuroscience, nor can we look to neuroscience as a guide to improve educational practice and policy. Our fascination with the brain leads us to overlook and

underestimate what behavioral science can already provide to improve policy and practice. The neuroscience and education argument may be theoretically appealing, but scientifically, it's a bridge too far. (Breuer 1997, p. 5)

Teachers, their administrators, and professors would be better served through the maintenance of a critical consciousness that carefully examines "new" approaches to teaching and learning in light of what we already know about classroom practice. The latest fad cannot replace the persistence of good teaching.

From a historical perspective, early childhood education for teachers and student teachers is made poignant by Mendel E. Branom in *The Project Method in Education*, written in 1919:

The teacher's work is a complex project. The good teacher in a significant degree "is not born but is made." Native ability must be present, but the social viewpoint requires a long period of careful training, while the problem of proper adaptation of material to each child is ever present. After a student teacher has undergone a certain amount of training, her project becomes greatly intensified when she takes charge of a group of pupils. She continues to make a study of herself, of the children, of society in general, and of materials, but a larger responsibility has been given her. As long as she is a teacher, her project-complex is never solved, but situations demanding the best reaction of which she is capable constantly are arising. The capable, energetic person, stirred by an aspiration to serve others, will find a large field of opportunity in teaching. (p. 266)

Throughout this text, experience is recognized as fundamental to knowledge acquisition in school, at home, and in the community. Learners gain experience through formal and informal settings and spontaneity. It is well documented that children learn a great deal from each other.

Much recent attention has been focused upon violence in schools. Despite the fact that research reports that childhood violence is more likely to occur outside of school, professionals and the general public continually focus on the school to address these complex issues. Lev Vygotsky has called our attention to the power of social experiences and language in personality development of children. Children acquire knowledge of personal characteristics from their family, their neighborhood, and their country.

Since acts of childhood violence occur more often outside of school, more attention should be focused upon out-of-school experiences. For example, when parents, teachers, and counselors inform children about situations where conflict might arise, children are encouraged to act in a nonviolent manner, and to try to resolve disagreements through discussions. Some schools have formed conflict resolution groups made up of students who act on the spot during in-school peer conflicts. Children expect adults to provide guidance and appropriate modeling of acceptable behavior, but how often does proper modeling occur?

On the one hand, if children are harmed or their work destroyed, they are told not to respond with violence, but to report such incidents to their teacher or nearby adult. On the other hand, our country has been known to attack countries suspected of committing terrorist acts, as well as attacks on countries like Panama, Grenada, Cambodia, and Vietnam, for political reasons. The United States is the only country to use atomic weapons to kill civilian populations. While children are advised to talk through their conflicts and resolve them using nonviolent means, their country seldom does.

In their neighborhoods children often witness long-standing family feuds and adult conflicts over what others might consider minor issues. These mixed messages from neighborhood adults can leave children confused and bewildered. We should not be surprised when young children consider violence an appropriate means for resolving *their* conflicts.

Early childhood education has been the most successful level of education to define a cooperative role for the family in the lives of their schoolchildren. Human service agencies and leaders in education appear to recognize and accept this phenomenon; they turn to early education to improve family life. The goals of philanthropists were defined by the needs of poor European families during the immigration period of the late 1800s.

The needs of these families helped to define the free kindergarten movement. During times of war, when the labor of women was deemed necessary by industry, some mothers from this group were employed in childcare centers, and modest training was paid for by government and industry. During the great depression and the inauguration of Head Start by President Lyndon Johnson, child care was central to the "war" on family poverty.

Professionals involved in the study and care of young children continue to educate mothers by making early childhood principles known to the general public through parenting magazines and educational programs on television. Early childhood education continually provides new career opportunities for thousands of young people who bring new energy and wisdom to the entire field of education.

Each new generation of early childhood teachers brings fresh ideas about child growth and development with them to their first teaching appointment, and, in turn, they invigorate and inspire thousands of colleagues throughout all school grades. For many of their children, this will be their first teacher. And early childhood teachers are always remembered, because they inspire childhood imagination that enables children to form memories that last a lifetime.

REFERENCES

Ashton-Warner, S. 1964. *Teacher*. New York: Bantam Books.

Atkinson, R. C., & Shiffrin, R. M. 1968. "Human Memory: A Proposed System and Its Control Processes." In K. W. Spence and J. T. Spence (eds.), *Advances in the Psychology of Learning and Motivation*, vol. 2. 90–195. New York: Academic Press.

Branom, M. E. 1919. *The Project Method in Education*. Boston: R. G. Badger.

Breuer, J. T. 1997. "Education and the Brain: A Bridge Too Far." *Educational Researcher* 16(8): 4–16.

Burt, C. 1958. "The Inheritance of Mental Ability." *American Psychologist* 13 (1): 1–15.

Gardner, H. 1987. "The Theory of Multiple Intelligence." *Annals of Dyslexia* 37 (1): 19–35.

Gardner, H., & Hatch, T. 1989. "Multiple Intelligences Go to School: Educational Implications of the Theory of Multiple Intelligences." *Educational Researcher* 18 (8): 4–10.

Guilford, J. P. 1967. *The Nature of Intelligence*. New York: McGraw-Hill.

Hacker, A. 1994. "White on White." *The New Republic* (October 31): 13–14.

Hechinger, F. F. 1979. "Further Proof the IQ Data Were Fraudulent." *The New York Times*, January 30, p. C4.

Herrnstein, R. J., & Murray, C. 1994. *The Bell Curve: Intelligence and Class Structure in American Life*. New York: Free Press.

Hunt, J. McV., Mohandessi, K., Ghodessi, M., & Akeyama, M. 1976. "The Psychological Development of Orphanage-Reared Infants: Interventions and Outcomes." *Genetic Psychology Monographs* 94: 177–226.

Kamin, L. 1974. *The Science and Politics of I.Q.* Potomac, MD: Lawrence Erlbaum Associates.

———. 1995. "Behind the Curve." *Scientific American* 272 (2) (February): 99–103.

Peabody, E. 1862. "Kindergarten—What Is It?" *Atlantic Monthly* (November).

Sternberg, R. J. 1991. "Death, Taxes, and Bad Intelligence Tests." *Intelligence* 15: 257–269.

Stone, D. (producer). 1997. *Intelligence: The Study of Human Behavior*. New York: Insight Media.

Selected Bibliography

Acredolo, L., & Evans, D. 1980. "Developmental Changes in the Effects of Landmarks on Infant Spatial Reference System." *Developmental Psychology* 16: 312–318.

Ainsworth, M. 1975. *Infancy in Uganda*. Baltimore: Johns Hopkins University Press.

———. 1979. "Infant-Mother Attachment." *American Psychologist* 34: 932–937.

Allen, V. 1976. *Children as Teachers: Theory and Research on Tutoring*. New York: Academic Press.

Anderson, L. 1989. "Classroom Instruction." In M. Reynolds (ed.), *Knowledge Base for the Beginning Teacher*. New York: Oxford University Press.

Annett, M. 1985. *Left, Right, Hand, and Brain: The Right-Shift Theory*. Hillsdale, NJ: Erlbaum.

Anthony, M., & Cohler, B. J. (eds.). 1987. *The Invulnerable Child*. New York: Guilford Press.

Apgar, V. 1953. "A Proposal for a New Method of Evaluation in the Newborn Infant." *Current Research in Anesthesia and Analgesia* 32: 260.

Archer, S. L. 1982. "The Lower Age Boundaries of Identity Development." *Child Development* 53: 1551–1556.

Archer, S. L., & Waterman, A. S. 1988. "Psychological Individualism: Gender Differences or Gender Identity?" *Human Development* 31(2): 65–81.

Aries, P. 1962. *Centuries of Childhood: A Social History of Family Life*. Translated by Robert Baldick. New York: Alfred A. Knopf.

Backward, T. J. 1984. "Twins Reared Together and Apart: What They Tell Us About Human Diversity." In S. W. Fox (ed.), *Individuality and Determinism*. New York: Plenum Press.

Backward, T. J., & McGee, M. 1981. "Familial Studies of Intelligence: A Review." *Science* 212: 1055–1059.

Bailyn, B. 1960. *Education in the Forming of American Society: Needs and Opportu-nities for Study*. New York: Vintage Books.

Bandura, A. 1977. *Social Learning Theory*. Englewood Cliffs, NJ: Prentice-Hall.

Barker, R., & Wright, H. 1955. *Midwest and Its Children*. New York: Harper & Row.

Barnett, M., Howard, J., King, L., & Dino, G. 1980. "Antecedents of Empathy: Retrospective Accounts of Early Socialization." *Personality and Social Psychology Bulletin* 6: 361–365.

Baugh, J. 1983. *Black Street Speech: Its History, Structure, and Survival*. Austin: University of Texas Press.

Baumrind, D. 1967. "Child Care Practices Anteceding Three Patterns of Preschool Behavior." *Genetic Psychology Monographs* 75(1): 43–88.

——— 1971. "Current Patterns of Parental Authority." *Developmental Psychology* 4(1): 1–103.

Bayley, N. 1969. *Bayley Scales of Infant Development*. New York: Psychological Corporation.

Beard, R. 1969. *An Outline of Piaget's Developmental Psychology*. London: Routledge & Kegan Paul.

Beck, R. 1978. *Motivation: Theories and Principles*. Englewood Cliffs, NJ: Prentice-Hall.

Becker, W., Peterson, D., Lurie, A., Shoemaker, D., & Helimer, K. 1962. "Relations of Factors Derived from Parent Interviews to Ratings of Behavior Problems of Five-Year-Olds." *Child Development* 33: 509–535.

Belsky, J. 1980. "Child Maltreatment: An Ecological Integration." *American Psychologist* 35: 320–335.

———. 1988. "The 'Effects' of Infant Day Care Reconsidered." *Early Childhood Research Quarterly* 3: 235–272.

Belsky, J., Gilstrap, B., & Rovine, M. 1984. "Stability and Change in Mother-Infant and Father-Infant Interaction in a Family Setting: One-to-Three-to-Nine Months." *Child Development* 55: 706–717.

Belsky, J., Lerner, R., & Spanier, G. 1984. *The Child in the Family*. Reading, MA: Addison-Wesley.

Belsky, J., & Steinberg, L. 1978. "The Effects of Daycare: A Critical Review." *Child Development* 49: 920–949.

Bem, S. 1974. "The Measurement of Psychological Androgyny." *Journal of Consulting and Clinical Psychology* 42: 155–162.

———. 1977. "On the Utility of Alternative Procedures for Assessing Psychological Androgyny." *Journal of Consulting and Clinical Psychology* 45: 196–205.

———. 1981. "Gender Scheme Theory: A Cognitive Account of Sex Typing." *Psychological Review* 8 (8): 354–364.

Berk, L. 1985. "Why Children Talk to Themselves." *Young Children* 40(5): 46–52.

Block, J. 1973. "Conceptions of Sex Role: Some Cross-Cultural and Longitudinal Perspectives." *American Psychologist* 28: 516–526.

———. 1978. "Another Look at Sex Differentiation in the Socialization Behaviors of Mothers and Fathers." *Merrill-Palmer Quarterly* 22: 285–308.

Bloom, L., Hood, L., & Lightbown, P. 1974. "Imitation in Language Development: If, When, and Why." *Cognitive Psychology* 6: 380–428.

Boles, S., & Jaunts, H. 1976. *Schooling in Capitalist America*. New York: Basic Books.

Borland, J. 1988. "Cognitive Controls, Cognitive Styles, and Divergent Production in Gifted Preadolescents." *Journal for the Education of the Gifted* 11(4): 57–82.

Bower, T. G. R. 1977. *The Perceptual World of the Infant*. Cambridge, MA: Harvard University Press.

———. 1981. *Development in Infancy*. San Francisco: Freeman.

———. 1989. *The Rational Infant*. New York: Freeman.

Bower, T. G. R., & Paterson, J. 1973. "The Separation of Place, Movement, and Object in the World of the Infant." *Journal of Experimental Psychology* 15: 161–168.

Brazelton, T. B. 1979a. "Behavioral Competence of the Newborn Infant." *Seminars in Perinatology* 3(1): 35–44.

———. 1979b. *The Infant Neonatal Assessment Scale*. Philadelphia: Lippincott.

———. 1983. *Infants and Mothers: Differences in Development*. New York: Delacorte.

Bredekemp, S. 1986. *Developmentally Appropriate Practice in Early Childhood Programs Serving Children from Birth Through Age 8*. Washington, DC: National Association for the Education of Young Children.

Bremner, J., & Bryant, P. 1977. "Place Versus Response as the Basis of Spatial Errors Made by Young Infants." *Journal of Experimental Child Psychology* 23: 162–171.

Brennan, J. 1985. *Patterns of Human Heredity*. Englewood Cliffs, NJ: Prentice-Hall.

Bridges, K. 1933. "A Study of Social Development in Early Infancy." *Child Development* 4(1): 36–49.

Brierly, J. 1987. *Give Me a Child Until He Is Seven: Brain Studies and Early Childhood Education*. London: Falmer Press.

Brigham, M. 1965. "Peer Group Deterrents to Intellectual Development During Adolescence." *Educational Theory* 15: 251–258.

Bronfenbrenner, U. 1970. *Two Worlds of Childhood: U.S. and U.S.S.R.* New York: Russell Sage.

———. 1979. "Context of Child Rearing: Problems and Prospects." *American Psychologist* 34: 844–850.

Brophy, J. 1983. "Research on the Self-fulfilling Prophecy and Teacher Expectations." *Journal of Educational Psychology* 75: 631–666.

———. 1986. "Teacher Influences on Student Achievement." *American Psychologist* 41: 1069–1077.

Brown, C. 1984. *The Many Facets of Touch*. Skillman, NJ: Johnson & Johnson.

Brown, R. 1973. *A First Language: The Early Stages*. Cambridge, MA: Harvard University Press.

Bruner, J. 1983. *Child's Talk: Learning to Use Language*. New York: Norton.

Bruner, J., Oliver, R., & Greenfield, P. 1966. *Studies in Cognitive Growth*. New York: Wiley.

Bumpass, L. L. 1984. "Children and Marital Disruption: A Replication and Update." *Demography* 21(1): 71–82.

Burck, G. 1964. "Knowledge—the Biggest Growth Industry of Them All." *Fortune* 70: 128–131.

Burgess, R., & Conger, R. 1978. "Family Interaction in Abusive, Neglectful, and Normal Families." *Child Development* 49: 1163–1173.

Buss, A. H., & Plomin, R. 1984. *Temperament: Early Developing Personality Traits.* Hillside, NJ: Erlbaum.

Butterworth, G. 1977. "Object Disappearance and Error in Piaget's Stage 4 Task." *Journal of Experimental Child Psychology* 23: 391–401.

Bybee, R. 1979. "Violence Toward Youth: A New Perspective." *Journal of Social Issues* 35(2): 1–14.

Calfee, R., & Drum, P. 1986. "Research on Teaching Reading." In M. Wittrock (ed.), *Handbook of Research on Teaching* (3rd ed.). New York: Macmillan.

Carey, S. 1985. *Conceptual Change in Childhood.* Cambridge, MA: MIT Press.

Caron, A., Caron, R., & Carlson, V. 1979. "Infant Perception of the Invariant Shape of Objects Varying in Slant." *Child Development* 50: 716–721.

Cazden, C. 1988. *Classroom Discourse.* Portsmouth, NH: Heinemann.

Chance, P. 1986. *Thinking in the Classroom.* New York: Teacher's College Press.

Chen, C., & Stevenson, H. 1989. "Homework: A Cross-Cultural Examination." *Child Development* 60: 551–561.

Chomsky, N. 1976. *Reflections on Language.* New York: Pantheon.

Clark, R. 1977. "What Is the Use of Imitation?" *Child Language* 3: 341–358.

Clarke-Stewart, K. A. 1989. "Day Care: Maligned or Malignant?" *American Psychologist* 44: 266–273.

Clifton, R., Morrongiello, B., Kulig, J., & Dowd, J. 1981. "Newborns' Orientation Toward Sound: Possible Implications for Cortical Development." *Child Development* 53: 833–838.

Cohen, D. 1983. *Piaget: Critique and Reassessment.* New York: St. Martin's Press.

Cohen, J., & Parmalee, A. 1983. "Prediction of Five Year Stanford Binet Scores in Preterm Infants." *Child Development* 54: 1242–1253.

Cohen, L., & Strauss, M. 1979. "Concept Acquisition in the Human Infant." *Developmental Psychology* 50: 410–424.

Cohn, J. F., & Tronick, E. Z. 1987. "Mother-Infant Face-to-Face Interaction: The Sequence of Dyadic States at 3, 6, and 9 Months." *Developmental Psychology* 23(1): 68–77.

Comer, J., & Poussaint, A. 1975. *Black Child Care.* New York: Simon & Schuster.

Constanzo, P. 1970. "Conformity Developments a Function of Self-blame." *Journal of Personality and Social Psychology* 14: 366–374.

Coopersmith, S. 1967. *The Antecedents of Self-Esteem.* San Francisco: Freeman.

Corea, G. 1986. *The Mother Machine.* New York: Harper & Row.

Cornell, E., & Gottfried, A. 1976. "Intervention with Premature Human Infants." *Child Development* 47(1): 32–39.

Cratty, B. 1979. *Perceptual and Motor Development in Infants and Children.* 2nd ed. Englewood Cliffs, NJ: Prentice-Hall.

———. 1986. *Perceptual and Motor Development of Infants and Children.* 3rd ed. Englewood Cliffs, NJ: Prentice-Hall.

Crawley, S. B., and Spiker, D. 1983. "Mother-Child Interactions Involving Two-Year-Olds with Down's Syndrome: A Look at Individual Differences." *Child Development* 54: 1312–1323.

Cremin, L. A. 1964. *The Transformation of the School: Progressivism in American Education, 1876–1957.* New York: Alfred Knopf.

———. 1965. *The Genius of American Education*. New York: Random House, Vintage Books.

———. (ed.). 1957. *The Republic and the School: Horace Mann on the Education of Free Men*. New York: Teachers College Bureau of Publications.

Crnic, K., Ragozin, A., Greenberg, M., Robinson, N., & Basham, R. 1983. "Social Interaction and Developmental Competence of Preterm and Full-term Infants in the First Year of Life." *Child Development* 54: 1199–1210.

Crockenberg, S. 1981. "Infant Irritability, Mother Responsiveness, and Social Support Influences on the Security of Infant-Mother Attachment." *Child Development* 52: 857–865.

Crockenberg, S. B., & McCluskey, K. 1986. "Change in Maternal Behavior During the Baby's First Year of Life." *Child Development* 57: 746–753.

Curtiss, S. 1977. *Genie: A Psycholinguistic Study of a Modern-Day "Wild Child."* New York: Academic Press.

Dale, P. 1976. *Language Development*. New York: Holt, Rinehart, & Winston.

Damon, W. 1977. *The Social World of the Child*. San Francisco: Jossey-Bass.

———. 1983. *Social and Personality Development: Infancy through Adolescence*. New York: Norton.

Damon, W., & Hart, D. 1982. "The Development of Self-understanding from Infancy through Adolescence." *Child Development* 53: 831–857.

Darwin, C. 1877. "A Bibliographic Sketch of an Infant." *Mind* 2: 286–294.

DeVillers, J., & DeVillers, P. 1977. *Early Language*. Cambridge, MA: Harvard University Press.

Dewey, J. 1897. "My Pedagogic Creed." *The School Journal* 54 (3): 77–80.

Dickinson, G. L. 1931. *Plato and His Dialogues*. Baltimore, MD: Penguin Books.

DiPietro, J. 1981. "Rough-and-Tumble Play: A Function of Gender." *Developmental Psychology* 17(1): 50–58.

DiSimoni, F. 1975. "Perceptual and Perceptual-Motor Characteristics of Phonemic Development." *Child Development* 46: 243–246.

Dodd, B. 1972. "Effects of Social and Vocal Stimulation of Infant Babbling." *Developmental Psychology*. 7(1): 80–83.

Donaldson, M. 1979. "The Mismatch Between School and Children's Minds." *Human Nature* 2(2): 60–67.

Dowd, J., & Tronick, E. Z. 1986. "Temporal Coordination of Arm Movements in Early Infancy: Do Infants Move in Synchrony with Adult Speech?" *Child Development* 57: 762–776.

Doyle, J. A. 1985. *Sex and Gender: The Human Experience*. Dubuque, IA: William C. Brown.

Drotar, D. (ed.). 1985. *New Directions in Failure to Thrive*. New York: Plenum Press.

Dunn, J. 1983. "Sibling Relationships in Early Childhood." *Child Development* 54: 787–811.

———. 1985. *Sisters and Brothers*. Cambridge, MA: Harvard University Press.

Dunn, J., & Kendrick, C. 1963. "The Arrival of a Sibling: Changes in Patterns of Interaction Between Mothers and First-Born Child." *Journal of Child Psychology and Psychiatry* 21: 119–132.

Dusek, J. (ed.). 1985. *Teacher Expectancies*. Hillsdale, NJ: Erlbaum.

Dweck, C. 1986. "Motivational Processes Affecting Learning." *American Psychologist* 41: 1040–1048.

Easterbrooks, M. A. 1989. "Quality of Attachment to Mother and Father: Effects of Perinatal Risk Status." *Child Development* 60: 825–830.

Easterbrooks, M. A., & Goldberg, W. A. 1985. "Effects of Early Maternal Employment on Toddlers, Mothers, and Fathers." *Developmental Psychology* 4: 774–783.

Eder, D., & Hallinan, M. 1978. "Sex Differences in Children's Friendships." *American Sociological Review* 43: 237–250.

Edwards, N., & Richey, H. G. 1947. *The School in the American Social Order: The Dynamics of American Education*. Boston: Houghton Mifflin Co.

Eifermann, R. 1973. "Social Play in Childhood." In R. Heffon and B. Sutton-Smith (eds.), *Child's Play*. New York: Wiley.

Eimas, P., & Miller, J. 1980. "Discrimination of Information for Manner Articulation." *Infant Behavior and Development* 3: 367–375.

———. 1981. "Organization in the Perception of Segmental and Suprasegmental Information by Infants." *Infant Behavior and Development* 4: 395–399.

Eisenberg, N., Lennon, R., & Roth, K. 1983. "Prosocial Development: A Longitudinal Study." *Developmental Psychology* 19: 846–855.

Eisenberg, R. 1976. *Auditory Competence in Early Life: The Roots of Communicative Behavior*. Baltimore: University Park Press.

Elias, M. F., Nicolson, N. A., Bora, C., & Johnston, J. 1986. "Sleep-Awake Patterns of Breast Fed Infants in the First Two Years of Life." *Pediatrics* 77: 322–329.

Elkind, D. 1987. *Miseducation: Preschoolers at Risk*. New York: Knopf.

Elkind, D., & Weiner, I. 1978. *Development of the Child*. New York: Wiley.

Elms, A. 1981. "Skinner's Diary Year and Walden Two." *American Psychologist* 36: 470–479.

Emde, R., Gaensbauer, T., & Harmon, R. 1976. "Emotional Expression in Infancy: A Biobehavioral Study." *Psychological Issues Monograph Series* 10(1): 37.

Emergency Nursery Schools During the First Year. (1933–1934). Report of the U.S. Advisory Committee on Emergency Nursery Schools. Washington, DC: U.S. Government Printing Office.

Emergency Nursery Schools During the Second Year. (1934–1935). Report of the U.S. Advisory Committee on Emergency Nursery Schools. Washington, DC: U.S. Government Printing Office.

Emery, R. 1982. "Interparental Conflict and the Children of Discord and Divorce." *Psychological Bulletin* 92: 310–330.

Engelmann, S. 1988. "The Logic and Facts of Effective Supervision." *Education and Treatment of Children* 11 (4): 328–340.

Erikson, E. 1968. *Identity: Youth and Crisis*. New York: Norton.

Fagan, J. 1973. "Infants' Delayed Recognition Memory and Forgetting." *Journal of Experimental Child Psychology* 16: 425–450.

Fagot, B. 1977. "Consequences of Moderate Cross-Gender Behavior in Preschool Children." *Child Development* 48: 902–907.

Fantz, R. 1963. "Pattern Vision in Newborn Infants." *Science* 140(3564): 296–297.

Farnham-Diggory, S., & Gregg, L. 1975. "Color, Form, and Function as Dimensions of Natural Classification." *Child Development* 46: 101–114.

Fein, G. 1981. "Pretend Play: An Integrative View." *Child Development* 52: 1095–1118.

Feiring, C., Fox, N. A., Jaskir, J., & Lewis, M. 1987. "The Relation Between Social Support, Infant Risk Status, and Mother-Infant Interactions." *Developmental Psychology* 23: 400–405.

Feld, S., Ruhland, D., & Gold, M. 1979. "Developmental Changes in Achievement Motivation." *Merrill-Palmer Quarterly* 25(1): 43–60.

Field, T. 1978. "Interaction Behaviors of Primary Versus Secondary Caretaker Fathers." *Developmental Psychology* 14: 183–185.

———. 1979. "Visual and Cardiac Responses to Animate and Inanimate Faces by Young Term and Preterm Infants." *Child Development* 83: 355–375.

Finkelhor, D. 1979. *Sexually Victimized Children*. New York: Free Press.

———. 1984. *Child Sexual Abuse: New Theory and Practice*. New York: Free Press.

Finkelhor, D., & Browne, A. 1985. "The Traumatic Impact of Child Sexual Abuse: A Conceptualization." *American Journal of Orthopsychiatry* 55: 530–541.

Fischer, D. C. 1912. *A Montessori Mother*. New York: Henry Holt.

Flavell, J. 1985. *Cognitive Development*. Englewood Cliffs, NJ: Prentice-Hall.

Flynn, J. 1987. "Massive IQ Gains in 14 Nations: What IQ Tests Really Measure." *Psychological Bulletin* 101: 171–191.

"For the Study of Young Children." 1922. *Journal of the American Association of University Women* 15: 147–148.

Fortney, V. 1983. "The Kinematics and Kinetics of the Running Pattern of Two-, Four-, and Six-Year-Old Children." *Research Quarterly for Exercise and Sport* 54: 126–135.

Foulkes, D. 1982. *Children's Dreams: Longitudinal Studies*. New York: Wiley.

Franciosi, R. 1983. "Perspectives on Sudden Infant Death Syndrome." In J. Schowalter (ed.), *The Child and Death*. New York: Columbia University Press.

Frank, L. 1938. "The Fundamental Needs of the Child." *Mental Hygiene* 22: 353–379.

———. 1962. "The Beginnings of Child Development and Family Life Education in the Twentieth Century." *Merrill-Palmer Quarterly* 8 (4): 7–28.

Freedman, D. 1979. "Ethnic Differences in Babies." *Human Nature* 2(1): 36–43.

Freeman, N. 1980. *Strategies of Representation in Young Children*. London: Academic Press.

Freud, S. 1965. *New Introductory Lectures in Psychoanalysis*. New York: Norton.

Friedrich-Cofer, L., & Huston, A. 1986. "Television Violence and Aggression." *Psychological Bulletin* 100: 373–378.

Furman, W. 1982. "Children's Friendships." In T. Field (ed.), *Review of Human Development*. New York: Wiley.

Furstenberg, F. F., Brooks-Gunn, J., & Chase-Landsdale, L. 1989. "Teenaged Pregnancy and Childbearing." *American Psychologist* 44(2): 313–320.

Gal, S. 1979. *Language Shift*. New York: Academic Press.

Galinsky, E. 1987. *The Six Stages of Parenthood*. Reading, MA: Addison-Wesley.

Gamble, T., & Zigler, E. 1986. "Effects of Infant Day Care: Another Look at the Evidence." *American Journal of Orthopsychiatry* 56(1): 26–41.

Gardner, H. 1980. *Artful Scribbles: The Significance of Children's Drawings*. New York: Basic Books.

Garvey, C. 1977. *Play*. Cambridge, MA: Harvard University Press.

———. 1984. *Children's Talk*. Cambridge, MA: Harvard University Press.

Gelles, R. 1978. "Violence toward Children in the United States." *American Journal of Orthopsychiatry* 48: 580–592.

Gelman, R. 1978. "Cognitive Development." *Annual Review of Psychology* 29: 297–332.

Genishi, C., & Dyson, A. 1984. *Language Assessment in the Early Years*. Norwood, NJ: Ablex.

George, C., & Main, M. 1979. "Social Interactions of Young Abused Children: Approach, Avoidance, and Aggression." *Child Development* 50: 306–318.

Geschwind, P. 1985. *Selected Papers on Language and the Brain*. New York: Reidel.

Gesell, A. 1923. *The Pre-School Child: From the Standpoint of Public Hygiene and Education*. Boston: Houghton-Mifflin.

———. 1943. *Infant and Child in the Culture of Today*. New York: Harper.

Gesell, A., & Thompson, H. 1929. "Learning and Growth in Identical Infant Twins." *Genetic Psychology Monographs* 6(1): 1–125.

Gibson, E. 1969. *Principles of Perceptual Learning and Development*. New York: Appleton-Century-Crofts.

Glaser, R. 1984. "The Role of Knowledge." *American Psychologist* 39(2): 93–104.

Godwin, A., & Schrag, L. (eds.). 1988. *Setting Up for Infant Care: Guidelines for Centers and Family Day Care Homes*. Washington, DC: National Association for the Education of Young Children.

Gold, D., & Andres, D. 1978. "Relations Between Maternal Employment and Development of Nursery School Children." *Canadian Journal of Behavioural Science* 10(1): 116–129.

Gold, M. 1985. "The Baby Makers." *Science* 85 (6) (April): 26–29+.

Goldberg, S., & DeVitto, B. A. 1983. *Born Too Soon: Preterm Birth and Early Development*. San Francisco: Freeman.

Goldberg, S., Perrotta, M., Minde, K., & Corter, C. 1986. "Maternal Behavior and Attachment in Low-Birth-Weight Twins and Singletons." *Child Development* 57(1): 34–46.

Goldenberg, C. N. 1987. "Low-Income Hispanic Parents' Contributions to Their First Grade Children's Word Cognitive Skills." *Anthropology and Research Quarterly* 18: 149–179.

Goldman, A., & Goldblum, R. 1982. "Anti-infective Properties of Human Milk." *Pediatric Update* 2: 359–363.

Golinkoff, R. (ed.). 1983. *The Transition from Preverbal to Verbal Communication*. Hillsdale, NJ: Erlbaum.

Gonzalez-Mena, J. 1986. "Toddlers: What to Expect." *Young Children* 42(1): 47–51.

Good, T., & Weinstein, R. 1986. "Schools Make a Difference: Evidence, Criticisms, and New Directions." *American Psychologist* 41: 1090–1097.

Goodenough, F. L. 1931. *Anger in Young Children*. Minneapolis: University of Minnesota Press.

Goodlad, J. 1984. *A Place Called School: Prospects for the Future*. New York: McGraw Hill.

Goodnow, J. 1977. *Children's Drawing*. Cambridge, MA: Harvard University Press.

Gottfried, A., Wallace-Lande, P., Sherman-Brown, S., King, J., & Coen, C. 1981.

"Physical and Social Environment of Newborn Infants in Special Care Units." *Science* 214: 673–675.

Grant, J. 1982. *The State of the World's Children*. New York: Oxford University Press.

Greenfield, P. 1982. "The Role of Perceived Variability in the Transition to Language." *Journal of Child Language* 9(1): 1–12.

————. 1984. *Mind and Media: The Effects of Television, Video Games, and Computers*. Cambridge, MA: Harvard University Press.

Greeno, J. 1989. "A Perspective on Thinking." *American Psychologist* 44: 134–141.

Greenspan, S., & Greenspan, N. T. 1985. *First Feelings: Milestones in the Emotional Development of Your Baby and Child*. New York: Penguin.

Griffiths, P. 1985. "The Communicative Functions of Children's Single-Word Speech." In M. Barrett (ed.), *Children's Single-Word Speech*. New York: Wiley.

Grimes, D., & Gross, G. 1981. "Pregnancy Outcomes in Black Women Aged 35 and Older." *Obstetrics and Gynecology* 58: 614–620.

Grolnick, W. S. & Slowiaczek, M. L. 1994. "Parents' Involvement in Children's Schooling: A Multidimensional Conceptualization and Motivational Model." *Child Development* 65: 237–252.

Grosjean, F. 1982. *Living with Two Languages*. Cambridge, MA: Harvard University Press.

Grubb, W. N. 1989. "Young Children Face the State: Issues and Options for Early Childhood Programs." *American Journal of Education* 94(3): 358–397.

Guardo, C., & Bohan, J. 1971. "Development of a Sense of Self-Identity in Children." *Child Development* 42: 1909–1921.

Guilford, J. 1967. *The Nature of Human Intelligence*. New York: McGraw-Hill.

Guttmacher, A., & Kaiser, I. 1984. *Pregnancy, Birth, and Family Planning*. New York: Signet.

Hall, C., Gregory, G., Billinger, E., & Fisher, T. 1988. "Field Independence and Simultaneous Processing in Preschool Children." *Perceptual and Motor Skills* 66: 891–897.

Hamilton, P. M. 1984. *Basic Maternity Nursing*. (5th ed.). St. Louis: Mosby.

Hardy, R., Eliot, J., & Burlingame, K. 1987. "Stability over Age and Sex of Children's Responses to Embedded Figures Test." *Perceptual and Motor Skills* 64: 399–406.

Hare-Muslin, R. T., & Mareck, J. 1988. "The Meaning of Difference: Gender Theory, Postmodernism, and Psychology." *American Psychologist* 43: 455–464.

Hareven, T. 1986. "Historical Changes in the Family and the Life Course: Implications for Child Development." In A. Smuts and H. Hagen (eds.), *History and Research in Child Development*. Monographs of the Society for Research on Child Development 50 (211). Chicago: University Press.

Harkness, S., & Super, C. 1987. "The Uses of Cross-Cultural Research in Child Development." *Annals of Child Development* 4: 209–244.

Harlow, H. 1959. "Love in Infant Monkeys." *Scientific American* 200(6): 68–74.

Harris, P. 1983. "Infant Cognition." In P. Mussen (ed.), *Handbook of Child Psychology* New York: Wiley.

Harter, S. 1982a. "Children's Understanding of Multiple Emotions: A Cognitive-

Developmental Approach." In W. Overton (ed.), *The Relationship between Social and Cognitive Development*. Hillsdale, NJ: Erlbaum.

———. 1982b. "A Cognitive-Developmental Approach to Children's Use of Affect and Trait Labels." In F. Serafica (ed.), *Social Cognition and Social Relations in Context*. New York: Guilford.

Hartup, W. 1974. "Aggression in Childhood: Developmental Perspectives." *American Psychologist* 29: 336–341.

Hartup, W. 1983. "Social Relationship and Their Developmental Significance." *American Psychologist* 44: 120–126.

Hersch, P. 1988. "Coming of Age on City Streets." *Psychology Today* 22(1): 30–32, 34–37.

Hetherington, E. M. 1979. "Divorce: A Child's Perspective." *American Psychologist* 34: 851–858.

———. 1984. "Stress and Coping in Children and Families." In A. Doyle, D. Gold, & D. S. Moskowitz (eds.), "Children and Families Under Stress." *New Directions for Child Development* 24 (June): 7–34.

———. 1989. "Divorce: A Child's Perspective." *American Psychologist* 44: 303–312.

Hetherington, E. M., & Arasteh, J. D. (eds.). 1988. *Impact of Divorce, Single-Parenting and Step-Parenting on Children*. Hillsdale, NJ: Erlbaum.

Hetherington, E. M., Cox, M., & Cox, R. 1979. "Play and Social Interaction in Children Following Divorce." *Journal of Social Issues* 35(4): 26–49.

Hinde, R., & Stevenson-Hinde, J. (eds.). 1973. *Constraints on Learning*. New York: Academic Press.

Hofer, M. 1987. "Early Social Relationships: A Psychobiologist's View." *Child Development* 58: 633–647.

Holwerda-Kuipers, J. 1987. "The Cognitive Development of Low Birth Weight Children." *Journal of Child Psychology and Psychiatry* 28: 215–228.

Honig, A. 1985. "High Quality Infant/Toddler Care: Issues and Dilemmas." *Young Children* 41(1): 40–46.

Honzik, M. P. 1957. "Developmental Studies of Parent-Child Resemblance in Intelligence." *Child Development* 28: 215–228.

Howard, J., & Barnett, M. 1981. "Arousal of Empathy and Subsequent Generosity in Young Children." *Journal of Genetic Psychology* 138: 307–308.

Howes, C. 1983. "Caregiver Behavior in Center and Family Day Care." *Journal of Applied Developmental Psychology* 4(1): 99–107.

Howes, C., & Stewart, P. 1987. "Child's Play with Adults, Toys, and Peers: An Examination of Family and Child-Care Influences." *Developmental Psychology* 23: 423–430.

Huesmann, L., & Eron, L. (eds.). *Television and the Aggressive Child: A Cross-National Comparison*. Hillsdale, NJ: Erlbaum.

Humphreys, L. G. 1988. "Trends in Levels of Academic Achievement of Blacks and Other Minorities." *Intelligence* 12: 231–260.

Hunt, J. M. 1964. "Revisiting Montessori: Introduction." In Maria Montessori, *The Montessori Method*. Translated by Ann E. George. New York: Schocken.

Hurley, L. 1980. *Developmental Nutrition*. Englewood Cliffs, NJ: Prentice-Hall.

Huston, A., Watkins, B., and Kunkel, D. 1989. "Public Policy and Children's Television." *American Psychologist* 44: 424–433.

Hutt, C. 1979. "Exploration and Play." In B. Sutton-Smith (ed.), *Play and Learning*. New York: Gardner.

Hyde, J. 1981. "How Large Are Cognitive Gender Differences?" *American Psychologist* 36: 892–901.

Hymes, J. L., Jr. 1944a. "A Social Philosophy from Nursery School Teaching. Kaiser Child Service Center Pamphlets for Teachers." No. 1. Carmel, CA: Hacienda Press.

———. 1944b. "Who Will Need a Post-War Nursery School? Kaiser Child Service Center Pamphlets for Teachers." No. 3. Carmel, CA: Hacienda Press.

Inhelder, B., & Piaget, J. 1958. *The Growth of Logical Thinking from Birth to Adolescence*. New York: Basic Books.

Itard, J. 1962. *The Wild Boy of Aveyron*. Translated by G. Humphrey & M. Humphrey. New York: Appleton-Century-Crofts.

Izard, C. E. 1982. *Measuring Emotions in Infants and Children*. New York: Cambridge University Press.

Jackson, P. 1968. *Life in Classrooms*. New York: Holt.

———. 1986. *The Practice of Teaching*. Chicago: University of Chicago Press.

Johnson, H. 1928. *Children in the Nursery School*. New York: John Day.

Kagan, J. 1973. "Meaning and Memory in Two Cultures." *Child Development* 44: 221–223.

———. 1979. "Structure and Process in the Human Infant: The Otogeny of Mental Representation." In M. Bornstein & W. Kessen (eds.), *Psychological Development from Infancy: Image to Intention*. Hillsdale, NJ: Erlbaum.

———. 1981. *The Second Year*. Cambridge, MA: Harvard University Press.

Kagan, J., & Moss, H. A. 1962. *Birth to Maturity: A Study in Psychological Development*. New York: Wiley.

Kagan, J., Reznick, J. S., & Snidman, N. 1986. "Biological Bases of Childhood Shyness." *Science* 240: 167–171.

Kalter, N. 1987. "Long-Term Effects of Divorce on Children: A Developmental Vulnerability Model." *American Journal of Orthopsychiatry* 57: 587–600.

Kane, B. 1977. "Children's Concepts of Death." *Journal of Genetic Psychology* 24: 315–320.

Kaplan, A., & Bean, J. (eds.). 1976. *Beyond Sex-Role Stereotypes: Readings Toward a Psychology of Androgyny*. Boston: Little, Brown.

Karniol, R. 1980. "A Conceptual Analysis of Imminent Justice Responses in Children." *Child Development* 51: 118–130.

Katz, P., & Zalk, S. 1978. "Modification of Children's Racial Attitudes." *Developmental Psychology* 14: 447–461.

Kilpatrick, W. H. 1914. *The Montessori System Examined*. Boston: Houghton-Mifflin.

Levitt, M. 1960. *Freud and Dewey on the Nature of Man*. New York: Philosophical Library.

Locke, J. 1968. *The Educational Writings: A Critical Edition*. Edited by J. L. Axtell. Cambridge: Cambridge University Press.

Machlup, F. 1962. *The Production and Distribution of Knowledge in the United States*. Princeton: Princeton University Press.

McMillan, M. 1919. *The Nursery School*. New York: E. P. Dutton.

Mowrer, A. H. 1960. *Learning Theory and the Symbolic Process*. New York: Wiley.

Mueller, E., & Vandell, D. 1978. "Infant-Infant Interaction." In J. Osofsky (ed.), *Handbook of Infancy*. New York: Wiley.

Muir, D., & Field, J. 1979. "Newborn Infants' Orientation to Sound." *Child Development* 50: 4431–436.

Murphy, L. 1937. *Social Behavior and Child Personality*. New York: Columbia University Press.

Mussen, P., & Eisenberg-Berg, N. 1977. *Roots of Caring, Sharing, and Helping: The Development of Pro-Social Behavior in Children*. San Francisco: Freeman.

Naeye, R. 1979. "Causes of Fetal and Neonatal Monality by Race in a Selected U.S. Population." *American Journal of Public Health* 69: 857.

Naeye, R., Blanc, W., & Paul, C. 1973. "Effects of Maternal Nutrition on the Human Fetus." *Pediatrics* 52: 494.

Nelms, B., & Mullins, R. 1982. *Growth and Development: Primary Health Care Approach*. Englewood Cliffs, NJ: Prentice-Hall.

Nelson, K. 1981. "Individual Differences in Language Development." *Developmental Psychology* 17: 170–187.

———. 1985. *Making Sense: Acquisition of Shared Meaning*. New York: Academic Press.

Noddings, N. 1984. *Caring*. Berkeley: University of California Press.

Norton, A. J., & Glick, P. C. 1986. "One Parent Families: A Social and Economic Profile." *Family Relations* 35(1): 9–18.

Nyhan, W. 1976. *The Heredity Factor*. New York: Grosset and Dunlap.

Okagaki, L. & Frensch, P. A. 1998. "Parenting and Children's School Achievement: A Multiethnic Perspective." *American Educational Research Journal* 35 (1): 123–144.

Omwake, E. B. 1963. "The Child's Estate." In A. Solnit and S. Provence (eds.), *Modern Perspectives in Child Development*. New York: International Universities Press.

Opie, I., and Opie, P. 1969. *Children's Games in Streets and Playgrounds*. London: Clarendon Press.

Orlick, T. D. 1981. "Positive Socialization via Cooperative Games." *Developmental Psychology* 17: 426–429.

Palincsar, A. 1986. "Metacognitive Strategy Instruction." *Exceptional Children* 53: 118–124.

Parke, R. D. 1981. *Fathers*. Cambridge, MA: Harvard University Press.

Parke, R., & Sawin, D. 1976. "The Father's Role in Infancy: A Re-evaluation." *The Family Coordinator* 25: 365–371.

Parmalee, A. 1986. "Children's Illnesses: Their Beneficial Effects on Behavioral Development." *Child Development* 57(1): 1–10.

Parten, M. 1932. "Social Play Among Preschool Children." *Journal of Abnormal and Social Psychology* 27: 243–269.

Pestalozzi, J. H. 1907. *Leonard and Gertrude*. Translated by E. Channing. Boston: D.C. Heath.

Piaget, J. 1963. *The Origins of Intelligence in Children*. New York: Nonon.

———. 1964. *The Moral Judgment of the Child*. New York: Free Press.

———. 1965. *The Child's Conception of the World*. Totowa, NJ: Littlefield, Adams.

Piaget, J., & Inhelder, B. 1967. *The Child's Conception of Space*. New York: Norton.

———. 1969. *The Psychology of the Child*. New York: Basic Books.

————. 1973. *Memory and Intelligence*. New York: Basic Books.

Plomin, R. 1986. *Development, Genetics and Psychology*. Hillsdale, NJ: Erlbaum.

Pollitt, E., Eichier, A., & Chan, C. 1975. "Psychosocial Development and Behavior of Mothers of Failure-to-Thrive Children." *American Journal of Orthopsychiatry* 45: 527–537.

Powell, D. 1986. "Parent Education and Support Programs." *Young Children* 41 (3): 47–52.

"Preschool and Parental Education." 1929. In *Twenty-eighth Yearbook of the National Society for the Study of Education*. Bloomington, IL: Public School Publishing Co.

Pringle, S., & Ramsey, B. 1982. *Promoting the Health of Children*. St. Louis: Mosby.

The Protection and Promotion of Mental Health in Schools. 1964. Mental Health Monograph 5. Washington, DC: U.S. Public Health Service.

Purkey, S., & Smith, M. 1983. "Effective Schools: A Review." *Elementary School Journal* 83: 427–452.

Rambusch, N. M. 1967. *Learning How to Learn: An American Approach to Montessori*. Baltimore: Helicon Press.

Rice, M. 1982. "Child Language: What Children Know and How." In T. Field (ed.), *Review of Human Development*. New York: Wiley.

Riese, M. L. 1987. "Temperament Stability Between the Neonatal Period and 24 Months." *Developmental Psychology* 23: 216–222.

Rist, R. 1973. *The Urban School: A Factory for Failure*. Cambridge, MA: MIT Press.

Roberton, M., & Halverson, L. 1984. *Developing Children: Their Changing Movement*. Philadelphia: Lea & Febiger.

Rogoff, B., & Morelli, G. 1989. "Perspectives on Children's Development from Cultural Psychology." *American Psychologist* 44: 343–348.

Roopnarine, J., & Field, T. 1982. "Peer-directed Behaviors of Infants and Toddlers during Nursery School Play." In T. Field (ed.), *Review of Human Development*. New York: Wiley.

Rosenberg, M. 1979. *Conceiving the Self*. New York: Basic Books.

Rosenberg, M. S., & Repucci, N. D. 1985. "Primary Prevention of Child Abuse." *Journal of Consulting and Clinical Psychology* 53: 576–585.

Rosenfeld, A. A., Wenegrat, A. O., Haavik, D. K., Wenegrat, B. G., & Smith, C. R. 1982. "Sleeping Patterns in Upper-Middle-Class Families When the Child Awakens Ill or Frightened." *Archives of Genetic Psychology* 39: 943–947.

Rousseau, J. 1762; 1911. *Emile, or, On Education*. London: Dent.

————. 1964. *Emile, Julie, and Other Writings*. Edited by S. E. Frost, Jr. Translated by R. L. Archer. Woodbury, NY: Barron's Educational Series.

Rubenstein, J. L., Howes, C., & Boyle, P. 1981. "A Two Year Follow-Up of Infants in Community Based Infant Day Care." *Journal of Child Psychology* 22: 209–218.

Rubin, K., & Krasnor, L. 1980. "Changes in the Play Behaviours of Preschoolers: A Short Longitudinal Investigation." *Canadian Journal of Behavioural Science* 12: 278–282.

Rubin, K., Maioni, T., & Hornung, M. 1976. "Free Play Behaviors in Middle and Lower Class Preschools: Parten and Piaget Revisited." *Child Development* 47: 414–419.

Rubin, K., Watson, K., & Jambor, T. 1978. "Free Play Behaviors in Preschool and Kindergarten Children." *Child Development* 49: 534–536.

Ruff, H. 1980. "Infant Recognition of the Invariant Form of Objects." *Child Development* 49: 293–306.

Ruhland, D., & Feld, S. 1977. "The Development of Achievement Motivation in Black and White Children." *Child Development* 48: 1362–368.

Ruopp, R., & Travers, J. 1982. "Janus Faces Day Care: Perspectives on Quality and Cost." In E. F. Zigler and E. W. Gordon (eds.), *Day Care Scientific and Social Policy Issues*. Boston: Auburn House.

Sachs, J. 1985. "Prelinguistic Development." In J. Gleason (ed.), *The Development of Language*. Columbus, OH: Merrill.

Saitz, E., & Brodie, J. 1982. "Pretend-Play Training in Childhood: A Review and Critique." In D. Pepler and K. Rubin (eds.), *The Play of Children: Current Theory and Research*. Basel, Switzerland: Karger.

Sameroff, A., & Cavanaugh, P. 1979. "Learning in Infancy: A Developmental Perspective." In J. Osofsky (ed.), *Handbook of Infant Development*. New York: Wiley.

Scarr, S. 1984. *Mother Care, Other Care*. New York: Basic Books.

Scarr, S., Phillips, S., & McCartney, K. 1989. "Working Mothers and Their Families." *American Psychologist* 44: 1402–1409.

Scarr, S., & Salapatek, P. 1970. "Patterns of Fear Development During Infancy." *Merrill-Palmer Quarterly* 16(1): 53–90.

Scarr-Salapatek, S. 1976. "An Evolutionary Perspective on Infant Intelligence: Species Patterns and Individual Variations." In M. Lewis (ed.), *Origins of Intelligence*. New York: Plenum Press.

Schachter, F. F., & Stone, R. K. 1985. "Difficult Sibling, Easy Sibling: Temperament and the Within-Family Environment." *Child Development* 56: 1335–1344.

Seefeldt, C. (ed.). 1987. *The Early Childhood Curriculum: A Review of Current Research*. New York: Teachers College Press.

———. 1990. *Continuing Issues in Early Childhood Education*. New York: Teachers College Press.

Seguin, E. 1886; 1907. *Idiocy: And Its Treatment by Physiological Method*. New York: Teachers College, Columbia University.

Selman, R. 1989. "Fostering Intimacy and Autonomy." In W. Damon (ed.), *Child Development Today and Tomorrow*. San Francisco: Jossey-Bass.

Shapiro, M. S. 1983. *Child's Garden: The Kindergarten Movement from Froebel to Dewey*. University Park: Pennsylvania State University Press.

Shattuck, R. 1980. *The Forbidden Experiment: The Story of the Wild Boy of Aveyron*. New York: Washington Square Press.

Singleton, L., & Asher, S. 1979. "Racial Integration and Children's Peer Preferences: An Investigation of Developmental and Cohort Differences." *Child Development* 50: 936–941.

Slade, A. 1987. "Quality of Attachment and Early Symbolic Play." *Developmental Psychology* 23(1): 78–85.

Slater, A., Morrison, C., & Rose, D. 1985. "Movement Perception and Identity Constancy in the Newborn Baby." *British Journal of Developmental Psychology* 3: 211–220.

Slaughter, D. 1983. "Early Intervention and Its Effects on Maternal and Child Development." *Monographs of the Society for Research on Child Development* 48(4): 1–91.

Snow, C., & Ferguson, C. (eds.). 1977. *Talking to Children*. Cambridge: Cambridge University Press.

Somerville, J. 1984. *The Rise and Fall of Childhood*. Beverly Hills, CA: Sage.

Spock, B., & Rothenberg, M. 1985. *Baby and Child Care*. New York: Pocket Books.

Stern, D. 1977. *The First Relationship: Infant and Mother*. Cambridge, MA: Harvard University Press.

Stevenson, D. L., & Baker, D. P. 1987. "The Family School Relation and the Child's School Performance." *Child Development* 58: 1345–1357.

Stewart, R. B., Mobley, L. A., Van Tuyl, S. S., & Salvador, M. A. 1987. "The First-born's Adjustment to the Birth of a Sibling: A Longitudinal Assessment." *Child Development* 58: 341–355.

Strauss, M. E., Lessen-Firestone, J. K., Starr, R. H., & Ostrea, E. M. 1975. "Behavior of Narcotics-Addicted Newborns." *Child Development* 46: 887–893.

Streissguth, A. P., Martin, D. C., Barr, H. M., Kirchner, G. L., & Darby, B. L. 1984. "Intrauterine Alcohol and Nicotine Exposure: Attention and Reaction Time in Four-Year-Old Children." *Developmental Psychology* 20: 533–541.

Sugarman, S. 1983. *Children's Early Thought: Developments in Classification*. New York: Cambridge University Press.

Super, C. 1981. "Behavioral Development in Infancy." In R. H. Munroe, R. L. Munroe, & B. B. Whiting (eds.), *Handbook of Cross-Cultural Human Development*. 181–270. New York: Garland STPM Press.

———. 1982. "Unpacking African Infant Precocity." In N. Warren (ed.), *Studies in Cross-Cultural Psychology*, Vol. 3. London: Academic Press.

Sutton-Smith, B. 1981. *A History of Children's Play*. Philadelphia: University of Pennsylvania Press.

———. 1986. *Toys as Culture*. New York: Gardner Press.

Taub, H., Goldstein, K., & Caputo, D. 1977. "Indices of Neonatal Prematurity as Discriminators of Development in Middle Childhood." *Child Development* 48: 797–805.

Thomas, A., & Chess, S. 1981. *Temperament and Development*. New York: Brunner/Mazel.

Trueba, H. T. 1988. "Culturally Based Explanations of Minority Students' Academic Achievement." *Anthropology & Education Quarterly* 19(3): 270–287.

Vandell, D. 1980. "Sociability with Peers and Mothers in the First Year." *Developmental Psychology* 16: 355–361.

Vandell, D., & Powers, C. 1983. "Day Care Quality and Children's Free Play Activities." *American Journal of Orthopsychiatry* 53: 493–500.

Vandenberg, B. 1978. "Play and Development from an Ethological Perspective." *American Psychologist* 33: 724–738.

Volterra, V., and Teaschner, R. 1978. "The Acquisition and Development of Language by Bilingual Children." *Journal of Child Language* 5: 311–326.

Vygotsky, L. 1962. *Thought and Language*. Cambridge, MA: MIT Press.

———. 1976. "Play and Its Role in Mental Development of the Child." In J. S. Bruner, A. Jolly, and K. Sylvia (eds.). *Play: Its Role in Mental Development and Evolution*. 537–544. New York: Basic Books.

Waddington, C. H. 1966. *Principles of Development and Differentiation*. New York: Macmillan.

Walker, L. 1984. "Sex Differences in the Development of Moral Reasoning: A Critical View." *Child Development* 53: 1330–1336.

Wallach, M. 1985. "Creativity Testing and Giftedness." In F. Horowitz & M. O'Brien (eds.), *The Gifted and Talented: Developmental Perspectives*. Washington, DC: American Psychological Association.

Wallerstein, J. 1983. "Children of Divorce: The Psychological Tasks of the Child." *American Journal of Orthopsychiatry* 53: 230–243.

––––––. 1987. "Children of Divorce: Preliminary Report of a Ten-Year Follow-Up." *American Journal of Orthopsychiatry* 57: 199–211.

Wapner, J., & Conner, K. 1986. "The Role of Defensiveness in Cognitive Impulsivity." *Child Development* 57: 1370–1374.

Washburn, R. W. 1944. "Re-education in a Nursery Group: A Study in Clinical Psychology." *Monograph of the Society for Research in Child Development* 9(2): 1–167.

Weinraub, M., Jaeger, E., & Hoffman, L. W. 1988. "Predicting Infant Outcomes in Families of Employed and Non-Employed Mothers." *Early Childhood Research Quarterly* 3: 361–387.

Weisner, T. S., & Gallimore, R. 1977. "My Brother's Keeper: Child and Sibling Caretaking." *Current Anthropology* 18: 169–190.

Wertsch, J. 1985. *Vygotsky and the Social Formation of Mind*. Cambridge, MA: Harvard University Press.

White, B. 1985. *The First Three Years of Life*. Englewood Cliffs, NJ: Prentice-Hall.

White, D. 1986. "Treatment of Mild, Moderate, and Severe Obesity in Children." *Canadian Psychology* 23: 262–274.

White, R. W. 1963. *Ego and Reality in Psychoanalytic Theory*. New York: International Universities Press.

Whiting, B., & Whiting, J. 1975. *Children of Six Cultures: A Psychocultural Analysis*. Cambridge, MA: Harvard University Press.

Williams, H. 1983. *Perceptual and Motor Development*. Englewood Cliffs, NJ: Prentice-Hall.

Zahn-Waxler, C., Radke-Yarrow, M., & King, R. A. (1979). "Child Rearing and Children's Prosocial Initiations Toward Victims of Distress." *Child Development* 50: 319–330.

Zigler, E. 1987. "Formal Schooling for Four-Year-Olds? No." *American Psychologist* 42: 254–260.

Zigler, E., & Finn-Stevenson, S. 1987. *Children's Development and Social Issues*. New York: Heath.

Index

About the Author

HARRY MORGAN is Professor of Early Childhood Education at the State University of West Georgia. He is the author of *Historical Perspectives on the Education of Black Children* (Greenwood 1995) and *Cognitive Styles of Classroom Learning* (Greenwood 1997).

ISBN 0-89789-594-0

90000>

EAN

9 780897 895941

HARDCOVER BAR CODE